European Television
in the Digital Age

European Television in the Digital Age

Issues, Dynamics and Realities

Stylianos Papathanassopoulos

Polity

First published in 2002 by Polity Press in association with Blackwell Publishers Ltd

Editorial office:
Polity Press
65 Bridge Street
Cambridge CB2 1UR, UK

Marketing and production:
Blackwell Publishers Ltd
108 Cowley Road
Oxford OX4 1JF, UK

Published in the USA by
Blackwell Publishers Inc.
350 Main Street
Malden, MA 02148, USA

A catalogue record for this book is available from the British Library.

Library of Congress Cataloging-in-Publication Data
Papathanassopoulos, S.
   European television in the digital age : issues, dynamics and
realities / Stylianos Papathanassopoulos.
      p. cm.
Includes bibliographical references and index.
   ISBN 0-7456-2872-9 (acid-free paper)—ISBN 0-7456-2873-7 (acid-free
paper : pbk.)
   1. Television broadcasting—Europe.   2. Digital television—Europe.   I. Title.
PN1992.3.E78 P37 2002
   384.55′094—dc21

                                                                2001004452

Typeset in 10½ on 12pt Plantin
by Graphicraft Limited, Hong Kong
Printed in Great Britain by MPG Books Ltd, Bodmin, Cornwall

This book is printed on acid-free paper.

Contents

Detailed Chapter Contents

Figure and Tables

Abbreviations

ABC	American Broadcasting Corporation
AP	Associated Press
API	application programme interface
APTN	Associated Press Television Network
APTV	Associated Press Television
ARD	Arbeitsgemeinschaft der Öffentlichrechtlichen Rundfunkanstalten der Bundesrepublik Deutschland
BBC	British Broadcasting Corporation
BIB	British Interactive Broadcasting
BNP	Banque Nationale de Paris
BNT	Bulgarian National Television
BRU	Broadcasting Research Unit
BDB	British Digital Broadcasting
BSkyB	British Sky Broadcasting
CBS	Columbia Broadcasting System
CCE	Christian Channel Europe
CDS	Canal Satelite Digital
CE	Council of Europe
CEC	Commission of the European Communities
CES	Comité Économique et Sociale
CFI	Court of First Instance
CLT	Compagnie Luxembourgeoise de Télédiffusion
CNBC	Cable NBC
CNE	Chinese News and Entertainment
CNN	Cable News Network

CNNI	Cable News Network International
CSA	Conseil Supérieur de l'Audiovisuel
CSD	Canalsatelite Digital
CSN	Canalsatellite Numérique
CT	Ceska Televise
CyBC	Cyprus Broadcasting Corporation
DF1	Digitales Fernsehen 1
DFS	Deutsches SportFernsehen
DT	Deutsches Telecom
DTH	direct-to-home
DTT	digital terrestrial television
DVB	Digital Video Broadcasting
DW	Deutsche Welle
EBN	European Business Network
EBU	European Broadcasting Union
EC	European Commission
EIM	European Institute for the Media
EPG	electronic programme guide
ERT	Elliniki Radiofonia Teleorasis
ERTT	Établissement de la Radiodiffusion Télévision Tunisienne
ERTU	Egypt Radio Television Union
ESPN	Entertainment and Sports Network
ESR	Ethniko Symvulio Radioteleorasis
EU	European Union
EWTN	Eternal Word Television Network
GATS	General Agreement of Trade in Services
GATT	General Agreement on Tariffs and Trade
GDP	gross domestic product
GMAF	Gestora de Medios Audiovisuales del Fútbol
HBO	Home Box Office
HMG	Holland Media Groep
HSN	Home Shopping Network
Idate	Institut de l'Audiovisuel et des Télécommunications en Europe
IDTV	Integrated Digital TV sets
IFPI	Producers of Phonograms and Videograms
IP	Internet Protocol
ISL	International Sports and Leisure Marketing
ISPR	International Sports Rights
ITC	Independent Television Commission
KEK	Commission for Media Concentration (Germany)
KNVB	The Royal Dutch Soccer Federation

KPV	The Royal KPV (Dutch Telecommunications Organization)
M6	Métropole 6
MPEG	Motion Picture Experts Group
MSG	Media Services GmbH
MSNBC	Microsoft NBC
MTA	Muslim Television Ahmadiyyah
MTG	Modern Times Group
MTV	Music Television
MTVE	MTV Europe
MTVNE	MTV Networks Europe
MUTV	Manchester United Television
NBC	National Broadcasting Company
NHK	Nippon Hoso Kyokai
NOS	Nederlandse Omroep Stichting
NRK	Norsk Rikskringkasting
NSD	Nordic Satellite Distribution
NT	Norsk Telekom
NVOD	near-video-on-demand
OFCOM	Office of Communications
OJEC	*Official Journal of the European Communities*
OMTV	Olympique de Marseille Télévision
ORF	Osterreichischer Rundfunk
OTC	over the counter
PBS	Public Broadcasting Services
PSB	public service broadcasting
PTDP	Plataforma de Televisão Portuguesa
PPV	pay-per-view
QVC	Quality Value Convenience
RAI	Radio Televisione Italiana
RTBF	Radio Télévision Belge de la Communauté Française
RTÉ	Radio Telefis Éireann
RTI	Reti Televisive Italiane
RTL	Radio Télévision Luxembourgeoise
RTP	Radio Televisão Portuguesa
RTVE	Radio Televisión Española
SBS	Scandinavian Broadcasting System
SECEMIE	Société Éditrice de la Chaîne Européenne Multilingue d'Information
SET	Sony Entertainment Television
SGAE	Sociedad General de Autores y Editores
SIAE	Società Italiana degli Autori et Editioni

SIC	Sociedade Independente de Comunicação
SMM	Strategic Money Management
SNG	satellite newsgathering
SOCEMIE	Société Opératrice de la Chaîne Européenne Multilingue d'Information
SSR–SRG	Swiss Broadcasting Organization
STV	Sveriges Television
TCC	The Children's Channel
TD	TeleDanmark A/S
TEN	The Entertainment Network
TMC	Télé Monte-Carlo
TPS	Télévision Par Satellite
TRT	Turkiye Radyo Televizyon
TVE	Televisión Española
TVR	Television Romania
TVS	TV Sport
UEFA	Union of European Football Associations
UPC	United Pan-European Communications
UPI	United International Pictures
VCR	video cassette recorder
Vía	Vía Digital
VOD	video-on-demand
VPL	Video Performance Limited
VTM	Vlaamse Televisie Maatschappij
VTR	Vlaamse Radio en Televisie
WAP	Wireless Application Protocol
WTN	World Television News
WWW	World Wide Web
YLE	Yleisradio Oy
ZDF	Zweites Deutsches Fernsehen

Acknowledgements

Many people helped in the making of this book. I would like to thank the National University of Athens for its financial assistance at various stages of my research in the last four years. My thanks also to the many media journalists for helping me to find relevant material and answering my questions, especially Paul Barker, Tim Westcott and Sarah Callard. I would also like to thank Dr Ralph Negrine and Professors Denis McQuail and Jeremy Tunstall for their thoughts on earlier versions of some of the material found here. I would also like to thank Dr Korina Patelis for her comments on the whole book as well as the two anonymous readers at Polity for their valuable comments and thoughts on my typescript. My special thanks go to John Thompson and the people at Polity who have enthusiastically supported the whole project. I would like to express my sincere thanks to Pamela Thomas and Hilary Walford, who have shown patience and professionalism throughout the process of putting this book together. Needless to say, all responsibility for shortcomings and inaccuracies are mine.

Finally my grateful thanks to my wife, Katia, and my two kids, Thanassis and Aphrodite, for their continuous support, good humour and patience.

Stelios Papathanassopoulos
Athens, May 2001

Introduction
European Television in the Digital Age

The twenty-first century has brought with it a new era of television change and this book traces the financial dynamics and realities of such changes as a key to understanding the years to come. Developments in communications technology have significantly altered the potential of television transmission. Digital compression and the universality of the TV set have created the prospect of a world market for both hardware equipment and programmes. Within this context, the European countries have tried, as they did in the mid-1980s, to advance their television systems. Indeed, since the mid-1980s West European television has entered a period of tremendous and continuous change, following the developments in television technology and the implementation of public policies favouring the deregulation, privatization and commercialization of television systems. But these changes have created many problems for electronic media. The restructuring of the West European television systems has brought about an increase in the number of private channels in operation and, consequently, has changed the relationship between the private and the public broadcasting sectors. Where once a few channels existed, there are now many, and many more to come.

At the beginning of the twenty-first century the effects of broadcasting deregulation are being felt across Western Europe, with new commercial players and forces coming into play, although the processes of deregulation and the impact of change have varied from country to country. The new audio-visual landscape has led to an increase in competition and an increase in demand for programmes, while the existing broadcasters (both private and public) have been forced to meet the challenge of the newcomers in order to retain their audiences. Moreover, the effects of these changes on the television sector will clearly depend on the financial position of the competing bodies, and, as funding is usually scarce, the impact on programming quality and diversity will soon be felt.

What is equally important is that private media companies, telecommunications operators and PC companies have all taken advantage of the new possibilities that the new media environment has offered. The arrival of digital television has slowly begun to alter the media landscape, even though it has not penetrated all markets as fully and as deeply as its proponents had hoped.

The rapid pace of technological and political change will continue to alter the television landscape, though few are brave enough to predict what those changes are going to be. Television, especially with the development of interactive digital applications, is directed to new forms of communications, perhaps moving towards the delivery of more specific programme material to individual households and away from the more traditional delivery of signals to a mass audience. Such a move – in reality only one amongst many possible future developments – highlights the ways in which the broadcast media will need to tailor their services to a plethora of individual, local, regional, national and international viewers. At the same time, it indicates the ways in which different sources of funding such as subscription and pay-per-view will be exploited, and will influence the nature of broadcasting systems in the future. In fact, technology and economics are driving much of the change, but there is also a social agenda to consider, since the gap between the 'haves' and 'have nots' in the 'pay-per-view society' will widen rather than decrease.

Whilst such changes are likely to have a global impact, that impact will be felt across European countries in many different ways. As this book will try to show, Europe is made up of many different countries, each with particular mixes of media. Nevertheless, some common issues will confront all those who have an interest in the media in Western Europe. Some of these issues are very general but others have a more specific European dimension. These include: the increasing commercialization of the media, the fragmentation of both audiences and advertising expenditure and the reliance on new methods of funding, such as subscriptions and PPV.

Moreover, the trend towards a complex form of cooperation between media, information technology and telecommunications groups in Europe has raised fears of an excessive concentration of ownership. Mergers, acquisitions and common shareholding have created a web of common interests across West European media, though even here the pattern is not uniform. The interest of the European Union (EU) signals a concern with the economic forces behind media and the risks these pose for diversity and pluralism. But the EU has failed to introduce common-ownership regulations for the European media. Nor have governments and politicians managed to tackle the owner-ship issue, since, in the age of television dominance, the electronic media in Europe have become central to the conduct of politics. In the 1990s, European politicians were ready to criticize the media and to threaten them with a law that would place them under a more restrictive legal framework. However, these threats have never been carried out.

Finally, the advent of digital television has forced both governments and the media industry to reconsider the place of public broadcasters in the new media age. As with cable and satellite, each new technology forces old problems to be viewed in the light of new ones.

The structure of this book

This book attempts to describe the issues, dynamics and realities of West European television in the digital age by synthesizing the hard facts. It moves away from normative debates about what the audio-visual scene should be like and presents a detailed account of the contemporary television process, focusing on digital TV and the rise of thematic channels in Europe. An analysis of the ways in which the West European audio-visual landscape has responded to a set of common problems at a European level complements the presenta-tion of financial trends and market fragmentation in operation. How the changes at stake intertwine with domestic forces and markets is analysed in detail. This book first assesses the problems associated with the new market developments in West European television, and then describes what has happened since the mid-1990s in the Euro-pean audio-visual landscape, centring on the development of niche markets, localization and the crisis of demand. The book is organized into two interrelated parts: the first provides an overview of the issues and dynamics of European television at the beginning of the twenty-first century. The second focuses on the new ways television content is delivered to the viewers.

The first chapter discusses the processes and effects of the deregula-tion that took place in European television systems during the 1980s and 1990s. The second chapter looks at the development of the digital television market in Western Europe. This chapter describes the players and the outcomes of the coming television age. It argues that, as in the case of analogue cable and satellite television in the 1980s, the development of digital television, cable, satellite or terrestrial, is associated more with hype than with realistic estimates. However, it predicts that digital television will become reality in the years to come, as the industry is looking at ways to exploit new forms of television transmission, hardware and software.

The third chapter deals with the challenges public broadcasters are facing in a competitive digital television market from a neglected point of view: the future of funding. It reviews existing policy, focusing on the challenges public broadcasters are facing in maintaining their dual funding (advertising and public aid). It deems that public broadcasters face the most difficult challenge of their long history. This is because not only do most of the public policies for the new digital era give preference to the private sector, but also because public broadcasters are not allowed to use their funding mechanisms to enter digital markets strategically.

The fourth chapter explores the changes in the traditional funding of television. It looks at the prospects and the role of advertising, sponsorship and barter in the European television systems, and examines the EU policy to harmonize advertising across Europe. It also looks at the new forms of subscription of television channels, especially PPV, near-video-on-demand (NVOD) and video-on-demand (VOD), as well as the development of pay-TV in Western Europe. It also examines the evolving model of television revenue in the next decade and the issues associated with it. It considers that, even though advertising will remain the main source of revenue, subscription funding or pay-TV will also increase considerably in the first decade of the twenty-first century. However, it concludes that the fragmentation of audiences will complicate matters further.

The fifth chapter discusses the problems associated with the concentration of media ownership at the EU level, and argues that deregulation, while aiming to cement an internationally competitive European industry, has in fact unleashed the pressure for large firms and concentrated power in all European industrial sectors, including mass media. It challenges the view according to which EU or individual governments, on the eve of technological and media convergence, can really control media concentration and media ownership, particularly if their policies favour the development of larger communications groups.

The sixth chapter discusses the prominent role of television and refers to changes in the political domain. This chapter examines the relationship between television and politics. It suggests that the growing indifference of the public towards politics is related more to the decline of politics in a new post-cold-war era than to the dominance of television. It also reviews the role of television in contemporary election campaigning in Europe and the effects of television on politicians. It argues that the rise of a 'modernized' relationship between the media and politics does not seem to be making a positive contribution to the health of democracy.

Chapter 7 introduces changes in television output and focuses on the rise of thematic channels. It presents data showing that television in Europe is becoming a specialist medium. The traditional general-entertainment family television channel model is gradually becoming an endangered species. In fact, none of the European channels that have been planned since the late 1990s aim to follow the traditional format. The chapter describes the arrival of thematic channels in Europe, most of which have come from the USA. It discusses the issue of rationalization or localization as a strategy for commercial viability, showing that in reality there is no channel with an international strategy that has not tailored its content and schedule in order to fit local differences.

Chapter 8 looks at the news channels that have sprung at international and local levels. It notes that the rise of news channels was one of the most significant developments of television journalism in the 1990s but argues that, despite this, the financial rewards involved in newscasting are still limited, since there is more supply than demand for international news channels. On the other hand, it notes that the news channels reconfirm the dominance on the international news front of the large Western operations (agencies and broadcasters), which can restructure, expand and differentiate themselves, and invest heavily in new technologies, new channels and new formats.

Chapter 9 describes the advent of the pay-TV and PPV sports channels in Europe. It examines the inflation of TV sports rights and the association of subscription channels to sport. It also discusses the side effects on both soccer and television, especially the efforts at regulation, the subordination of sports to television and the effects on viewers and TV viewing.

Chapter 10 looks at the ongoing popularity of music channels and the intense competition in music television. There were more than twenty domestic music channels across Europe at the beginning of the twenty-first century and several more were scheduled to be developed as a result of digitalization. This chapter looks at the strategies adopted by the music channels for localization and rationalization and their entry into the Internet age. Chapter 11 focuses on channels targeting children. It notes that the growth of children's channels, again originating from the USA, is adding to the popularity of all children's programmes, but especially animation. On the other hand, US children's channels have to localize their output, if they want to be successful. Thus, there is increased international co-production with local operators and producers. So there are more local children's channels across Europe, while US-originated channels try to establish strong brands and compete with local channels. This chapter describes and discusses the development of children's channels in Europe and their strategies. It also discusses the increased volume of co-productions, especially animation production and the issues of programming and content. Finally, it looks at the entry of children's channels on the Internet and how they use it as a promotional tool for their activities in general.

The final concluding chapter looks at the convergence in the television and Internet industries. It also discusses what the new pay and PPV channels mean for the viewers, and their social implications. It deems that the process started in the 1980s has come to completion at the beginning of the twenty-first century. The European viewer has gone from being silent in the era of state monopoly to being a valuable consumer in the digital era of private oligopolies. But this has led to a new societal cleavage. This chapter argues that only the resistance of citizen viewers can change the plans of large corporations, but that these already dominate the field and classify their viewers according to their purchasing power. This points to a more general argument, with which the book concludes. The development of digital TV has been driven by supply. What seems absent in this new laissez-faire equation is demand. In theory, the viewer seems to remain king, but, in practice, he is still looking for his kingdom.

Part I
The Issues

1
The Effects of Deregulation
An Overview

From the early 1980s, West European broadcasting systems entered a period of rapid change. This period was associated with changes in broadcasting policy as well as a series of technological developments, which, either directly or indirectly, had an influence on policy choices towards television. In reality, there is no simple explanation for the complex processes of change; each and every country dealt with the issues and the pressures for change in different ways. What united them was the sense that the issues and pressures were common to all. These included: uncertainty over the direction of future techno-logical change in respect of the 'new media'; the spiralling costs of programme production and administration at a time of pressure on licence fees; the emerging demand for the liberalization of previous monopolies, particularly in the field of telecommunications; growing political and economic pressure for the reconceptualization of broad-casting as a marketplace rather than as a cultural entity; and concern over the effect of inward and outward investment on broadcast-ing and communications systems (Dyson and Humphreys 1986; McQuail and Siune 1986; De Bens and Knoche 1987; Negrine and Papathanassopoulos 1990; Noam 1991; Thompson 1995).

The changes that have taken place came about as a result of many interconnecting factors. But, as Herbert Schiller (2000: 116–17) has pointed out: 'The banner of capital, in its push toward total social unaccountability, proclaims "deregulation". With deregulation, one sector of the economy after another is "liberated" to capital's unmon-itored authority. The very existence of a reality called the "public interest" is contested. Public functions are weakened or eliminated.'

The aim of this introductory chapter is to explain the processes and effects of the deregulation that took place in European television systems in the 1980s and 1990s. Most of the themes outlined in this chapter are dealt with in some detail in the subsequent chapters of this book.

Deregulating European television

The pressure for change in broadcasting in the 1980s could also be accounted for by the growing interest in, and attraction of, the so-called information technology revolution and the convergence of communications technologies. Different technologies such as satellites, cable and telecommunications systems could no longer be seen as separate technologies, but rather as different parts of an increasingly complex and converging whole. In some cases convergence created new forms of communications, such as PPV, but in other cases the technologies became an interchangeable means of achieving essentially similar objectives. Thus, cable and satellite services could replace terrestrial broadcasting systems and, if nothing else, this meant that the scarcity of terrestrial television could no longer be used as an obsolete justification for maintaining strict state regulation of broadcasting.

The growing convergence of technologies had implications that extended beyond technology (Thompson 1995: 161). First, new technologies necessitated the formulation of policies to manage and exploit them. Secondly, it became obvious that regulatory changes in one sector had a ripple effect on the other sectors: policies towards cable impacted on policies towards, and the structures of, terrestrial broadcasting. Thirdly, pressures to deregulate television (directly or indirectly through the liberalization of new media) ultimately led to the creation of a global market in television. Under a deregulated or liberalized regime, television companies are free to pursue the dictates of the market both domestically and internationally and they too become tradable commodities in themselves. This can often lead to a greater concentration of media power, which, in turn, requires the attention of domestic and international regulators.

In the broadcasting sector, the most obvious manifestation of that change was the transformation of the monopolistic public service broadcasting (PSB) corporations from being sole broadcasters to being only one amongst many in a more competitive broadcasting market. In hard contrast to the approach of US broadcasting, which had been developed within a competitive framework with private, commercially funded companies running the broadcasting services, European countries mostly favoured some form of state control over broadcasting. This not only avoided the chaos in the airwaves that was characteristic of an unregulated system, but also answered the concerns of most European countries relating to the power of broadcasting (see Missika and Wolton 1983; Dyson and Humphreys 1986; McQuail and Siune 1986; Rolland and Ostbye 1986; Sassoon 1986; Humphreys 1990; Negrine and Papathanassopoulos 1990; Noam 1991; Syvertsen 1991; Hofmann-Riem 1992; Mazzoleni 1992; Wolton 1992; Smith 1995; Thompson 1995). Kuhn (1985: 4) has suggested that PSB comprises the following characteristics (see also BRU 1985: 2):

• a universal service available to all irrespective of income or geographical location;
• a commitment to a balanced output and to balanced scheduling across different programme genres;
• a balanced and impartial political output; and
• a degree of financial independence from both governmental and commercial bodies.

In practice, no public broadcaster would claim that it had (always) adhered to all the values that these definitions embrace, although the definitions had often acted as a guide to broadcasting practices. Nonetheless, the models of broadcasting that eventually developed in European countries reflected both individual political, economic and cultural arrangements and attempts to uphold the imprecise 'public interest'. In some instances, only public broadcasting organizations were permitted to operate; in others, private – that is, profit-making – organizations were permitted to participate to varying degrees, but still within a framework established by the state. A diversity of structures was apparent: some of the broadcasting organizations were state owned and/or state controlled, some were publicly funded or funded by the body of users, and some were funded by a combination of public and private (that is, commercial) funds. In spite of their similarities and/or differences, European television systems all confronted a similar set of fundamental and recurring problems in this period. Five problems in particular stand out.

• Problems of how to organize and control the broadcasting system were particularly severe in countries that experienced major political dislocations or a readiness on the part of politicians to interfere in all aspects of broadcasting.
• Pressure to introduce commercial broadcasting services brought problems from about 1950. By the 1970s, with a few exceptions,

most European broadcasting systems had embraced some element of competition, adopting commercial practices in terms of either funding and/or programming.

• Recurring funding problems were particularly relevant for the public service broadcasters, whose funding from the licence fee never quite managed to match the resources of the commercial broadcasters. At the same time, there was often pressure to supplement (or entirely replace) licence funding with advertising revenue.

• Problems arose introducing regional diversity into systems that had been created as monopolistic institutions with monopoly rights to transmit a universal service. Countries with linguistic and cultural differences, e.g. Belgium, created a broadcasting system that served those different communities, but, on the whole, the template for European broadcasting systems was that of a unitary, centralized and universal service.

• Problems arose related to the scarcity of frequencies. These had informed early policies on the creation of broadcasting organizations. Under conditions of scarcity, it had been possible to justify monopolies as 'natural', but, once the scarcity had been eliminated, other justifications needed to be found. Alternatively, the monopolies had to be abandoned.

With the challenge from cable and satellite and the advancement of new ideas about how broadcasting systems could be organized in a different technological era, these problems became more acute. Moreover, new ways of thinking about broadcasting and regulatory frameworks were being developed in the USA (Tunstall and Machin 1999: 5), and pressure from the advocates of the new technologies was to change the face of European broadcasting within a few years (Curran 1986; Tracey 1998: 17). Furthermore, the pace of change meant that the issues and problems had to be confronted whilst the audio-visual landscape was itself changing.

The pace of change in the age of globalization

As we have seen, technology was a necessary condition of the deregulation of the European audio-visual landscape. Deregulation of broadcasting or 'regulatory reform' (Wheeler 1997: 193) suggests the relaxation of the rules governing the state-controlled broadcasting monopoly system. But deregulation is more than the simple removal or relaxation of certain rules and regulations. It is central to the broader neo-liberal strategy for modernizing the economy by privatization and engendering an 'enterprise culture' around the globe. It is also seen as a device to reduce alleged bureaucratic inefficiency and financial profligacy in public enterprises (such as public broadcasting organizations). Deregulation is a response to the imperatives of increasing international competition and the globalization of television markets as well as a political prescription motivated by partisan and commercial interests (Dyson and Humphreys 1990: 231–3). Technological developments such as cable and satellite created further pressure for the deregulation of European broadcasting and, more generally, communications systems as a whole.

One source of the critique for regulatory change came from the academic world (Burgelman 1986; Curran 1986). Another came from the business world, whose favoured solution was to reduce or eliminate regulatory activity and simply let the marketplace dictate the level and the nature of services (see also Veljanovski 1990; Humphreys 1996: 161–4). The idea to reduce or eliminate regulatory activity came from the USA (Tunstall 1986), but proponents of a neo-liberal ideology in Western Europe also articulated such a view. They also pointed out forcefully that consumers would be protected only if they were allowed to make their own choices, according to their needs and requirements, rather than have their choices dictated to them by regulations. In this respect, the attraction of the USA as a point of reference became quite important; it was a model to be copied in the development of new policies (Tunstall and Palmer 1991) and particularly in respect of 'new' media such as cable television (Negrine 1985). By and large, as Wheeler (1997: 192) notes, there was 'A general consensus between politicians, policy makers and the media industry that deregulation would benefit both the national and the international economy . . . [while] the technological revolution meant that major transformations within the distribution of communications were available for business and domestic use.'

This context was not wholly congenial to public broadcasters. First, their position was under attack from within. In 1981, in the then Federal Republic of Germany, the Constitutional Court ruled that 'private broadcasting was constitutional' within a model of 'external pluralism' between competing private channels (Hofmann-Riem 1992). In France in 1982 the government abandoned the state monopoly of broadcasting partly as a way of redressing the weaknesses of the traditional system (Wolton 1992; Kuhn 1995).

Secondly, television penetration had reached saturation point in many countries and consequently funding from the licence fee had levelled off. The politicians could not accept the sorts of amounts desired by the broadcasters since they often feared the electoral consequences of large increases.

Thirdly, broadcasters were also finding it difficult to adapt to the cultural and moral pluralism, which seemed to undermine the traditional idea of a universal service.

Fourthly, governments were becoming aware of what their neighbours were doing, and sometimes benefiting from.

Finally, broadcasters had to contend with the challenge of the new technologies of cable and satellite television. Though analogue cable and satellite television in the 1980s developed more slowly than initially promised, their high profile forced policy-makers to act and broadcasters to respond to the challenge of their control over the airwaves being questioned. Furthermore, the significance of converging technologies for the economic and industrial development of individual countries could neither be overlooked nor ignored. It called for the development and implementation of communications policies and so for a while the focus of broadcasting policy shifted towards much larger industrial questions. Thus, after the mid-1980s broadcasting policies became entwined with more general questions about information technology and the industrial and technological development of countries themselves.

The outcome of change

In these changing circumstances, new commercial broadcasters came into existence. For example, in 2000 the number of channels in Europe exceeded 580 compared to 220 in 1996 and less than 90 in 1989. Moreover, three-quarters of the 580 channels were private. Some took advantage of the new technologies by broadcasting through satellite or cable. Others took advantage of a more liberal approach to broadcasting, which allowed for the development of terrestrial television systems. But all, one way or another, took advantage of the more liberal set of rules that were now governing the audiovisual landscape: rules, for example, that allowed commercial broadcasters to carry just entertainment or merely to broadcast large quantities of imported material. And so what had initially been a fairly closed, state-controlled system characterized by a small number of public broadcasters now became a large competitive environment, and this had a knock-on effect on the nature of the public broadcasters, on funding systems, on cultures, and so on.

The pace of broadcasting deregulation in Europe followed various waves (table 1.1). According to Tunstall and Machin (1999: 190), there were several waves of what they call 'injudicious deregulation', while the main beneficiaries were the US interests:

- The initial wave of injudicious deregulation included Italy, Luxembourg, France and Germany; all four countries had committed themselves to massive deregulation by 1986.
- The second wave (around 1988–92) included Britain and some heavily cabled nations such as the Netherlands and Belgium.
- Next came most of the smaller nations of Scandinavia and the Mediterranean including Sweden, Greece, Portugal and Spain. This wave occurred in the early 1990s.
- The final wave involved a number of newly independent and newly ex-communist nations in eastern and east-central Europe. (Tunstall and Machin 1999: 190)

Table 1.1 The pace of deregulation on European terrestrial television

Country	Year of TV deregulation	Number of available national analogue and digital channels in 1998	Number of terrestrial national channels[a]	
			Public	Private
UK	1954	13	2	3
Italy	1976	10	3	6
Spain	1982	9	2	3
Germany	1984	37	5	9
France	1986	17	3	3
Denmark	1987	17	3	2
Belgium	1988	34	3	2
Greece	1989	9	3	6
Netherlands	1989	33	3	6
Finland	1991	9	2	2
Norway	1991	8	2	3
Portugal	1992	10	2	2
Sweden	1992	14	2	3
Austria	1999	29	2	1

[a] with at least 3% share.

Sources: based on Beardsley et al. (1997); Siune and Hultén, (1998); Idate (2000).

The effects of deregulation

By 2000 some of the effects of television deregulation were already being felt in diverse countries around Western Europe with new commercial players and forces coming into play. But, as noted above, the processes of change and the impact of that change varied from country to country. There are, however, some common effects. These are summarized in turn below.

Effects on programmes

As new channels have developed, there has been an increase in competition and an increase in demand for programmes. In fact, the proliferation of channels has resulted in a sharp increase in the total volume of broadcast hours (Siune and Hultén 1998: 30). Moreover, the cost of content rights has increased, owing both to increased competition and, especially, the aggressive competition policy of pay-TV channels for certain programming content such as films and sports. In macroeconomic terms, the total value of film and programme content acquired by European broadcasters from the USA stood at $2.5 billion in 1995. This represents 30 per cent of all US filmed entertainment sales to Europe, with the remaining 70 per cent coming from cinema and video distribution. Out of the $2.5 billion TV total, $630 million were spent on pay-TV rights, and the remaining $1.87 billion on free-TV rights (Godard 1997: 7). Rights used to be licensed exclusively for a flat fee (that is, unencrypted) and for subscription rights. But the development of PPV services, as we shall see in chapter 4, has given rise to new arrangements, such as non-exclusive rights, revenue sharing and equity stakes. Increased competition has forced free-to-air channels to make volume commitments to Hollywood studios rather than inflate costs. For pay-TV channels, the increase in costs has been evident (Godard 1997: 8–11). Sport differs from other programming. But, as we shall see in chapter 9, TV sports rights have increased dramatically in recent years.

Additionally, European television is entering the multichannel environment with the advent of a plethora of digital channels. But, as the market for thematic channels becomes more competitive, broadcasters, especially international ones, are being forced to adapt to the needs of different local markets (see chapter 7). This is because European viewers prefer to watch domestic channels (be they public or private), and programmes with a local content remain the key to winning large audiences in Europe. For example, locally produced programmes comprised 70 per cent of the top rating successes of 1999, which indicates a continued decline in the number of foreign hit programmes (Mediametrié 2000). Moreover, programmes that cross national and cultural frontiers are increasingly requiring a local flavour to do so. For instance, the Belgian show *FC de Kampionen* was successfully remade as *Clube de Campeos* for the Portuguese audience.

Effects on programming imports

Although the USA remains the world leader in TV-programming exports at the beginning of the twenty-first century, adaptations of American entertainment shows (such as *Wheel of Fortune* or *Jeopardy*) are losing ratings, while game-show formats originating from Europe such as *Who Wants to be a Millionaire?* have made inroads into the North American market for the first time.

Concern over American imports in the light of the deregulation of broadcasting post-1980 was expressed in the context of the 1993 negotiations of the General Agreement on Tariffs and Trade (GATT) Uruguay Round agreement, and especially in respect of the trade in cultural goods and programmes as well its successor the General Agreement of Trade in Services (GATS), which started in 2000 under the general liberalization of online services (Wheeler 2000). As far as many European governments are concerned, this issue cannot be detached from the whole issue of national or political sovereignty and cultural sovereignty (see EIM 1988; Lange and Renaud 1989; Collins 1990). As Tunstall and Machin (1999: 3) note, Europe 'is much the most lucrative export market for US media'. In fact, in the EU, the annual EU trade deficit with the USA in this sector is approaching Euro 7 billion. US productions account for between 60 and 90 per cent of Member States' audio-visual markets (receipts from cinema ticket sales, video cassette sales and rentals, and sales of television fiction programmes), whilst the corresponding European share of the US market is of the order of 1 or 2 per cent. The concern noted above was evident in the conclusions of the working group of the 1998 European audio-visual conference in Birmingham, since European-originated television programming suitable for exploitation in more than one market was rarely made available to potential buyers in sufficiently large volume and in competitively priced packages.

Overall, the export performance of the EU audio-visual creative content industries to third countries has remained disappointingly low since the mid-1980s. In view of this imbalance, in 1993 the EU asked for a 'cultural exemption' – that is, the exclusion of the film and television sector from the trade pact. After many negotiations, both sides agreed in 1993–4 to leave this issue to one side for later negotiation.

However, the fourth report on the implementation of the provisions of the well-known EU Directive *Television without Frontiers* with regard to the broadcasting of European works – the report covers the period 1997 and 1998 – notes that the aims of the Directive have generally been achieved. According to the fourth report, the weighted average for the transmission of European works by the major channels varied between 53.3 and 81.7 per cent, with the exception of Portugal, where the proportion was 43 per cent (CEC 2000). The main German, French and Italian channels broadcast approximately 70 per cent European works. More generally, there was a noticeable increase in the broadcasting of European works during the period 1997–8 compared with the preceding period. With regard to the percentage of independent productions, the vast majority of channels were complying with the provisions of the Directive. However, as Els de Bens (1998: 31) notes, the quota system may be misleading, as all programmes apart from news, sports, games and advertising may be counted, so that, 'practically all channels comply with the norms set by Article 4'. (Article 4 states that the majority of the transmission time of the EU television stations should be fictional programmes of European origin.)

On the other hand, in December 1999 the Commission decided to continue the Media programme for four more years. The new Media programme, called 'Media Plus', was introduced in 2001 and focuses on the transnational circulation of European audio-visual works, within and outside the EU. It reinforces the link between market performance and support mechanisms (that is, training and distribution). It is intended to be flexible enough to provide support for new projects arising from the development of digital technologies. Furthermore it sets out to take greater account of the specific needs of countries with a low audio-visual capacity and/or a limited language market. Media Plus will provide complementary support to national audio-visual support systems and will also be implemented alongside other Community measures such as the Fifth Framework Programme for research (1998–2002) and 'e-Europe' (financing start-ups in the audio-visual sector through risk capital). The budget for the Media Plus programme is Euro 400 million for the period 2001–5.

Commercialization and decline in quality

The effects of competition on programme content can be seen not only with respect to the level of programme imports and the cost of programmes, but also in relation to the quality and range of programmes on offer (see Blumler 1992b; Achile and Miège 1994). Initially there was a reliance on the 'tried and tested', on entertainment, on imports, but the real question is whether that pattern will change as the new broadcasting systems 'mature'. In effect, it seems that, regardless of the differences, there has been a general tendency in European television, especially on commercial channels, to link the costs of programming to TV ratings and advertising revenues, which has led to the marginalization of minority TV genres. Broadly speaking, a television culture led by market forces tends towards the maximization of profit and the minimization of financial risk, resulting in imitation, blandness and the recycling of those genres, themes and approaches regarded as most profitable (McQuail 1998: 119–20; Ouellette and Lewis 2000: 96).

In the search for larger audiences, broadcasters have not refrained from using whatever means they can to increase the popularity of their offerings. Both public and commercial broadcasters are now engaged in fierce competition for revenues and for audiences, since they feel that their very survival is at stake, and this is gradually leading to the possibility of a convergence between the public and the commercial system with respect to their programming output (Pfetsch 1996: 428–9). This is most evident on prime time (de Bens 1998: 27). According to research conducted by Arthur Andersen, European public broadcasters have argued that commercial broadcasters tend to broadcast a high proportion of cheap imported content, particularly in the start-up phase of their activities, and to invest less in original productions (in Davis 1999: 54).

McQuail (1998: 120) has provided the main points to consider when analysing the effects of commercialization and competition on content.

- The absolute and relative share of television time, especially prime time, given to information, education and culture, usually with reference to increased 'entertainment' content.
- The performance of public service television, especially in respect of traditional obligations and degree of convergence on the commercial sector in programming policy.
- Programme diversity.
- Reliance on foreign programmes and on 'second-hand' content.
- Standards of 'quality' with particular reference to sex and violence or creativity and originality.

Violent television programmes, in particular, seemed to increase in most European television systems in the 1990s, especially with the commercialization of broadcasting (Wiio 1995; Carlsson and Feilitzen 1998; Papathanassopoulos 1999b). On the other hand, 'content will be the king' for the development of the new digital channels, since they offer tangibly different content from existing analogue TV output to stimulate and retain consumer interest, and this will require huge investments in programming. This does not mean, however, that the content will be of higher standards. For example, European television drama and comedy production reached record levels in 1999, according to the annual Eurofiction report (*TV International* 2000e), since total new product broadcast in the region's largest five markets rose to 5,193 hours in 1999 from 4,120 in 1996. But cheaper products such as soap operas – for example, *Medico di Famigla* (Italy) and *Cap des Pains* (France) – made for off-peak broadcast times largely fuelled the market growth. Higher-quality content for prime time was decreased. In fact, growth between 1996 and 1999 was rarely for prime time. In 1996, 89 per cent of production was broadcast in prime time against only 77 per cent in 1999 (*TV International* 2000e: 1–2).

Tabloidization of news

One of the effects of the intense competition of commercial television channels has been the proliferation of TV news programmes. Since the late 1980s news programming has undergone a revolution. New methods, new technologies, new companies and new channels have emerged; even old-style broadcasters have re-examined their news output. Competition at the international, regional and local level has mushroomed (see chapter 8), and news output has expanded considerably. All of these developments give the impression that in the era of globalization the world wants news. Whereas viewers once had no option how they received their information, news and current affairs have become a ratings battleground like any other form of programming.

While broadcasters are feeling the pressures of the market, they have nevertheless been slow fully to take on board the necessity of marketing. And news and information services are not exempt: content may take precedence over style, but journalists have to pay more attention than they used to do to the way they present themselves to their audience both on and off the air.

The changing structures and technologies of television have been accompanied by an equally significant change in the very nature of television journalism. In an era of intensive competition, broadcasters have come to realize that news is an important link with their viewers. News and current affairs programmes seem to represent the identity of a channel, much more so than entertainment and sports programmes. In effect, as most TV schedulers agree, news provides a powerful vehicle on which to build TV viewer loyalty.

Since news has become an important, if not distinctive, element of most channels, even for the ratings-driven commercial broadcasters, the main preoccupation of most schedulers is how to sell or to market it to the public. Compared to that of the past, the news of the twenty-first century has much more 'value added': not only do channels inform viewers of the facts; they are also preoccupied in how to sell the information to them. In other words, news has become more valuable than ever. And TV channels pay more attention to news presentation and less to the content of news. Nowadays, not only are popular anchors important, since familiarity is essential in the news programmes, but graphics and visual presentation also play an equally important role.

In effect, the face of European television news is changing fast. International news stories are making way for local coverage and news on politics is gradually giving way to human-interest items (*Television Business International* 1997; Thussu 1998; Paterson 2000; Biltereyst 2001). In an intensively competitive environment, it seems that broadcasters are placing more emphasis on local, human-interest stories. On the other hand, international news becomes important once in a while, either because a big personality is involved as in the death of Princess Diana or because of a big event like a bomb exploding in the centre of a capital. Whereas in the past, and during the era of state monopoly, in most of Europe the main television news bulletin used to be the chief source of information for the average European viewer, nowadays news bulletins and news programmes have become commonplace in most TV schedules.

Bob Franklin (1997: 49) notes that 'journalism has changed radically in recent years'. As he points out (Franklin 1997: 4):

> Journalism's editorial priorities have changed. Entertainment has superseded the provision of information; human interest has supplanted the public interest; measured judgement has succumbed to sensationalism; the trivial has triumphed over the weighty; the intimate relationships of celebrities from soap operas, the world of sport or the royal family are judged more 'newsworthy' than the reporting of significant issues of international consequence. Traditional news values have been undermined by news values; 'infotainment' is rampant.

In the past, the format of the programme was simple and rigid and remained unchanged for many years; nowadays the format changes with almost every television season. In the past, the majority of news was on politics and economy; nowadays there are more police and crime-related stories, as well as sport and consumer stories on the main news bulletins (Papathanassopoulos 1999a; Barnett *et al.* 2000). In the past, there was a regular supply of news on cultural items; nowadays these items hardly appear on the main news TV bulletin. In effect, news on culture and arts has been replaced by news on fashion and medicine. Television news has traditionally been regarded as national in scope, but nowadays most European national TV networks have pushed international news further down their news agenda and have gradually given it an increasingly lower priority.

The 'tabloidization' of TV news or 'infotainment' can be seen as the direct result of the commercialization and deregulation of the broadcasting system, an obsession with TV ratings and pressure from advertisers for larger audiences. 'Tabloidization' itself is not new (McQuail 2000: 106, 339–40). In fact, as Frank Esser (1999: 292) notes: 'It began to appear about one hundred years ago when newspapers started adding sections emphasising sports and entertainment, illustrations and sensations that appealed to wider audiences.'

But tabloidization on European television news is a new phenomenon. This is because, in most European TV systems during the state monopoly, information took priority over entertainment, substance over presentation. The new approach has fewer long stories, and more short ones with pictures; a decrease in news on politics and economics and an increase in news such as scandal, sensation and police or crime stories. For the first time in the history of European TV news, news bulletins seem to look increasingly for 'scandals' and 'political crises' and 'crimes' in their coverage, presumably prompted by extended competition. However, as Kees Brants (1998: 329) notes, the arrival of commercial television may 'have resulted in somewhat more human interest stories and sensationalism, but hardly so in political reporting'.

Even some of the most prestigious TV channels in Europe, such as the BBC and ITV in the UK, appear to give a growing emphasis to the 'sensational, the shallow and the parochial'. As Barnett, Seymour and Gaber (2000: 12) reveal in their research on UK television news 'there has undoubtedly been a shift in most bulletins towards a more tabloid domestic agenda, a decline in political stories'. They conclude (Barnett *et al.* 2000: 13) that 'we are not wholly optimistic that ten years from now television news will have maintained its current balanced and diversified approach'.

There has also been a rise in new television genres, such as 'reality television' and talk shows, in which traditional distinctions between information and entertainment have collapsed. As van Zoonen, Hermes and Brants (1998: 4–5) note:

Journalism in its broadcast but also in its print form has become market driven and guided by – as it is sometimes called – what is interesting rather than what it is important, by an audience orientation rather than an institutional logic. As a result of these developments themes formerly hidden from the public eye have become generally visible; this is clear, for instance, in the obsessive search of contemporary journalism for scandal in the private lives of public officials, or in the incredibly intimate confessions of people appearing in talk shows or in sensationalist reality genre. The once more or less taken for granted social responsibility of journalism has been undermined and a pressing question is whether market logic allows for an ethical journalistic practice.

Effects on financing

The economics of European television have changed dramatically. With more competition in television, advertising revenue has to be shared out amongst even more broadcasters. On the one hand, more competition for programmes increases the costs of programme acquisitions, but, on the other hand, it also increases the power of advertisers to negotiate for better prices and a greater range of audiences. Deregulation has brought with it an enormous increase in television revenues. But building up audience reach and frequency over a greater number of channels risks pushing up overall TV advertising and programming costs. It is not surprising, therefore, to find private broadcasters in Europe challenging public broadcasters for carrying advertising, as we shall see in chapter 3. At the same time, private channels and interests have put pressure on regulatory agencies to relax the framework surrounding television advertising, sponsorship and bartering. It is likely then that in the years to come sponsorship, PPV and subscription will complement conventional advertising revenue (see chapter 4).

Effects on public broadcasters

Public broadcasters have faced erosion of both their viewing share and their revenue; that erosion has been more severe for some than for others. As we shall see in chapter 3, a number of European public broadcasters have responded to the challenge from commercial broadcasters by pursuing commercial opportunities of their own such as co-productions, international sales or joint ventures, within the limits of national and EU regulations. They have also launched new thematic channels and have used their brands to develop a strong presence in the digital era. However, their future will rest in their way of funding. This, in close association with the digital threats, will be the most important issue for European public broadcasters, as we shall discuss in chapter 3.

Effects on media ownership

The deregulation of television has led to the creation of larger and fewer dominant groups and as a result the sector is becoming more concentrated and populated by multimedia-multiconnected conglomerates, as we shall discuss in chapter 5. The trend towards a complex form of cooperation between media and telecommunications groups in Europe has raised fears of excessive concentration of ownership. Mergers, acquisitions and common shareholding, led in most instances by telecommunications groups, have created a web of common interests across the European media, though even here the pattern is not uniform. Although the EU has failed to harmonize ownership regulations for the European media, its interest in this area indicates a concern with the economic forces behind media and the risk these pose for diversity and pluralism. It seems clear that any attempt to tackle the issue of media ownership and concentration at a European level at this stage is unrealistic. The industrial imperatives of the information society and the new opportunities, stakes and interests of the convergence of the media, telecommunications and information society seem not to allow any attempt to harmonize, or even to tackle, the issue of concentration at this stage. As Peter Humphreys (1996: 304) notes: 'There is every sign that oligopolistic developments in the mainstream European industry are the price to be paid for the sector's growth and for the development of new technologies.' Moreover, it seems that the trends towards consolidation and diversification in response to the new opportunities opened up by the liberalization of EU and world markets, and with a view to the opportunities offered by convergence, will go on (Siune 1998: 24). This picture, as we shall discuss in chapter 5, becomes more and more real. In the digital era, as Peter Golding (2000: 179) has noted: 'The growth of vertical integration strategies which this trend represents places the audiovisual sector in a key position, as distribution becomes the next priority for Internet commercialisation.' Certainly, it is more than urgent that Europe needs a kind of re-regulation, especially on ownership status, as well as on the 'relationship between the state and the production and the distribution of information and communication goods and services' (Golding

2000: 180). But, as Herbert Schiller (2000: 126) has pointed out, 'with the deregulation imposed across all continents, the state has a reduced capability to intervene and socially manage the system'.

The rise of 'proximate television'

The deregulation, privatization and commercialization of television have had implications not only nationally but also internationally and locally. Although regional and local television is not new in Europe, deregulation has brought a multiplication of regional and local private channels in most countries. As Moragas Spa and López (2000: 43) note, in contrast to the past, 'What it is observed nowadays in Europe is a panorama of multiple forms and models of stations trying to adapt themselves and give an answer to the existent diversity (cultural, linguistic, political, demographic, geographic).'

Moragas Spa and López (2000: 44–8) give the following classifications:

- regional centres of public corporations (such as the BBC (UK), TVE (Spain), RAI (Italy) and delegations of private broadcasters);
- television companies with their own personality, officially independent, private or public, which operate in a regional reference territory (such as the regional companies of the ITV in the UK or the ARD in Germany or S4C in Wales);
- the television entity of a 'small state' that extends its coverage to one or more regions from a neighbouring country (such as RTL in Luxembourg or TeleMontecarlo in Monaco);
- local television with regional outreach (metropolitan areas) – i.e. local television stations of local–urban character that extend their coverage beyond the strict borders of the urban character in terms of both technical reach and journalistic coverage;
- 'small local television' – i.e. local television channels of local scope, from small and medium cities, even boroughs and small villages.

The advent of regulatory authorities

The deregulation of broadcasting in the 1980s has led to new formalized procedures – for example, the foundation of new regulatory bodies and procedures to license new (mainly commercial) broadcasters and to oversee their behaviour. This has often led to different rules (sometimes stricter, sometimes less strict) being enacted.

In fact, there is a great diversity among these regulatory authorities. Broadcasting regulation usually encompasses the power to license broadcasters, to monitor whether broadcasters are fulfilling their legal obligations, and to impose sanctions if they fail to carry out those obligations. To these traditional functions can be added those of organizing and coordinating the broadcasting landscape. Since 1998 regulatory authorities have started cooperating in order to coordinate their approaches and avoid divergent policies. They also have meetings, at least once a year.

Broadcasting regulation may be exercised by governmental administrative authorities or by courts (for example, for issues regarding the protection of fundamental rights). Moreover, in some countries such as the UK and Germany, public service broadcasting may be subject to a form of self-regulation. However, the most common organizational form in Europe is that of the independent regulatory authority, which is not part of the actual structure of governmental administration and which has apparatus that does not serve any other body. Generally, the rise of independent regulatory authorities coincided with the decline of public service monopolies in the 1980s.

The function, structure and jurisdiction of such authorities vary too. In most countries there are separate regulatory bodies for supervising broadcasting and telecommunications. Some countries, such as Italy with the Autorità per le Garanzie nelle Comunicazioni, have a single regulatory body whose remit encompasses both broadcasting and telecommunications. While most of the regulatory bodies in Europe regulate both the public and private sector (for example, the French Conseil Supérieur de l'Audiovisuel (CSA) or the Dutch Commissariaat voor de Media), others, such as the UK Independent Television Commission (ITC) or the German *Landesmedienanstalten*, are responsible only for the regulation of private broadcasting. In terms of power, three basic categories can be identified: the administration of the broadcasting sector (for example, the award of broadcasting licences), supervision (for example, programme monitoring) and rule making (for example, the imposition of codes of practice). Once again, the range of powers varies considerably. For instance, most authorities have the power to award licences but some can only make recommendations addressed to the ministry responsible for the communications sector. Moreover, there is a great variety regarding their structure. In Germany and Belgium, broadcasting is in the remit of federal states, resulting in a number of regional regulatory bodies. Finally, the number of personnel the European regulatory authorities employ varies too, according to the size of the country and of the national media landscape (from approximately ten for the smallest bodies to over 400 for the biggest) (Robillard 1995; Hoffmann-Riem 1996; Molsky 1999).

The French CSA consists of a board of nine members chosen by the President of the Republic, the Speakers of the Senate and the National Assembly. The CSA employs approximately 400 people and plays a vital role in overseeing the public and commercial broadcasting sector. It controls compliance with broadcasting laws, mission statements and quotas by monitoring television programmes. It manages and allocates frequencies and television licences, and appoints the directors of public broadcasters. It can impose sanctions against broadcasters that violate regulations, imposing fines or even shortening or cancelling their licences. It advises Parliament and other public bodies such as the Culture Ministry or the Competition Council.

In Germany, the twelve regional state media authorities (*Landesmedienanstalten*) are responsible for the licensing and supervision of public and commercial broadcasters. The federal character of the German systems can become a source of conflict, as the federal government is also, for example, signing agreements in audio-visual matters at the EU level.

In Italy, the Autorità per le Garanzie nelle Comunicazioni (Authority for Equal Protection of Communications) was established in July 1997. The Autorità is a fully independent body. It is made up of nine members appointed by the Senate and the Parliament (four members each), while the Prime Minister nominates its chairman. The Autorità has a permanent staff of about 260, and comprises two commissions: one for the infrastructures and networks, the other for products and services. The authority also advises the government on legislative measures related to broadcasting and supervises the sector on the application of the regulatory framework. It also verifies the financial statements and data provided by the broadcasters and monitors compliance with the legislation banning dominant positions in the sector.

In the UK, the ITC is responsible for the regulation of private television and grants licences to private channels, ensures compliance with the legislation and has the power to impose fines or even to revoke the licences. Generally, it oversees the sector to ensure that there is fair competition. Since the 1996 Broadcasting Act, the ITC has also overseen the commercial services provided by the BBC. Moreover, another body, the Broadcasting Standards Commission, investigates complaints about the content of programmes. In October 2000, the UK government published the *Communications White Paper* recommending the creation of a single regulatory authority called the Office of Communications (OFCOM). OFCOM will be responsible for the economic regulation of the whole communications sector, content regulation and spectrum management.

In Austria, the law has set a number of bodies with a regulatory and supervisory role to play in the running and operation of the public broadcaster, Osterreichischer Rundfunk (ORF). In Denmark, a satellite and cable committee, appointed by the Ministry of Culture, supervises cable and satellite television and advises the Ministry on the licensing of broadcasters, while the technical aspects of broadcasting are supervised by a national telecommunications authority. In Finland, the Ministry of Transport and Communications is responsible for the broadcasting sector. Moreover, the Telecommunications Administration Centre supervises compliance with the law and other regulations, with the exception of the ethical principles of advertising, teleshopping and the protection of minors, which are the responsibility of the Consumer Ombudsman.

In Greece, the regulatory body is the Ethniko Symvulio Radioteleorasis (ESR), which was formed in 1989. The political parties select the ESR's members. In theory, it is responsible for the allocation, suspension and cancellation of broadcasting licences and the supervision of the programmes. Its role concerning TV licences is to recommend to the Ministry of the Press and the Media as well as the Ministry of Transport and Communications which candidates are suitable to hold licences. In Ireland, the Independent Radio and Television Authority, a body appointed by the Ministry of Culture to oversee programming and grant licences for private channels, supervises private broadcasting.

In the Netherlands, the Commissariaat voor de Media, set up in 1988, supervises the functioning of broadcasters and compliance with the provisions of the Media Act governing programming and advertising. It deals with both public and private channels as well as cable. It can also impose penalties and fines on those channels that have not followed the legislation. In Portugal, the Alta Autoridade para a Comunicação Social (Higher Authority for Social Communication) has increased its powers with the 1998 law. Thus, it is responsible for granting licences to new operators, both public and private, as well as for programmes.

TV consumption and measurement

As television has become the dominant medium, households across Europe continue to experience the most spectacular growth in product penetration. Television reaches impressive daily penetration rates throughout Europe. However, a more detailed analysis of television consumer habits among viewers points to numerous far-reaching differences. From a general point of view, this is a time of media consumption, where peak times vary considerably. These differences are also to be seen in regard to viewing duration. Southern European countries are well ahead of the rest. It is also worth noting that viewers in France spend 30 per cent more time viewing than Germans. Moreover, Southern Europeans spend more time looking at television than Northern Europeans.

Generally speaking, viewing time rose when audiences were first offered an alternative to the state fare. In 1999 the average daily television viewing time was 199 minutes, much lower compared to North America (236 minutes) and Latin America (220 minutes), but higher compared to the Middle East (196 minutes), Pacific Asia (151 minutes) and Africa (130 minutes) (Mediametrié 2000).

One significant change in the European television household has been the transition from collective family viewing of two or three generalist channels to the situation where individual family members view alone. Moreover, with a much broader range of channels on offer, European viewers have become less loyal to channels as a result of the almost absolute penetration and heavy use of remote controls. Additionally, more and more European TV households now own two or three TV sets.

Although TV viewing time and programme preferences differ throughout Europe, European viewers seem to give preference to sports (especially soccer), news, films (in most cases US films), sitcoms and serial fiction. Moreover, the annual reports of Mediametrié (1996–2000) show that the best performing programmes, such as sports, films and news, have presented a relatively high stability and the same shows have often dominated the rankings.

On the other hand, the expansion of commercial television and intense competition has raised the profile of the audience measurement industry (Syfret 1998). This is because TV ratings are a determining factor in the location of advertising expenditure, programming schedules, purchasing rights and so on. In fact, TV ratings and their 'peoplemeters' (the gadgets on which viewers push a button to state their viewing preferences) have become the 'buzzwords' of the European television industry.

In Europe about 30,000 peoplemeters were installed by 1998; the UK, Belgium, Switzerland and Greece were early adopters of this electronic audience measurement system. As the television industry has needed more accurate figures, most audience research companies have gradually upgraded the peoplemeters and increased their panel sizes (for example, in Belgium, Germany, Austria, Italy and Greece).

The television channels, especially the smaller ones, and advertising agencies have questioned and criticized the data provided by the electronic audience measurement systems. For example, a controversy over the reliability of the television measurement system flared in Greece at the end of 1996. In an era of intense competition and TV revenue stability, audience measurement has become a determining factor for broadcasting.

In the eve of digital television and the new multiplication of channels, audience measurement companies are looking for ways to improve the quality and scope of their figures and are exploring new horizons such as measuring digital packages, new services, and so on. From a political economy perspective, however, one could say that electronic audience measurement represents the logic of commodification, where people ultimately become undifferentiated from products, are standardized by advertising and television companies into interchangeable units of consumption, and are studied and segmented into computerized profile samples, according to tastes, values, attitudes and lifestyles (Gandy 1990; Jhally 1990; Sussman 1999).

The smaller states follow the larger ones

The developments in the audio-visual field cannot easily be followed by the European states that are smaller in terms of power, resources and market size (Burgelman and Pauwels 1992; Meier and Trappel 1992). In fact, they have shown a considerable time lag in terms of the development and implementation of media policy, lack of coherence in implemented policy and poor execution in policy (Traquina 1998). It is argued that the smaller European countries face both external and internal problems in their effort to formulate and implement their broadcasting policies. This is because the globalization of the audio-visual economy and the integrative action of the EU eventually promote the marginalization of both production and culture in smaller countries. Thus, the latter, which have a limited market for their national products – which in turn poses an obstacle for the profitability and survival of their small audio-visual industries – have very limited possibilities to be credible and profitable in a European single market (Burgelman and Pauwels 1992: 171–5). Moreover, the smaller states face internal difficulties that are a consequence of internal structural weakness, resulting in inadequate national policies, with plenty of irrationalities and para-doxes (Burgelman and Pauwels 1992).

In effect, small states have to act and react to new developments in very different conditions from those found in larger states (Meier and Trappel 1992: 129–34). The policies of smaller states have to take into account the policies of larger countries, rather than the other way round. This is because their resources are limited, their market size is small for production and consumption, and their markets do not usually represent a worthwhile target for multinational corporations. As Tunstall and Machin (1999: 247–9) note, the small countries and their media industries have to face, not only the Anglo-American media, but often also the inescapable presence of a larger neigh-bouring country that speaks the same language. According to Tunstall and Machin (1999: 254), despite the tremendous changes since the mid-1980s, 'the smaller countries of Western Europe continue on their traditional paths which emphasise (1) idiosyncratic media na-tionalism; (2) imports of both policies and programming from the Anglo-Americans; and only (3) some modest interest in, and defer-ence towards, the European continent'. The result is that in most cases small states have gained little or nothing from the changes in the European television landscape (Meier and Trappel 1992: 129). On the contrary, they have to follow and implement policies that they do not really need. This can result in extremely negative effects on their industries, such as heavy cross-ownership by local domin-ant groups or a sharp decline in the ratings and advertising revenue of their public broadcasters.

A new deregulation of European television

If deregulation has been the force that weakened public broadcasters, it is also the force that will ensure that commercial channels of the future will have to contend with more competitors (Bughin and Griekspoor 1997: 14). Since the late 1990s, European television has entered a new deregulatory wave, again led by technological develop-ments. The advent of digital television has brought a second wave of deregulation of the already deregulated television environment, re-gardless of the side effects of the first wave in the 1980s. In fact, the number of television channels in Europe doubled every three years between 1985 and 2000 and this trend has not ended yet, because of the arrival of digital transmission. Not only have new channels entered the European television universe, with a number of new channels preparing their launch; television consumption is also expected to increase. Moreover, while the average capacity of European cable networks in the mid-1990s used to be about twenty-seven channels, their capacity in the early years of the twenty-first century is almost unlimited, thanks to digital compression. The result of this new deregulation is that television is moving into an apparently far more competitive and market-driven environment (Graham and Davies 1997).

Additionally, the advent of digital television and the growth of digital television services have raised new regulatory issues and new players. In fact, huge, global telecommunications operators, which can take advantage of the technological convergence, are moving beyond their traditional role as mere carriers to become true multimedia and global conglomerates (Moragas Spa and López 2000: 38). Since content is the king and 'distribution the key to this kingdom' (CEC 1998a), it is easy to understand the telecommunications operators' expanding multimedia strategy.

As in the 1980s, this can also be seen at the EU level. While, in the 1980s, the regulatory concern of the European Union was for a *Television without Frontiers*, in the late 1990s and at the beginning of the twenty-first century it is on the *Convergence of the Media*. Concerns include the conditional access to digital set-top boxes and the need to prevent control over these set-top boxes acting as a bottleneck to the providers of digital television and other services entering the market. Moreover, the EU, with the stated aim of ensuring competition, is striving to regulate the digital services markets, just as it regulated Europe's analogue pay-TV market. It aims to prevent companies from extending existing dominant positions or excluding competitors, and to use competition rules to block the creation of new monopolies (Davis 1999: 81). Whether the new EU policy initiative will be a success remains to be seen.

The full implications of the digitalization of television are still the subject of much speculation, hype and uncertainties. As the history of European television has shown us, the successful development of any new technology and form of television has to do with the content and the perceived value added that they offer to the viewers. In the following chapters of this book, an account of these new dynamics of European television is offered.

2
Going Digital
The Advent of Digital Television in Europe

In the 1980s and 1990s, technological change was viewed as an opportunity to expand the range of services available to viewers. First cable, then satellite, and then digital television – all these technologies constituted a way of promising an increase in range and diversity. As Chalaby and Segell (1999: 352) note: 'Digitization is transforming not only the way we watch television, and the way we use television, but also the way television is made.' Since the mid-1990s reports and articles in the press have predicted a new multiplication of television channels thanks to the advent of digital compression. But has this promise materialized?

This chapter discusses the development of digital television in Western Europe since the mid-1990s and traces the players and the outcomes of the new television revolution. It argues that, as with the case of analogue cable and satellite television in the 1980s, the development of digital television – cable, satellite or terrestrial – has been associated more with hype than with realistic estimates, and, most importantly, has not taken the reaction of the viewers into account.

A new TV revolution

The digital television revolution is based on the compression of signals. By using compression technology, such as Moving Picture Experts Group (MPEG), digitization maximizes the use of bandwidth. This allows more channels to be broadcast in the same bandwidth used for the transmission of a single analogue programme – up to twelve times as many channels can be broadcast in the space that a single analogue channel occupies. Digital compression transmits only the digits that change between one frame and the next, which enables a better use of the available spectrum, while those digits representing repetitive or redundant information are discarded. Superior sound and image can then be broadcast in the space currently transmitting only one analogue programme. Thus, the threat of spectrum scarcity, a characteristic of analogue broadcasting, is receding. Additionally, the MPEG transport system is encrypted, or scrambled, in order to prevent unauthorized access by non-subscribers (Peters 1995; Davis 1999: 7; Papathanassopoulos 1998a; Sankey 1998; Molsky 1999: 13).

Analysts estimate that the cost of transmission is set to fall by about 90 per cent (Davis 1999). In other words, the extra bandwidth created by digital technology will not only reduce the cost of owning or leasing a bandwidth, but will also allow broadcasters to target smaller audiences, including small geographical areas and special interest groups.

In technological terms, digital technology revolutionizes the way that television works on the frequencies, whether cable, satellite or terrestrial. This is because the more efficient use of the frequency spectrum allows the introduction of a number of new television services such as PPV, NVOD, home shopping, home banking and niche channels that were not financially viable in the past (Molsky 1999: 14). Additionally, digital technology allows a certain degree of interactivity, which will make some of the new services more attractive to viewers.

The technological advantage of digital television

Initially, all digital transmissions are received via a digital set-top box, which provides an interface between a domestic TV set and media received from outside the home via cable, satellite or terrestrial delivery methods. Issues surrounding digital set-top box technologies are of interest not only to service providers, but also to equipment suppliers, such as consumer companies and regulators. The digital set-top boxes used in Europe are all quite similar in their specifications. The vast majority are based on the Digital Video Broadcasting Group's standard, DVB MPEG-2. A set-top box contains a telephone or cable modem, flash memory and other features that are necessary to support interactive television and other interactive services. The European Broadcasting Union (EBU) set up the DVB group. In 1997, the initial aim was for DVB to establish international standards for digital broadcasting. By 1998 it had become an industry body that combined representatives from more than 250 member organizations from thirty countries – that is, almost all the relevant industry players. The European Commission (CEC 1999c) in the Cable Directive of 1999 points out that this approach has contributed to the success of European standardization in this field, which is now widely adopted beyond the EU market.

Digital transmission and its interactivity are also related to some other technical but important dimensions that affect the way that television works – in particular, the distribution of content and the use of the TV set. These are electronic programme guides, the multiplex, conditional access and application programme interfaces.

- *Electronic programme guides* (EPGs) are navigational aids similar to browsers in the PC world. EPGs will become increasingly import-ant for users as the number of digital channels increases. In other words, EPGs allow operators to 'guide' viewers through the maze of programmes and services, including moving from one channel to another. In many households across Europe, EPGs will be at the heart of the digital revolution, since their use will be essential but also an enjoyable experience in its own right (Engelbrecht and Engelbrecht 1998). The new generation of EPGs will host new features and will transform the way people use their TV sets. EPGs will offer more sophisticated ways to search programmes, the ability to personalize listings according to taste, and also access to non-broadcast services such as games, shopping and banking. By and large, EPGs will become like an Internet portal (Davies 2000).
- The *multiplex* is the frequency spectrum allocated to operators on which they decide which programmes to carry.
- The *conditional-access* mechanism unscrambles the signal, but is not standardized. This will prevent hackers from developing systems to circumvent the mechanism. Broadcasters need to maintain ·control over their conditional access and prevent competing broad-casters from using the same set-top box. In other words, the owner of the conditional access can decide which pay-TV pro-gramme to encode and provide to viewers. Conditional-access systems are generally incompatible, often forcing viewers to opt for one service only, which restricts their choice. However, the DVB has introduced a common scrambling algorithm, which provides the basis for the conditional-access standards, 'Multicrypt' and 'Simulcrypt'. These make it possible for installed set-top boxes

to decode transmissions from multiple broadcasters, thereby redu-
cing the strategic advantage of being the first broadcaster to market.
- The *application programme interface* (API) is the software platform
  of the set-top box. The API can be either the proprietary system
  of the operators or embedded as an integral part of the other com-
  ponents of the set-top box (Sankey 1998). Early generations of
  decoders did not contain APIs, only simple operating systems. An
  API is, however, an essential prerequisite for offering an EPG. The
  API also plays an essential role in on-demand services and electronic commerce services running on set-top boxes. But, as the
  European Commission notes (CEC 1999c: 22), none of the existing APIs 'is compatible with each other, so applications have to be
  rewritten or possibly converted using a suitable algorithm in future'.

A costly technology

The introduction of digital television is extremely costly, since it
requires a new infrastructure for both operators (transmission equipment, studios, etc.) and consumers (purchase of new TV sets and
set-top boxes). Broadly speaking, four ingredients constitute digital
television:

- attractive, preferably exclusive programming;
- an encryption system and corresponding decoding software in
  set-top boxes;
- a system for sending out decoder cards and subscription bills,
  including creditworthiness checks;
- outlets, whether satellite, cable or terrestrial transmitters.

As noted above, digital television can be transmitted by cable, satellite or terrestrial frequencies. According to Davis (1999: 8–10), each
of them has its advantages and disadvantages.

- *Satellite* is the easiest way to transmit a large number of services and
  thus a wide range of choices, but it is limited by the number of
  homes under the satellite footprint, and further limited by the number of homes with receiving dishes. In fact, digital satellite television requires the installation of a dish, which some consumers
  dislike, even for the analogue satellite television subscribers, who
  also have to buy and install new set-top boxes and satellite aerial.
  Moreover, satellite transmission is also dependent on the weather
  – for example, downtime can result from very rainy weather.

- Digital *terrestrial* television (DTT) is potentially universally available (given appropriate TV sets) because it works with standard TV aerials, but it is more restricted than satellite in terms of its spectrum. The entry, however, of DTT makes the longer-term replacement of analogue terrestrial distribution television technology inevitable. With DTT, a significant incentive will be offered for the mass-market general public to upgrade to digital when the time comes to replace their old TV sets. The replacement cycle of TV sets will be a major driver for the penetration of DTT, since new TV sets will increasingly be capable of receiving DTT broadcasts automatically.
- Digital *cable* is positioned somewhere between digital satellite and terrestrial in terms of the number of channels it can offer. Since, from their beginning, cable systems were designed as multifunctional networks offering their customers television and telephony services, they are better suited to provide interactive applications such as home banking, home shopping and computing, but they require a large investment in broadband fibre-optic cabling.

Since the late 1980s the EU has been pressing to open the cable and telecommunications markets of its member states to competition. In 1999 the Commission adopted a Cable Directive, which requires telecommunications operators to separate their cable television operations in a structurally separate company. This will aid the development of the cable television sector in the EU and will encourage competition and innovation in local telecommunications and high-speed Internet access. The Commission considers this the first step towards the convergence of communications technologies and the introduction of high-speed Internet access and other broadband services over both types of network in the local loop (CEC 1999c).

As we shall see in this chapter, in some countries digital satellite television has had a head start (the UK, France and Spain). In others, such as the Netherlands and Germany, with high cable TV reach, either DTT or digital satellite entry was small, while some other countries (the UK, Sweden and Spain) have started digital television either by satellite, cable or terrestrial frequencies.

The development of digital television in Western Europe

In the early 1990s, it was foreseen that the new digital channels would develop mainly on a pay-TV or PPV basis. It would also revolutionize the economics of television and would allow television companies to raise revenues directly from the viewers, freeing the industry from its traditional dependence on advertising. It would also allow channels with small audiences, incapable of attracting much advertising, to become profitable. In this new scenario, European media groups and producers appeared to be ready and keen to push their way into Europe's TV markets as broadcasters too. In effect, large European media companies announced their plans for digital satellite pay-TV channels. They formed alliances to maximize clout in buying programme rights, to share encryption technology and to spread the financial risk.

It was also predicted that competition would be fiercest in Germany and France. Germany, with its $5.5 billion TV advertising revenue and its thirty-three million homes in 1995, was seen as one of the most valuable markets in Europe. The reason for considering Germany to be the 'powerhouse' of Europe, as far as the television industry is concerned, was simple and obvious. The European market is much too fragmented. Thus, large European media companies that wanted to expand into other markets considered that, if they could 'conquer' the largest market in the EU, they could expand their operations to other markets as well. Therefore, Europe's main media players, such as British Sky Broadcasting (BSkyB), Canal Plus, Bertelsmann, Kirch and Compagnie Luxembourgeoise de Télédiffusion (CLT), entered the 'magic circle' in the mid-1990s by agreeing to merge their activities in the television of the future.

It was assumed not only that the future of television was digital, but also that to be digital was to be better and therefore to be the leader of the market. The whole issue was about being first. What was at stake in Germany was the so-called 'battle of the boxes', the system of decoding the digital satellite channels. It is an unwritten law of media that two delivery systems cannot survive in a single market. Kirch's consortium was backing a system called 'd-box', and Bertelsmann was hoping its 'Media-box' product would dominate the market. The winning system could well be rolled out into all the other European territories. The battle was looking expensive, even before its launch.

In June 1996, media companies became involved in the 'digital rush', but they failed to agree on a common decoder box. What, in effect, they agreed to develop was a so-called common interface, a plug-like connection device that would link digital TV decoder boxes. In April 1996, the French pay-TV service Canal Plus became the first broadcaster in Europe to launch digital TV, Canalsatellite Numérique. In mid-1996, out of the 250–plus satellite transponders being used in broadcast services across Europe in diverse formats,

Table 2.1 Major West European digital television markets (forecasts)

Country	Digital TV homes in 2003 (m)	Penetration of DTV (%)	Digital TV homes in 2005 (m)	Penetration of DTV (%)
Germany	15.1	40	15.7	42
UK	12.3	52	19.5	83
France	6.7	29	10.4	45
Spain	3.6	30	4.9	41
Italy	2.7	13	9.1	44
Overall Western Europe	50.8	33	71.3	47.8

Note: Includes cable, satellite and terrestrial digital television.
Sources: 2003: Jupiter Communications Inc. 2000; 2005: Informa Media Group, in TV International (2001: 5).

seventeen were already transmitting in digital video. In September 1996, CLT and Bertelsmann decided to scrap their digital plans because they thought that free TV would remain the dominant form of television in the medium term. By the end of 1997, there were over 200 digital television channels in Europe, and France accounted for about half of the European total of some two million installed digital set-top boxes. By the end of 2000, the West European total for digital television households was over sixteen million. Forecasts indicate a spectacular growth of the digital market, particularly pay-TV services by the year 2005. For example, according to recent researches, one in three homes in Western Europe will receive digital television by 2003 or approximately one in two homes will receive digital television by 2005 (table 2.1). As other forecasts estimate digital television would emerge as one of Europe's leading interactive platforms alongside mobile phones and PCs.

Past experience, however, has shown that similar forecasts have been way off the mark. Consequently current forecasts may also prove too optimistic. Although the growth of digital television in Europe is faster than in the USA and Japan, the European television sector, as noted in chapter 1, is not only fragmented, but is made up of individual markets with specific particularities. According to IDATE (2000: 22–3), the EU countries differ in terms of analogue TV reception modes, methods of financing the TV sector and the richness of the analogue TV offering. Also according to IDATE (2000: 23), they form two distinct groups:

- countries where the terrestrial reception mode dominates (France, Greece, Italy, Portugal, Spain, UK, Iceland and Finland);
- countries where cable infrastructure is the dominant mode (Sweden, Denmark, Benelux countries, Germany and Austria).

In the following pages we will try to describe the development of digital television in the larger and smaller West European countries in terms of resources and market size at the dawn of the twenty-first century.

Digital television in the larger European countries

The development of digital television in the larger European countries, i.e. France, Germany, Italy, Spain and the UK, saw a lot of hype, strong competition and ambivalent results (see table 2.2).

France

Digital television in France is transmitted mainly through satellite, although in September 1998, following a government initiative, Télédiffusion de France, the national transmission operator, started DTT trials in north-western France. The government wants the terrestrial frequencies to be replaced by digital by 2015 at the latest. One must note, however, that, although 30 per cent of French households subscribe to pay-TV services, only 12 per cent had a satellite dish by the end of 2000. France also has three cable satellite platforms (France Télécom, Lyonnaise Câble and NC Numéricâble), but cable's penetration is small. France is considered the strongest digital market in Europe. The digital satellite television market is shared between three services.

Canalsatellite Numérique was launched in April 1996, owned by pay-TV operator Canal Plus (with a 70 per cent share), French Group Pathé (20 per cent) and US Time Warner (10 per cent). In 1999 the group Vivendi acquired 49 per cent of the shareholding of the company, after purchasing shares from Pathé, the group Richemont and the stockmarket. In January 2000, Groupe Lagardère formed an alliance with Canal Plus, acquiring a 34 per cent stake in Canalsatellite Numérique. In 1998 it had 864,000 subscribers, and by June 2000 it had attracted 1.6 million subscribers.

Télévision Par Satellite (TPS), launched in December 1996 as a joint venture between the public company France Télévision Enter-

Table 2.2 Digital platforms in Western Europe, mid-2000

Country/Region	Number of subscribers	Platform	Date of launch
France			
Canalsatellite Numérique	1,611,000	DTH	1996
Télévision Par Satellite	900,000	DTH	1996
AB Sat	325,000	DTH	1996
Lyonnaise Câble	100,000	CTV	1994
NC Numéricâble	72,815	CTV	1997
TOTAL	3,008,815		
Belgium			
Le Bouquet	31,178	DTH	1999
Canal Digitaal	28,789	DTH	1999
TOTAL	59,967		
Germany			
Premiere World	2,500,000	DTH	1996
ARD Digital	n.a.	DTH	1998
TOTAL	2,500,000		
Italy			
Telepiu/D+	1,143,000	DTH	1998
Stream	580,000	DTH/CTV	1998
TOTAL	1,723,000		
Netherlands			
Canal Plus Digital Nederland	312,637	DTH	1998
TOTAL	312,637		
Scandinavia			
TeleDanmark	38,000	CTV	1998
Telia (Sweden)/ViaSat	293,000	CTV	1999
Sweden PTT	50,000	DTT	1999
Canal Digital (pan-Scandinavian)	328,592	DTH	1998
TOTAL	709,592		
Spain			
Canalsatelite Digital	904,401	DTH	1997
Vía Digital	550,000	DTH	1997
Onda Digital		DTT	1999
TOTAL	1,454,401		
Greece			
Nova	65,000	DTH	1999
TOTAL	65,000		
UK			
BSkyB	4,510,000	DTH	1998
ONdigital	740,000	DTT	1998
TOTAL	5,250,000		

Note: n.a. = not available.
Sources: based on data collected by *Cable and Satellite Europe* (1996); Davis (1999);
Molsky (1999); TV Express (2000b); *TV International* (2000b).

prises (a joint venture of France Télécom and public broadcaster France Télévision) (25 per cent share); the private TV channels TF1 (25 per cent) and M6 (25 per cent), and utility company Suéz Lyonnaise des Eaux (25 per cent). The latter with a 35 per cent stake and CLT-Ufa with 42 per cent are shareholders of M6. In June 2000, TPS had attracted 900,000 subscribers.

AB Sat, launched in December 1996 by Grouppe AB, is the smallest operator. Canalsatellite Numérique is trading on the success of premium movies and sports channels and offers a large number of channels. TPS launched with exclusive digital carriage of the main terrestrial channels that make up its main shareholders – TF1, M6 and France Télévision. It also offers several other new channels, including three film channels (TPS Cinéma), a sports channel (Superfoot), a children's channel (Télétoon) and interactive services (TPS Services). AB Sat has positioned itself as a complementary offering to those of the existing platforms and has created eighteen low-budget niche channels. Strong competition exists between TPS and Canalsatellite Numérique. This has led to a reduction in the cost of subscriptions and increased the value of strategic film and sports rights. The TPS package is considered less expensive than Canalsatellite Numérique, and so reaches a target that is less affluent and more provisional (*TV International* 2000d). Most Hollywood studios have exclusive deals with Canal Plus, but these expire in 2001, while TPS is understood to have non-exclusive agreements. If it can increase its PPV output, TPS will increase its movie channels.

Pay-TV consumers have a broader range of thematic channels and they can choose between different formats (16:9 wide-screen format; PPV); they can also experiment with interactive services. The two platforms increasingly compete through innovative kinds of services, including interactive advertising and home banking via DTV decoders, employing return channel technology.

Germany

Germany has proved to be an extremely difficult market for pay-TV, since the thirty or so free channels have dampened demand for PPV channels. On the other hand, at the beginning of the twenty-first century the penetration of cable TV is high, since 51 per cent of TV households rely on cable and have access to more than thirty channels. Moreover, 37 per cent of households use satellite and only 12 per cent receive their TV signals through the terrestrial frequencies. The telecom operator Deutsche Telekom dominates German cable

television, but after the 1999 decision of the EU is looking for partners. Additionally, the German government plans to switch off analogue by 2010 – assuming that by that time 95 per cent of TV
households are able to receive digital transmissions (Becker 2000).

The Kirch Group, after the failure of its joint project with Deutsche
Telekom and Bertelsmann in 1994 to form the 'Media Service
Gesellschaft' – technical and administrative services for digital tele-
vision (Holznagel and Grünwald 2000) – started its Digitales
Fernsehen 1 (DF1) platform in July 1996 with ambition. BSkyB, 40
per cent owned by News Corporation through its UK subsidiary
News International, was supposed to acquire 49 per cent of the Kirch
Group's DF1, shouldering part of the estimated $300 million start-
up costs. But the take-up for DF1 was disappointing. Instead of the
target of 200,000 subscribers by mid-1997, only 30,000 subscribed.
Moreover, it was estimated that Kirch and BSkyB had to spend up
to $800 million before the service would turn to profit. This situ-
ation apparently made BSkyB withdraw from its digital alliance with
Kirch. In March 1997, the two companies announced that they
would not proceed further.

Kirch's launch projections for DF1 were for three million subscribers by the year 2000. But, despite a heavy marketing campaign,
DF1 failed to meet the projected goals and the Kirch Group faced
pressure from all sides. The shortfall was because Kirch did not have
the projected access to Deutsche Telecom (DT)'s seventeen million
cable homes. Moreover, DT was reluctant to allow DF1 to provide
PPV over its network (Watson 1997). This forced DF1 to abandon
plans to place its decoder box in the homes of cable households,
with a consequent decrease in the price of the decoders, since Kirch
had a commitment to buy one million decoders from NOKIA.

In 1997, Kirch, Bertelsmann (through its television unit CLT Ufa)
and Deutsche Telekom reached a comprehensive agreement for the
adoption of Kirch's 'd-box' as a set-top box for Germany. They also
agreed on the merger of DF1 with Premiere – a competing pay-TV
joint venture, available by both satellite and cable, between Bertelsmann and Canal Plus, and in which Kirch also owned a stake – into
a new joint Premiere digital pay-TV operation. This alliance provoked
many fears amongst their rivals, who considered that Premiere would
be able to secure an overwhelming advantage in the purchase of
sports and film TV rights. The European Commission, the German
Commission for Media Concentration (KEK) and six of the sixteen
federal states in Germany shared these concerns. In October 1997
they blocked the plans of Bertelsmann and Kirch to increase their
stakes in Premiere to 50 per cent each on the grounds that it would

give them unchallenged control over the pay-TV market. In May 1999, the EU, through the Commissioner Mr Van Miert, pointed out that 'the creation of a decoder infrastructure on the basis of a d-box is one of the substantial consequences of the intended merger. The anticipated use of the d-box by Premiere would create a substantial fait accompli' (see Holznagel and Grünwald 2000).

In the meantime, in November 1998, the public broadcaster ARD launched a free digital platform, ARD Digital, via an ASTRA satellite. The platform included the national ARD first channel, ARD1, three special programmes, 1MuXx, 1 Etra and 1 Festival, the eight ARD regional programmes, the two channels co-produced with public broadcaster ZDF, Kinderkanal and Phoenix, and two cultural channels co-produced with ZDF and foreign partners, 3Sat and Arte. A multimedia channel, ARD Online Kanal, completed the offer.

In March 1999, Bertelsmann, through its television unit CLT-Ufa, sold its 45 per cent of Premiere to Kirch for $870 million, raising Kirch's stake to 95 per cent, while CLT-Ufa retained only 5 per cent of the shares in order to ensure a foothold in the German pay-TV market. The restructuring was approved by KEK, and reports were claiming that Kirch was looking to sell part of its 95 per cent stake to a third party.

At the end of 1999, Kirch relaunched its DF1 platform to Premiere World and reapproached Rupert Murdoch, while broadcasters ARD and ZDF reacted against this partnership and filed a complaint with the European Commission. But the Commission authorized (in a decision on 21 March 2000) the participation of BSkyB in KirchPay TV. In the view of the Commission, BSkyB is not likely to enter the pay-TV market in Germany in the short to medium term. On the other hand, the Commission admitted that the operation would have strengthened KirchPay TV's dominant position in the German pay-TV and digital market, making its d-box a standard decoder in Germany for interactive services.

BSkyB's investment in the Kirch Group's pay-TV operations (KirchPayTV GmbH & Co.) was nearly £1 billion. According to the agreement, BSkyB took a 24 per cent stake in KirchPay TV, for DM 2.9 billion (£942 million). Moreover, BSkyB paid £320 million in cash and gave Kirch Group 78 million new BSkyB shares, worth about £622 million. The transaction left Kirch with a 4.3 per cent stake in BSkyB. What is interesting, however, is that, as part of the bargain, BSkyB would get a majority stake in the company after 2001 if it fails to meet targets specified in the agreement. In the meantime, Premiere World added more than half a million new customers, and the number of digital subscribers rose to 1.5 million in 2000. Premiere

World has four multichannel packages: The Movie World package, which comprises eight channels, including the Premiere premium channel; the eight-channel Family World, which includes Disney, Discovery Channel and Planet; the five-channel Sports World; and Extras, with special interest channels.

With respect to DTT, public broadcasters consider it as a means to enhance their distribution and to develop interactive and data services on the new digital frequencies, while commercial channels seem unwilling to spend money to develop it.

Italy

The digital market of Italy is dominated by Telepiu/D+, 98 per cent of which is owned by France's Canal Plus. Italian company Fininvest ceded the 10 per cent share it held in Telepiu/D+, after it had decided not to exercise its option to acquire the stake. The public broadcaster Radio Televisione Italiana (RAI) owns the remaining 2 per cent. RAI has an option to increase its stake by 10 per cent in five years. In June 2000, Telepiu/D+ had attracted approximately 1.1 million subscribers.

A rival digital satellite TV service is provided by Telecom Italia's cable and satellite TV unit Stream (launched in October 1998), which had about 580,000 subscribers in June 2000. Initially, News Corporation Europe controlled Stream with a 35 per cent stake. The other partners of Stream were: Telecom Italia (film producer and distributor as well as the owner of national terrestrial channels TMC and TMC2) (35 per cent), Cecchi Cori (18 per cent) and a newly formed venture set up by Serie A soccer teams (Roma, Lazio, Parma and Fiorentina), Società Diriti Sportivi (12 per cent). In February 2000, News Corporation and Telecom Italia agreed to a capital increase for Stream from L400 billion to L940 billion ($200 million to $471 million). Cecchi Cori sued News Corporation and Telecom Italia, arguing that the change had been made without informing the minor shareholders, but they lost the case. The saga ended in April 2000, with Telecom Italia and News Corporation Europe agreeing to buy out Cecchi Cori's stake. Società Diriti Sportivi also sold its stake. Thus, News Corporation Europe and Telecom Italia each held 50 per cent of Stream. The transaction cost the companies a total of approximately L380 billion ($118 million).

One has to note that, since 1998, both platforms have shown a strong inclination to merge or to collaborate on a single technical platform, since the cost of maintaining two separate platforms is high. In 1998 the EU warned against the establishment of a single, common digital platform, considering that infrastructure competition was feasible in the Italian market. On the other hand, the Italian government was reluctant to see News Corporation invest in Stream. But, after the EU's intervention, the Italian government back-pedalled. In December 1998 News Corporation Europe signed a deal to buy 80 per cent of Stream and again the Italian government called for limitations on ownership of soccer rights (60 per cent), which are considered as the key to pay-TV success in Italy. Eventually, after a new round of negotiations, in April 1999 News Corporation Europe acquired 35 per cent of Stream. The issue of a common digital platform is still on. The two services have agreed to simulcrypt their packages from April 2001, thus making them available to each other's subscriber base. Italy also plans to introduce digital terrestrial television, according to the government by 2006, but this will be associated with the new broadcasting bill, which has been discussed in the Parliament since 1998, while cable is negligible.

Spain

Canalsatelite Digital (CSD) was launched in July 1997, and Vía Digital in September 1997. Both share the digital television market of Spain of only 2.1 million subscribers or 17.5 per cent of Spain's 12 million TV households. CSD is owned by Sogecable (83 per cent) – which in turn is owned by Prisa (19.74 per cent), France's Canal Plus (19.74 per cent), Group March (13.39 per cent), BBVA bank (10.29 per cent), Caja Madrid Bank (3.95 per cent) and Bankinter Bank (3.95 per cent), with the remaining shares, 24.99 per cent, placed on the stockmarket. The rest of the capital of CSD is owned by Warner Bros. (10 per cent), Prisa (4.5 per cent) and Antenna 3 (controlled by Telefónica) (2.5 per cent) (Del Valle 2000). In June 2000, it had attracted 904,000 subscribers.

Vía is owned by the Spanish telecommunications operator Telefónica (48.6 per cent), the Dutch investment fund company Strategic Money Management (SMM) (15.95 per cent), the Mexican company Televisa (10 per cent), the US operator Direct TV (6.9 per cent), the content distributor Media Park (5 per cent), the telecom company Recoletos (5 per cent) and other smaller investors (regional channels, Itochu and others) (3.6 per cent). In June 2000, it had attracted 550,000 subscribers.

The development of digital satellite television in Spain is coloured by strong competition between the two platforms. In 1996 Antonio

Asensio, then president of Antenna 3, started the so-called 'soccer war'. Securing soccer rights – until then shared by Canal Plus and the regional channels – became the essential goal, especially for the launch of PPV channels. At the end of 1996 Prisa – the Spanish media empire containing Canal Plus España, Sogecable and CSD – reached an agreement with Asensio, allowing CSD access to all important football rights for its launch. Then the 'digital war' started. Fearing Prisa would monopolize pay-TV, the Spanish government promoted Vía. The government tried to block CSD's launch by disallowing its decoder by a law, but the European Commission intervened and forced it to amend the law (*Television Business International* 1998: 134).

In 1997, the two digital platforms were embroiled in a price war. Vía was offering its digital platform of forty channels (in 2001 it offers 53 TV channels and forty-six other audio services) free of charge from its launch date 15 September 1997 until 31 December 1997, in an attempt to attract subscribers. Subscribers had only to pay the connection fee of Pta 5,000 (£21) to have access to the offer. CSD retaliated on 19 September 1997 with a new marketing offer. Subscribers to the terrestrial Canal Plus España were able to access the CSD platform (a basic package that included thirty-five channels and forty-three audio services for Pta 1,000 (£4) (Johnson and Tremlett 1997). This offer lasted until August 1998 and included some discounts for other thematic channels. In 1998 the 'digital war' seemed to have come to an end. The two platforms decided to merge on a 50:50 basis and both would share the management. But, in January 1998, Telefónica announced that these merger talks with Sogecable had failed, since they disagreed over the financial assessment of their digital platform, especially on the 1998–2002 pay-TV football rights. The European Commission also raised serious doubts regarding the proposed merger, considering it as an abuse of dominant position. In June 1999 the two rivals signed an agreement to share pay-TV football rights until 2008 and agreed to set up a joint company to market rights over the Internet. At the beginning of 2000 the terrestrial platform Onda (see below) lodged a complaint before the European Commission accusing Vía and CSD of abuse of a dominant position. Onda argued that the soccer deal was breaking competition legislation and asked the European Commission to intervene to open Spanish soccer TV rights to other broadcasters. The European Commission (12 April 2000) decided that the agreement infringed EC competition rules (see chapter 9).

In 1998, both platforms jointly incurred losses of around Pta 28.4 billion (£110.6 million). Regardless of their heavy losses, the market has a strong potential for growth, owing to strong demands for sports programmes and the limited capacity of Spanish free-to-air offerings. CSD is broadcast through the Astra satellite system and Vía through the Spanish, Hispasat, satellite system. The digital satellite TV is to strengthen with the launch of a third Hispasat satellite, 1C.

In June 1999, the Spanish government awarded the first DTT licence to the consortium called Onda Digital (Onda). Its main investors were Retevision (49 per cent), Media Park (15 per cent), several banks (12 per cent), the telecom company Euskatel (15 per cent) and the British company Carlton (7.5 per cent). In November 1999, Onda began broadcasting its platform consisting of fourteen digital channels and five audio channels in Madrid and Barcelona, reaching 2.6 million households – that is, 20 per cent of the Spanish population. In April 2000, Onda was relaunched to Quiero Television and chose Nagravision as its conditional access and, like Vía, Open TV for its interactive services. It also announced that it covered 58 per cent of the Spanish population, with, however, a low subscription rate. In November 2000, the Spanish government granted two new digital terrestrial licences to Veo Television, backed by publishing companies Recoletos and Unedisa, publisher of the newspaper *El Mundo*, and Net TV, which is owned by Prensa Española and others. Each is expected to begin broadcasting by 2002.

Thus, Spain has become the third country in the world to introduce DTT after the UK and Sweden. Some analysts are worried about a possible digital 'war' between DTT and satellite platforms (Davis 1999). Hardware manufacturers, TV operators and even the government called for all digital operators to use a compatible open decoder. The government originally set 2010 as its target for the end of Spain's analogue-to-digital migration for a number of reasons, including the need to renew licences for private TV stations and to allow for new licences to be granted. The date has since been revised to 2012 or 2013.

United Kingdom

On 1 October 1998, BSkyB, 40 per cent of which is owned by News Corporation, started its 140-channel Sky Digital satellite service. It spent £60 million on a marketing campaign to promote the launch. By March 2001, BSkyB had attracted 5.3 million digital subscribers, exceeding market forecasts. Moreover, total revenue in the first quarter of 2001 increased by 20 per cent to £1.8 billion and direct-to-home (DTH) revenues surpassed £1 billion for the first time, growing by 21 per cent to £2.2 billion driven by a 13 per cent increase in the average number of subscribers. In 2000 DTH revenues grew by £28 million to £51 million and cable revenue increased by £19 million (C. Doherty 2000).

A month after the launch, on 15 November 1998, ONdigital, a joint venture of ITV licence-holders, Carlton Communications and Granada, launched the world's first DTT service offering a thirty-channel service including all the free-to-air UK channels as well as pay-TV channels. This service reached 70 per cent of homes in the UK at launch and 90 per cent by the end of 1999. Six multiplex channels were allocated to the UK's DTT service – three to existing terrestrial providers and three to ONdigital. Subscription charges start at £7.99 for a choice of six primary channels. In its first three months, 75 per cent of the company's customers were new to multichannel TV, while the rest had converted from satellite or cable. In December 2000, ONdigital had attracted 1 million subscribers. On 25 April 2001, Carlton and Granada announced plans for a new partnership to align ITV and ONdigital to create an integrated free-to-air, pay-TV and online media platform, which was renamed as ITV Digital. The latter aims to attract 1.7 million subscribers by 2003–4.

Initially the prices for BSkyB's and ONdigital's services were similar. Set-top boxes cost £200 and monthly subscription packages started at under £10. Sky charged only £160 for a set-top box to customers upgrading from its existing analogue service. Both ventures started out by subsidizing the cost of set-top boxes by about 50 per cent, so a viewer interested in receiving only free-to-air programmes had to pay twice as much to buy a set-top box. Premium channels, including the most popular offerings of analogue satellite TV and news services, entailed the payment of separate monthly subscription fees.

The cable TV industry has since mid-1999 started offering digital services. The industry is dominated by three large groups: CWC (the cable division of Cable & Wireless), NTL and Telewest. Either through merger (NTL bought up CWC) or new partnerships (Telewest with Microsoft and Flextech), cable companies plan to offer their customers not only digital television, but also high-speed interactive applications in many areas of the UK.

According to Davis (1999: 21), the UK is the first country to have digital television in three different forms – satellite, cable and terrestrial. The predictions concerning the development of digital television in the UK vary, but most of them agree that it will have a considerable growth before 2010. However, the growth of digital TV in the UK in 1999 was strongly associated with the 'price war' of the set-top boxes between BSkyB and ONdigital. In April 1999, BSkyB announced plans to cut the price of the set-top decoder box needed to receive digital TV on analogue sets by half, from £200 to £99. In May 1999, BSkyB decided to offer new subscribers a free set-top box together with free satellite dishes to receive its digital services on the condition that they signed a one-year contract and paid a one-off £40 installation fee. BSkyB also offered subscribers free Internet access via PCs from June 1999 and a 40 per cent discount on British Telecom phone calls (White 1999c).

ONdigital had no option but to do the same. Initially, it offered free set-top boxes to customers spending £199 on purchases (not necessarily TV equipment) in retail outlets. With the May offer of BSkyB, ONdigital did exactly the same – that is, free set-top boxes to new subscribers. It also promised customers savings of up to 40 per cent on standard British Telecom phone rates from July 1999 and added that it would scrap its £20 connection charge.

On the other hand, BSkyB said that now the customers would have the chance to make a direct comparison between the content and services offered by the two digital providers. The main arm of BSkyB was not the movies, but the exclusive TV rights of the Premier League, which holds up to 2001.

This 'price-cut war' was in fact a major incentive for the development of digital TV in the UK, mainly by making it a low-cost new service. This development also led the UK government, through the then Minister of Culture, Media and Sport, Mr Chris Smith, in October 1999 to consider a switch-off date of analogue between 2006 and 2010. On 11 July 2001 ONdigital was rebanded to ITV Digital, which integrates it fully into the Independent Television (ITV) network.

The development of digital television in the smaller European countries

Smaller European countries and their public and private media companies have attempted to accommodate the developments of digital television. Some have attempted to keep up with the developments of larger European countries; others have adopted a 'wait-and-see' approach.

The Benelux countries

In the Benelux countries (Belgium, the Netherlands and Luxembourg) the development of digital television is strongly associated with cable TV. In fact, in these countries the penetration of cable TV is the highest in Europe (90–95 per cent), and appears to be the primary means of the transmission and distribution of television services. This means that digital television in these countries will come through cable. But, most of the cable systems require substantial upgrading of their infrastructure to provide digital services. The Canal Plus operates digital satellite services in the Benelux countries and the French-speaking Le Bouquet in Belgium, which offered twenty thematic channels to some 30,000 households in mid-2000.

With regard to the penetration of DTT, the high cable development hampers prospects of growth. These are complicated further by the socio-linguistic/cultural divisions. However, analogue switch-off could be achieved quickly, because of the cable factor.

In the Netherlands, there are also some DTT plans by a consortium called Digitenne. Digitenne is formed by the public broadcaster Nederlandse Omroep Stichting (NOS), Canal Plus Nederland, the association of Dutch commercial broadcasters Vestra and the transmitters facility company Nozema. Moreover, the main cable operator Mediakabel, a consortium of eight cable companies, plans to launch a digital cable TV service offering fifteen thematic channels.

Portugal

A government-backed report in 1998, entitled 'The Introduction in Portugal of Digital Terrestrial Television – DVB-T', which dealt with technological matters like the spectrum management, proposed five multiplexes – three to be national services, one for regional broadcasters and one for use at local level. In 2001 the Portuguese authorities selected the Plataforma de Televisão Portuguesa (PTDP) consortium to operate the country's digital terrestrial television platform. DTT services are set to launch in April 2002.

Ireland

The government considers DTT to be the best broadcasting delivery solution for Ireland. Like the Nordic countries, Ireland has a small population spread widely across remote rural areas, making cable or multipoint microwave distribution systems unsuitable. The government aims to license all six available multiplexes to a single operator, Digico, the transmission company owned by the public broadcaster Radio Telefis Éireann (RTÉ).

Scandinavia

Digital television has had a relatively slow start in Scandinavia. Of the region's 10 million TV households, 54 per cent have access to cable and 15 per cent have satellite dishes, while only 100,000 households receive digital television services. In Denmark, the tele-communications operator TeleDanmark launched a digital cable service in 1998, while a call for tender to issue DTT licences is scheduled for 2001, with the public broadcasters having already secured two channels each.

Sweden is the only Scandinavian country where DTT services have already been launched (April 1999), with two regular channels of public broadcasting, SVT and SVT24, while a number of commercial channels have been allocated digital licences. In effect, licences have been awarded to individual channels rather than to multiplex operators, and priority was given to free-to-air channels. Digital satellite television in Scandinavia is operated by Canal Digital–Canal Plus (50 per cent) and Telenor (backed by Modern Times Group's ViaSat).

In Finland the four existing terrestrial national channels introduced DTT services in August 2000. DTT is expected to reach 70 per cent of the country's TV households by the end of 2001. As in Sweden, the licences were awarded to individual free-to-air channels instead of multiplex operators.

Norway is also planning DTT services, through the transmission company Norkring, a unit of the telecommunications company TeleNor, and the country's DTT platform is to be launched in 2002.

Greece

Digital satellite television officially commenced in December 1999, when the Greek government signed the licence for the Nova platform owned by Multichoice Hellas. Digital satellite television in Greece became a reality after about eighteen months of negoti-ations, a new law (2644 of 1998) and hard bargaining.

The fifteen-year contract is the first that the Greek state has signed with a television company. It entails the payment of 0.5 per cent of the company's gross annual profits, to be adjusted every two years. The service provides a wide variety of Greek and international chan-nels as well as interactive services. Each household subscribing to Nova has to pay a subscription of 15,500 drachmas. The cost of the reception equipment (a satellite dish of 60 cm in diameter, access card, decoder and instalment) costs 149,000 drachmas. Multichoice Hellas is a joint venture between Myriad Development (40 per cent stake), Tiletypos (the owner of the private TV station Mega Channel) (40 per cent), Cypriot TV company LTV (18 per cent) and Sun Spot Leisure (2 per cent). By March 2001, Nova had attracted 175,000 subscribers. A second digital satellite platform, Alpha Digital, led by private television company Alpha started operations in October 2001, while the Greek telecom operator OTE announced in September 2000 that it would not be involved as a shareholder in any digital television platform.

The uncertainties of the digital market

As noted above, most forecasts indicate a spectacular growth of the digital television market, particularly of pay-TV services, by 2010 (see Foley 1998; Renaud 1998; BNP Equities 1999). However, experience shows that similar forecasts concerning the respective shares of free-to-air, satellite or cable delivery, or of Internet and digital television, have been way off the mark in the past and that current forecasts may also prove too optimistic. In fact, a number of uncertainties still surround the future of the digital television market. Chalaby and Segel (1999: 352–4) relate the process and impact of the digitization of television to Ulrich Beck's theory on 'risk society', since the digitization of television has considerably increased the sources of uncertainties and the level of risks for the rapidly expanding number of players involved in the field. Let us consider some of these uncertainties:

Financial uncertainties

Economic considerations often seem to be ignored when projections are made regarding the transition to digital. The huge capital costs associated with the launch of digital services not only bring higher prices for programmes but also make people think twice before entering new digital ventures. Some suggest that digital TV is no more risky than the sudden rush to launch free TV in the 1980s. For example, Kirch's DF1 was said to be losing 1 billion DM a year (*European Television Analyst* 1997). In 1999 Telepiu/D+ had losses of L360 billion, and Stream of L458 billion. As noted above, the two Spanish digital satellite platforms incurred enormous losses. France's Canal Plus is believed to have invested around FFr1.5 billion in its digital platform in 1996–2000, while TPS has revealed that losses since its launch over the same period had spiralled to FFr1.8 billion (Bruneau 1999). Britain's BSkyB and ONdigital have heavily subsidized their set-top boxes by giving them free to their potential subscribers.

In fact, Western television industry is not as it used to be in the 1970s and the 1980s, when many private TV channels were launched. The prices paid were not huge, but distributors had an interest in building up competition to the monopoly state broadcaster. Additionally, the current cost of analogue devices, television sets and VCRs is considerable, particularly in what has become a multiset world. These are not necessarily compatible with digital technology, and the cost of acquiring digital compatible services, plus that of subscription services, could prove too high for many households, who may opt for free-to-air digital services only when analogue is finally switched off (Molsky 1999: 23). The new digital services will have to offer tangibly different content to stimulate and retain consumer interest, and this will require large investments in programming. The relatively slow growth in the numbers of subscribers to digital services in Europe since they were launched in 1996 is ascribed mostly to a lack of compelling original and innovative content in many of the new channels they offer.

Market and consumer uncertainties

Where digital services have been introduced into markets with a large number of channels available offered free to air (for example, Germany and Italy), they have failed to attract the viewers and their growth has been slow. This brings us to another uncertainty: viewers are not so willing to subscribe at this stage to pay-TV services, especially when the platforms offer a limited number of interactive services. A significant part of the population may not be willing to pay for subscription-only services. Another part may not be interested in the first place and is quite satisfied with the free-to-air offer. More than this, it appeared that companies have ignored the realities of household economics.

First of all, the potential customers (households) appeared not to be persuaded to take up new ventures, since they not only had to acquire a digital decoder to receive the new channels, but also had to pay a subscription fee. Those who want to pay from only a limited audience share, even for the most wanted programmes such as newly released films, and sports will carry premium charges. For example, in the UK, which is the most advanced market in digital

TV, non-adopters 'are in no particular hurry to go to digital', according to a Consumers Association survey (Digital TV Group 2001).

Secondly, one has also to take into account that the partners in the consumption of audio-visual and multimedia products are changing. In the USA trends indicate that time spent watching television is declining, with more time being spent surfing the Internet or using other multimedia services. Broadcasters are trying to meet this challenge by broadening the scope of their services and expanding their activities into the Internet and multimedia areas. As far as Europe is concerned, market research indicates that consumers may accept digital TV, but their basic viewing habits will not change. They do not want to watch many more channels and will pay for TV services only if that is the only way to get the content they require. Furthermore, consumers are reluctant to make much more use of the interactive facilities of digital TV, preferring instead passive entertainment. The notion of a combined TV/PC is still some years from mass consumer acceptance. Consumers are in principle indifferent as to how they receive their TV signals – provided the content they want is available (Foley 1998).

Thirdly, there is great uncertainty as concerns the platforms the customers should subscribe to, since the set-top boxes remain incompatible. Moreover, the growth of digital satellite, the aggressive launch of digital cable, and ambitious interactive and e-commerce services – primarily on other digital TV platforms – have overshadowed the prospects for DTT. Digital pay-TV operators will have to encourage digital take-up by subsidizing (or giving away) set-top boxes and by moving premium content in their services to stimulate the market. Additionally, technology and services mean that buyers of new decoders or interactive TV sets risk being left with expensive but obsolete products. The cheaper, flexible, risk-free option is to buy a set-top box that can be replaced at minimal cost when upgraded services are introduced. On the other hand, service providers need to build audiences quickly, without waiting for consumers to replace their old TV sets, and are therefore likely to encourage sales of set-top boxes. In fact, differences in standards make interoperability a problem. Sidecars may allow users to access services from more than one platform, but differences in conditional access, APIs and EPGs can lead to compatibility problems (Page 1998). In effect, 'Integrated Digital TV' sets seem to be the best solution, but are being manufactured slowly and are at high prices. Thus, consumers are encouraged to buy set-top boxes, which may be useless later on. This makes consumers think twice, unless, as in the case of BSkyB and ONdigital, they are provided free.

Additionally, as Idate (2000: 14, 84) notes:

- Prices charged by most digital European pay-TV platforms are still relatively high.
- For certain EU countries, the 'innovative nature' of digital TV remains rather difficult to demonstrate. In certain countries, the digital TV offering is seen as a pale derivative of the analogue service; the 'national component' in the digital offering may, in the case of the smaller countries, be non-existent. Many of the apparently new channels are rehashes of existing channels or repeats.

New and old players

Media conglomerates, however, have been scrambling hard to mark out territory and establish a firm foothold as digital content providers. It has been assumed that digital pay-TV will bring about a Darwinian shake-out among Europe's leading media empires. On the other hand, the range of roles that they must undertake in the digital television market dictates that it is extremely unlikely that any one company will be able to fulfil them all, or be willing to bear the risks posed by spiralling development costs. Thus, one observes that the large media groups have tried to form a kind of alliance (although shaky) to overcome the financial risk. In fact, an increasing number of strategic alliances of larger groups have sought to ensure that they form part of the competitive content and service offering. The strategic logic for TV operators to merge or vertically to integrate is clear: the advantage of owning a distribution system means that a TV service provider will have a secure outlet for programmes and/or TV channels (di Piazza 1997). This coupling of media giants is certain to cause new problems in terms of media ownership and concentration. Media groups like News Corporation, Kirch, Canal Plus, Bertelsmann, Vivendi, and so on have most readily sought to occupy the space for new entrepreneurial activity that new technologies have opened up in the audio-visual domain.

News Corporation

In November 1998, the chairman of News Corporation, Rupert Murdoch, announced the formation of News Corporation Europe. The new subsidiary was based in Milan in Italy and it was to investigate and manage media investments in continental Europe. As noted above, after negotiations, News Corporation Europe eventually secured its presence in the Italian TV market in an effort of the parent company to expand in some major activities in Europe according to its global plans. Success in Europe may also compensate to some extent for losses that News Corporation has incurred in Latin America, Australia and the USA, which in 1998 led to an 18 per cent drop in first quarter net profits to £118 million (Davis 1999: 68). News Corporation's formal move to Europe followed earlier contacts that the company had had with Canal Plus in France, with the Kirch Group and with Italy's dominant commercial broadcaster Mediaset, all of which had had no result (Davis 1999: 68).

In effect, News Corporation had been trying to expand into continental Europe for several years to fill a gap in a media empire spanning the USA, the UK, Australia and the Far East. In 1995–6, as noted above, it tried unsuccessfully to form a 'grand digital alliance' in Germany and to buy Kirch's commercial channel Sat 1 – however, it has a 49 per cent in the TV channel Vox and 66 per cent in the Munich TV station TM3. News Corporation also twice tried unsuccessfully, in 1995 and in 1998, to seize control of Mediaset in Italy.

In 1999 there were also preliminary talks between BSkyB and Canal Plus for a possible merger – talks that ranged from a full merger to specific cooperations on TV rights for films and sports. A possible alliance between the two groups sparked a political storm in France (Vulser and Callard 1999). The merger talks eventually stalled over the issue of control, with Canal Plus insisting on having a dominant position in a combined group (Davis 1999: 69). The talks for a possible merger in another form may resume, since, as noted above, the French utilities and communications group Vivendi owns 49 per cent of Canal Plus and 22.7 per cent of BSkyB. Vivendi, which has become a major player of European digital television, aimed to see 'synergies' between the two groups, especially on football and film TV rights. Although, in December 2000, the chairman of Vivendi, Mr Jean-Marie Messier, announced that the company had decided against a long-term alliance with Rupert Murdoch, talks are still on. Finally, as noted above, the new deal between News Corporation and the Kirch Group will certainly strengthen Murdoch's presence in Europe and in Germany.

Canal Plus

Canal Plus has become the leader in European pay-TV. From organic growth and a merger with the Dutch-based NetHold, in

2000–1 it had over ten million subscribers in Belgium, Denmark, Finland, Italy, the Netherlands, Sweden, Spain and Poland. Canal Plus was created in 1984 in France and was the first over-the-air subscription channel in Europe and until 1996, when TPS was announced, the only buyer of pay-TV rights. TPS made clear it was in the market for exclusive pay-TV and PPV rights, and started courting Hollywood and output deals. Canal Plus responded in kind by agreeing a series of long-term deals during the winter 1996–7. By the late 1990s Canal Plus had signed all the major Hollywood studios except Paramount and MGM (Godard 1998). At the end of 1999, Groupe Lagardère, born out of the merger between technology-company Matra and media group Hachette, formed an alliance with Canal Plus. The various deals include the acquisition by Lagardère of a 34 per cent stake in Canalsatellite as well as 27.4 per cent stake in the cable and satellite channels holding company Multithématiques for the sizeable sum of FFr7.3 billion. This deal was presented as a 'global alliance' between the two groups in digital television and interactive services (Bruneau 2000).

Vivendi

As noted above, in 1999 a new player emerged in the digital TV market – the utilities and communications group Vivendi, which owns 24.5 per cent of BSkyB and 49 per cent of Canal Plus. In fact, in January 1999, it purchased a 16.7 per cent stake in BSkyB from Pathé and in July 1999 agreed to pay Pearson and Granada £825 million for their combined stake in BSkyB, making it the second largest shareholder in the British satellite TV operator. Additionally, in 1999 Vivendi became the main shareholder of Canal Plus, buying first the 34 per cent stake of Pathé and later increasing its shares to 49 per cent after a transaction with Swiss-based luxury goods and tobacco group, Richemont. In mid-2000, Vivendi bought up or merged with Seagram, at a cost of $34 billion, creating a new company called Vivendi Universal. The company plans to buy the 51 per cent of Canal Plus it does not already own, except for the domestic pay-TV business, where it is restricted by French law.

Consolidation in the European television business, as we shall see in chapter 5, is changing the landscape, and Vivendi is keen to take advantage. In fact, it has a larger stake in European television than Murdoch. Vivendi aims to merge the two leading pay-TV operators in Europe. This merger is not necessarily to be formal. For Vivendi, synergies and economies of scale could be achieved without a formal merger. It is possible that Canal Plus and BSkyB could instead establish a joint venture to purchase film and sports rights (along the lines of Kirch and Mediaset's venture).

Kirch and Mediaset's Epsilon

On 19 March 1999, after negotiations lasting more than five months, Kirch and the Italian broadcaster Mediaset announced the creation of a pan-European strategic alliance, called Eureka, to coordinate commercial television activities and rights trading. Eureka would operate in the German, Italian and Spanish television markets, which represent more than 50 per cent of continental Europe's television advertising and a potential audience of 200 million viewers (Cappucio 1999). The alliance received formal authorization from the EU in August 1999. In March 2000, it was renamed Epsilon Media Group.

Kirch and Mediaset each owns 13 per cent of Epsilon – estimated at a value of around DM2 billion. In terms of the agreement, Fininvest (Mediaset's parent company, which owns 48.4 per cent of it and which is controlled by Silvio Berlusconi) will buy a 3.19 per cent stake in KirchMedia for $164.3 million and has an option to increase its stake significantly in coming years. Saudi Arabian investor Shaykh Walid Bin Talal Abd al-Aziz will also buy 3.19 per cent of KirchMedia; he already owns 2.3 per cent of Mediaset, while Kirch owns 1.3 per cent and Canal Plus 6.4 per cent. Other main companies include Mediaset, KirchMedia, the Spanish private channel Telecinco (in which Mediaset and Kirch own a 25 per cent share) and Fininvest's Medusa film production arm (Davis 1999: 70). The main areas of activity of this umbrella group include broadcasting, advertising, production, acquisition and distribution of activities throughout Europe via various subsidiaries.

US cable, software and telecommunications companies in the European digital environment

Digital technologies are creating new opportunities for new entrants as well, since the convergence of communications technologies has created a window of opportunity for companies new to the television sector to invest in the field (Chalaby and Segell 1999). But, as mentioned in chapter 1, these new opportunities seem to be mainly for the benefit of the US interests that have taken advantage of the fragmentation of the European markets and of telecommunications operators, which, because of their financial and economic strength, have taken a strong position in the digital television universe. This is also related to the fact that no one leading European media group has emerged to dominate the European digital television landscape.

In other words, this means that Europe is still open to non-European players – mostly US companies, such as Direct TV, the digital satellite TV service owned by Hughes Electronics Corporation, the US telecommunications group NTL and Microsoft. The developments in the European telecommunications sector with the entry of US companies could be seen as indicative of the future of new digital media in Europe. For example, in May 1999, NTL, which is the largest cable operator in the UK, acquired Cablelink, Ireland's largest cable provider. It also announced its first broadband venture in continental Europe by acquiring the 1G networks owned by France Télécom and operated by France Télécom Câble.

The same month, Microsoft announced its intention to buy, with Liberty Media Corporation, a subsidiary of AT&T, almost one-third of the UK's second largest cable company, Telewest Communications, as part of a broader £3.1 billion alliance between Microsoft and US telecommunications operator AT&T. Moreover, Microsoft held talks with Bertelsmann jointly to acquire the cable systems of Deutsche Telekom. It is obvious that Microsoft has an interest in digital television because of its software, both at the cable-head end and more visibly in the digital set-top box. However, on 22 March 2000 the European Commission decided to open a full investigation into the proposed acquisition of Telewest, aiming to have a detailed assessment of the impact of the transaction on competition in various areas of the digital cable industry, especially the UK cable industry.

Additionally, the Netherlands-based cable operator United Pan-European Communications (UPC) – which was formed in 1995 as a 50:50 joint venture between US media investor UnitedGlobalCom, formerly United International Holding, and the Dutch, but nowadays multinational electrical company Philips Electronic – has plans for expansion in European cable systems, such as in France, Scandinavia, Austria, Israel and the Netherlands.

Moreover, the development of digital TV has brought a new wave of players into the broadcasting game: producers and owners of contents rights. Film producers and leading sports-rights owners, such as sporting federations, will be able to sell their content or pay-TV rights at higher prices. The existence of competing services such as Canalsatellite Numérique and TPS in France, CSD and Vía in Spain, and Telepiu and Stream in Italy, or within the German market, is of course a benefit for distributors, pushing prices up. For smaller distributors, making digital pay will also be a case of finding ways to recycle library products and to sell products, new and old, in flexible ways. Often, that will mean the creation of a secondary window between free-to-air and digital/pay channels, and, where competition exists, so much the better. Basically, they are after the same product and they want to push each other out of the marketplace (Westcott 1996; see also chapters 9 and 10 below).

It seems that the development of digital television and the convergence of technologies, as we shall see in chapter 5, are to be coloured by alliances, joint ventures and acquisitions. This is because, as with the development of cable and satellite television in the 1980s, it has been proven that a single although large, group cannot really bear the cost of developing new media. As Chalaby and Segell (1999: 366) note:

> As technology develops, so do risks for producers and uncertainties for investors. As competition increases between market players, so does the unpredictability of the broadcasting field. As the field globalizes and becomes dominated by transnational corporations and international consortia, which have the technological expertise to be competitive and the resources to afford the gamble, national public broadcasters are threatened by decline.

The diffusion scenario of digital television

By the end of the 1980s, it was believed that the 1990s would prove a watershed for TV. During the 1990s it was believed that the whole basis of transmission and viewing would change. In the 1980s, pundits were predicting the cable and satellite revolution. In the 1990s it was called the digital revolution. The argument surprisingly remains the same: new television will offer viewers greater convenience and personalization when they watch television. But, in effect, most of Europe's viewers still turn to the conventional free analogue terrestrial channels and most of the 'grandiose' digital plans are being reconsidered.

In practice, the 'consumer market development scenario' of digital television echoes the theoretical model of 'innovation diffusion' by Rogers (1983). In effect, companies and market research agencies believe that the development of digital television will pass through a series of stages before being widely adopted.

First, most consumers cannot see the point of digital television, but they will become aware of it, often through heavy information and marketing from the mass media.

Secondly, a small group of them, the so-called 'early adopters', will adopt and purchase the set-top boxes and relevant reception equipment and will become very keen on the multichannel environment.

At the third stage, more people will form an 'early majority', who will take an interest in the digital offering and may encourage their friends to do the same. Finally, after most consumers have adopted digital television, a group of 'laggards' or late adopters will be ready to make the change and to purchase digital TV sets as old sets need replacing. In the meantime, more digital services with more channels and interactive services will operate, while gradually the analogue services will cease to operate – by around 2010.

Just as diffusion theory had some unique drawbacks stemming from its application, so the development scenario of digital television has some disadvantages. Both facilitate the adoption of innovations that are sometimes not well understood or even desired by adopters.

An examination of viewing data shows that the most obvious discrepancy is in the level of analogue satellite penetration. Within multichannel homes, the share of viewing going to the new channels is reasonably in line with the expectations of all except the most partisan, but the total viewing figures are dragged down by limited penetration. Moreover, the analogue satellite channels could not increase competition in TV advertising. In effect, they failed to do this.

At first sight, the apparent failure of the satellite channels in total rating terms may appear difficult to explain and commercially disastrous. It was then thought, using as a model the success in France of Canal Plus and in the UK of BSkyB, that subscription might be a realistic option. To make pay-TV more attractive, they thought it would be better to offer 'bouquets of channels' based on digital technology. In other words, the promoters of digital television thought they could make a system profitable if they transported many channels of the current quality with a new transmission system.

What they did not take into account, once again, were the viewers. In hard contrast to the estimates, the number of viewers in Europe did not increase, regardless of the great proliferation of choice. Moreover, most programmes still depend on advertising money, and the average viewer largely continues to watch his or her favourite programmes on terrestrial channels, even when they have new channels available. Additionally, the average viewer does not seem prepared to pay extra for his or her television, as the new trends demonstrate. For example, in the UK, 66 per cent of non-adopters, according to the Consumers' Association, have not even considered switching to digital anyway. Moreover, early adopters to UK digital TV were not necessarily fanatical about watching TV (Landy and

Bridgewater 2001: 96). In other words, as Farrel Corcoran (1999: 67) notes:

> There is the danger, for early adopters especially, that disillusionment may set in as the rhetoric of abundance, pushed hard by the TV industry for so long, is confronted by viewer realization that 'multiplexing' is really synonymous with 'repeats', thus elevating the existing problem of viewer resistance to repeats in analogue to new heights.

This is because 'consumers do not react to a content offer in isolation; they decide whether it is valuable in comparison with alternatives' (Beardsley *et al.* 1997: 70). Viewers do not care whether they receive programmes by digital or analogue or whatever means.

Moreover, it must not be forgotten that in the 1950s there was plenty of time available for viewers to consume the new output. Nowadays, television occupies almost all leisure hours, so the same phenomenon cannot easily be repeated. Instead, the 500–1,000 proposed new digital channels – which need at least a slice of a large audience to be profitable – would target the present television audience. Despite the criticisms, there is no real evidence that the existing, mainly terrestrial channels, have downgraded their programme quality and diversity.

Last but not least, as noted above, the strong competition for set-top boxes and standards has created more confusion amongst viewers as to which delivery platform they should subscribe to. This makes the average consumer sceptical about becoming an adopter of this new innovation.

Summary

Technological developments will certainly change the television landscape, but the pace of this change may be slower than media pundits originally expected. Policy-makers, media pundits and companies should develop or better understand technology and its potential capacities and limitations. In the 1980s, emphasis of the technological characteristics such as cable and satellite television created false impressions, which led to overambitious decisions and a failure to appreciate the impact of the new television services. A similar scenario of hype is unfolding in the case of digital television.

Patrice Flichy (1999: 33) notes that historians of technologies would hardly be surprised to find more failures than success stories in this field. Certainly, there are many 'brakes' and 'accelerators' that are applied to technological innovation (Winston 1998: 11–15). But digital television, whether by satellite, cable or terrestrial, is here to stay and will play a growing role in bringing television to mass audiences around the world. This is because digital television follows the imperatives of the industry, not of the technology itself. Television industry needs to sell new products. New products have a critical mass when they come to replace old but similar products. As television arrived to replace radio, and colour television to replace black and white television, so digital television will replace analogue television. Industry needs to sell new products, and analogue TV hardware has come to the end of its 'life cycle', regardless of the fact that governments and politicians do not yet have 'a clear idea about what digital television as a social phenomenon will become' (Corcoran 1999: 69). The investments made by large corporations are huge and the EU believes that the switch-off of analogue by 2010 will be an 'important development' (CEC 1999c: 17).

3

Public Service Broadcasting in the Digital Age

Public broadcasters continue to dominate the broadcasting market of Western Europe, while their income accounts for a large proportion of the total West European broadcasting market value – 46 per cent in 1997–8. They are, however, going through probably the most important period in their long and distinguished history as a result of fundamental changes to socio-political and media environments as well as to an unprecedented technological development. This is because, on the one hand, the European audio-visual market is expanding tremendously, and, on the other, digital technology will further broaden the choice for viewers. In this situation public service broadcasters face new challenges and threats, since their operating costs are constantly rising while their revenues remain stable.

This chapter describes the challenges public broadcasting faces in an increasingly competitive digital television market. It provides an account of the situation of public broadcasters in Europe at the beginning of the twenty-first century. Then, it explores the two major challenges they are going to face, the fiscal crisis and the threats posed by digital television. Finally, it discusses the role of public broadcasters in the new European television landscape.

The effects of deregulation on public broadcasters

As noted in chapter 1, the position of the public service broadcasters has been challenged because of the deregulation of broadcasting systems as a whole or parts thereof. Since the mid-1980s, public broadcasters have been left behind, tied to providing traditional services whilst facing competitive pressures from private terrestrial broadcasters, cable and satellite delivery and pay-TV operators. At the same time, the adoption of a marketplace philosophy calls into question all those who wish to treat broadcasting as a cultural property with ideals and ambitions. In short, at the beginning of the twenty-first century public broadcasters face two severe threats concerning the future: the first is related to their source of income, and the second to their position in the new television landscape.

The effects on the audience

Public broadcasters have faced a severe stroke in terms of audience and revenues (Avery 1993; Achille and Miège 1994; Traquina 1998). The licence fee remains, in most countries, the primary source of revenue for the public broadcasters and over-dependence on advertising income is often considered a risk for the dynamics and even the very nature of the public service.

Although public channels have suffered, they retain, with a few exceptions, a sizeable share of viewing and advertising. Some European public broadcasters have managed to retain a considerable share of their national audiences. In Austria, Germany, Ireland, the Netherlands, Norway, Sweden and the UK, a combination of public broadcasters has managed to retain approximately 40 per cent of the audience.

But such figures do not entirely correspond to reality. Public channels such as Austria's Osterreichischer Rundfunk (ORF) and Ireland's Radió Telefis Éireann (RTÉ) – private TV came only in 1998 – face non-domestic competition only in the form of satellite service-delivered services or overspill from neighbouring countries. In other countries, public service audiences are spread across a number of national, regional and foreign public channels. In some European markets, individual public channels remain the ratings leaders, even if they do not have a correspondingly large share of the advertising market. In Germany, the public channels (Arbeitsgemeinschaft der Öffentlichrechtlichen Rundfunkanstalten der Bundesrepublik Deutschland (ARD) and Zweites Deutsches Fernsehen (ZDF)) remain the most-watched channels. For example, in 1994 the combined share of the public broadcasters was almost the same as the main private channels, but in the late 1990s their share was 16 per cent higher than the private share. In the UK, loss of TV share for the two channels of the British Broadcasting Corporation (BBC) was negligible (6 per cent). In the Netherlands, the three channels of Nederlandse Omroep Stichting (NOS) have decreased their viewing share in the 1990s. In Belgium, public broadcasters in both regions improved their TV market share in 2000. In Italy, regardless of the attacks by the channels of Silvio Berlusconi, Radio Televisione Italiana (RAI) managed to keep 48 per cent of the ratings in 2000. In France, the combined share of the public channels (France 2 and France 3) has increased since 1992 (about 8 per cent), largely as a result of the bankruptcy of La Cinq in 1992. However, in most cases public channels do not attract the same ratings as before. For example, in Spain, although Radio Televisión Española (RTVE) – TV1 or La Primera – has managed to retain its leadership in the market, its TV share has decreased to 22 per cent, and at the same time its hard competition from private channels has resulted in a significant increase in debts. In Portugal, Radio Televisão Portuguesa (RTP) has also lost a high percentage of its TV share points since the mid-1990s, because of the increased competition from private channels. In some cases, as in Greece, public television's audience has reduced dramatically (table 3.1).

Table 3.1 European public channels' combined audience share in their home markets, 1992–2000 (%)

Country	1992	1994	1996	1998	2000
Austria	72.7	62.3	63.1	50.0	56.5
Belgium, North	34.3	28.9	16.6	32.4	32.0
Belgium, South	18.2	17.0	25.0	18.0	24.5
Denmark	75.0	71.0	27.0	37.5	31.5
Finland	49.0	42.9	45.0	46.0	43.0
France	32.6	39.3	44.9	43.0	40.4
Germany	51.1	42.2	30.3	41.3	41.8
Greece	17.7	10.4	8.3	10.0	11.0
Ireland	63.0	57.0	53.0	52.0	45.6
Italy	46.3	46.5	40.0	48.1	48.1
Netherlands	47.7	43.6	43.6	36.6	37.4
Norway	57.0	48.0	43.7	41.0	41.0
Portugal	91.5	56.7	39.9	37.7	33.8
Spain	45.7	52.5	53.1	34.3	33.1
Sweden	67.0	54.0	49.0	48.0	44.0
Switzerland	28.0	29.0	28.0	34.0	36.1
UK	44.4	43.0	44.0	40.8	38.5

Sources: data based on IP Network (1994); Mediametrié (1995–8); Molsky (1999).

The effects on revenues

With the exception of fully licence-funded public broadcasters (such as the BBC), all European public broadcasters have experienced a decrease in their share of advertising revenue. This has been compounded by the fact that, even for the most successful public channels, the arrival of competition has reduced rates. This has especially hit Spain's RTVE and Portugal's RTP, which are almost entirely reliant on advertising income and public subsidies.

For the public broadcasters dependent on mixed funding, a decline in advertising revenue share has meant an increased reliance on licence fee funding or direct subsidies. In some countries, governments have accordingly granted increases in licence fees or have relaxed rules limiting the amount public broadcasters can raise from advertising. As concerns channels that are still solely reliant on licence fee income, the problems presented by audience erosion are more political than commercial.

Unfortunately, most European public broadcasters have inherited operating costs from the days of monopoly. Broadcasters (such as ARD, ZDF, BBC, France 2, RTVE, RAI) have been forced not only to review a process designed radically to restructure their organizational set-up, but also almost immediately to rationalize their costs, to cut some of their expenses and to make many of their employees redundant.

Funding arrangements of public broadcasters

The two main sources of revenue for public broadcasters are the licence fee and advertising (table 3.2). The total income attributable to public broadcasters in Western Europe totalled $24.2 billion in 1995. Their broadcast income (excluding other income such as publishing revenues) was $21.5 billion from a total television and radio market of $46.5 billion. Germany, the UK, France and Italy dominate in terms of public broadcasting revenues. Combined revenues of these public broadcasters account for 72 per cent of total public broadcasters' revenue in Western Europe. The dependence on the different sources of income varies between public broadcasters and, to a lesser degree, by regions within Europe (Chapman 1996). For example, in France, France 2 and France get 47 per cent and 58.3 per cent of their resources from the licence fee. In Germany, ARD is

Table 3.2 The funding of public broadcasters in the European Union, 2000

Public broadcasters	Way of funding
BBC (United Kingdom)	Licence fee
DR (Denmark)	Licence fee
VTR (Belgium)	Licence fee
YLE (Finland)	Licence fee
STV (Sweden)	Licence fee
ZDF (Germany) Advertising is allowed only after 20.00 and for 20 minutes per day	Licence fee and advertising
ARD (Germany) Advertising is allowed only after 20.00 and for 20 minutes per day	Licence fee and advertising
RTÉ (Ireland)	Licence fee and advertising
NOS (Netherlands)	Part of income tax and advertising
ORF (Austria)	Licence fee and advertising
TV2 (Denmark)	Licence fee and advertising
France Television (France)	Licence fee, public subsidies and advertising
RAI (Italy)	Licence fee and advertising
RTBF (Belgium)	Licence fee and advertising
RTP (Portugal)	State subsidies and advertising
RTVE (Spain)	State subsidies and advertising
ERT (Greece)	Licence fee (charged on the electricity bills) and advertising

Source: based on Oreja (1998).

mainly financed by the licence fee (97.3 per cent), as is ZDF (82 per cent). In Italy, the licence fee provides 53.5 per cent of RAI's total revenues. The licence fee wholly finances the BBC in the UK. In Austria, the licence fee provides 45 per cent of ORF's finances. In Belgium, Vlaamse Radio en Televisie (VTR) – the Flemish public broadcaster – receives 68.8 per cent of its resources from the licence fee, while for Radio Télévision Belge de la Communauté Française (RTBF) 65 per cent comes from the licence fee. In Denmark, Danmark's Radio, and in Sweden, Sveriges Television, are almost entirely financed by the licence fee. In Greece, public funds represent 91.8 per cent of revenues for Elliniki Radiofonia Teleorasis (ERT). In Ireland, the licence fee represents 35 per cent of RTE's revenues. In the Netherlands, NOS was financed by the licence fee, which provided around 70 per cent of its income.

By and large, a television licence exists in most of the EU Member States. Spain, Portugal,[1] Luxembourg and recently the Netherlands,[2] are the exceptions since a licence is not required. The terms of acquiring a licence fee vary from country to country. In some countries, like Belgium, the fee covers both radio and television, but in others, such as Finland, it is needed only for television. In some countries, such as the UK, Denmark and Sweden, the licence fee funds only public broadcasters.

As table 3.2 shows, most European countries have a system of mixed funding, combining revenue from a licence fee and advertising. In France, the public broadcasters are funded by a combination of licence fee, public subsidies and advertising. In some other countries, such as Spain, Portugal and the Netherlands, advertising and public funding or debt fund public broadcasters.

Receipts from the television licence fee increased in all EU Member States where the system was in use in the first half of the 1990s. Among the countries with the fastest growth were Sweden (+69 per cent), Germany (+59 per cent) and the UK (+56 per cent). By and large, the vast majority of Europeans paid an average of $185 in 1997 to their public service broadcasters, although the percentage of households paying varied (see also table 3.3). The income generated from advertising and/or sponsorship varies from country to country. In most countries, income from advertising and sponsorship amounts to several hundred million Euros. But advertising and sponsorship revenue still falls well below the revenue generated from the licence fee. In the 1990s, the total EU's public television income from advertising and sponsorship was about 48 per cent of the size of the total television revenue in the EU from the licence fee.

Threats on funding and the role of the European Union

Regardless of the decline in public broadcasters' revenue from advertising, public broadcasters still generate a significant share in television advertising. It is, therefore, easy to understand why private

---

[1]   In Portugal, the licence fee was abolished in 1991. However, RTP also receives annual state grants. From 1992 to 1995, the amount of the state grants represented about 15–18 per cent of RTP's annual revenues. In Spain, RTVE is financed from commercial sources. State grants represent about 12.9 per cent of RTVE's revenues.
[2]   In July 1999 the Dutch government announced that it would abolish the licence fee from 2000. It has been replaced by a contribution collected as part of income tax.

Table 3.3 The cost of public television across Europe, 1997–1999

Country	Population (m)	Licence fee in 1997 ($)	Licence cost per hour consumed, per person	1999 TV revenues ($m)
Austria	8.1	242	0.18	n.a.
Belgium	10.2	326	0.52	n.a.
Denmark	5.3	322	0.23	214.3
Finland	5.2	169	0.14	208.0
France	58.7	125	0.1	1,799.1
Germany	81.8	193	0.16	3,898.7
Greece	10.5	30	0.06	156.7
Ireland	3.6	100	0.05	212.7
Italy	57.6	91	0.05	2,505.9
Netherlands	15.7	91	0.1	n.a.
Portugal	10.0	n.a.	n.a.	n.a.
Spain	39.4	n.a.	n.a.	604.0
Sweden	8.9	194	0.21	423.4
UK	59.1	167	0.14	3,537.4

Note: n.a. = not available.
Sources: data based on Molsky (1999); Zenith Media (1999); *Cable and Satellite Europe*, (2000: 30).

broadcasters have debated whether their public counterparts should both receive a licence fee and compete for advertising. This debate goes back to 1988, when leading commercial broadcasters such as the French TF1 and Italian Fininvest asked for a breathing space to enable them to establish themselves in the increasingly fierce competition between private and public broadcasters. In effect, they argued that advertising should be the sole domain of private broadcasters. Resolving this issue is one of the most important issues in audio-visual policy.

The 'Protocol of Amsterdam'

Since the mid-1990s, the EU's Competition Directorate has received complaints from private broadcasters about their public rivals, which, they allege, enjoy an unfair competitive advantage, being funded by both public subsidies and advertising revenues. The private channels Spain, France, Germany, Denmark and Italy have complained to the European Commission over the dual funding of their public rivals.

In Amsterdam, on 2 October 1997, the EU Member States signed the well-known 'Protocol of Amsterdam', which is annexed to the EU Treaty of Amsterdam. The Protocol states:

> The provisions of the Treaty establishing the European Community shall be without prejudice to the competence of Member States to provide for the funding of public service broadcasting insofar as such funding is granted to broadcasting organisations for the fulfilment of the public service remit as conferred, defined and organised by each Member State, and insofar as such funding does not affect trading conditions and competition in the Community to an extent which would be contrary to the common interest, while the realisation of the remit of that public service shall be taken into account.

However, the pressures went on. In October 1998, the EU Competition Directorate unveiled a number of proposals suggesting stiff guidelines on European public funding for the television sector. Accordingly, the EU Member States would have to get clearance from the European Commission to grant subsidies to public service television channels.

The issue of public subsidies

Under the guidelines, public aid would be prohibited when subsidies, coupled with advertising revenues, exceed the costs of meeting public service obligations, which include 'information, educational and cultural services as well as programmes with a regional scope or directed at social and ethnic minorities'. The Commission would also be able to oppose the use of public subsidies to acquire broadcasting rights for sporting events and entertainment shows. The participation of public broadcasters in commercial ventures such as thematic channels and digital platforms would be allowed as long as they were not financed by public funds.

The proposed guidelines provoked the anger of both public broadcasters and EU governments, particularly in Germany, which noted that, according to the Amsterdam Treaty, public broadcasting is the sole responsibility of the Member States. The EU governments (20 October 1998) rejected the idea of guidelines on public aid to broadcasters, favouring a case-by-case approach. They also adopted a resolution reaffirming their right to control the remit and financing of public television. Moreover, a Council Resolution of EU Ministers of Culture (November 1998) stated that it is the competency of Member States to cover the financing of public service broadcasting to a degree where such financing is granted to the broadcasting bodies aiming to accomplish a public service mission, as conferred, defined and organized by each member state (*OJEC* 1999c).

In the meantime, the EC Audiovisual Directorate published a report by the 'High Level Group on Audiovisual Policy' headed by the responsible Commissioner, Mr Marcelino Oreja. The members of the Group, amongst their recommendations, identified a number of principles on which the funding of public broadcasting should be based (CEC 1998a).

• The funding of public broadcasting should respect the principle of proportionality, going no further than what is strictly necessary to fulfil the public service and be provided under conditions of complete transparency.
• Public funding should be used solely for fulfilling the public service remit, as defined by each Member State.
• When a public service broadcaster receives funding from sources other than the public sector to carry out its public service remit, and this broadcaster is involved in purely commercial activities – that is, activities that go beyond those defined as part of its public service remit – it must keep separate accounts.
• Public activities should primarily be funded from public sources. Use of advertising should remain secondary.

In a speech given by Commissioner Oreja in Madrid (11 December 1998), he also made clear what the 'Protocol of Amsterdam' meant. He noted that 'the funding of public broadcasting is entirely subject to the rules of competition . . . (and) . . . funding of public television by the member states does not distort competition in the common market to the detriment of the common interest' (Oreja 1998).

The intervention of the European Commission and the European Court of Justice

A little later, on 3 February 1999, the European Commission announced that it had decided to invite the French, Italian and Spanish governments respectively to provide information on the financing schemes in favour of public broadcasters (respectively, France Télévision, RAI, RTVE and the regional channel). The Commission justified its decision by stating that the European Court of Justice required it to obtain such information in cases where the

Commission has doubts as to whether a public measure constitutes existing aid within the meaning of Article 93(1) of the EC Treaty. The Commission noted that it was not opening a formal procedure within the meaning of Article 93(2) of the EC Treaty. In this announcement, the Commission noted that it had received the first complaint on the financing of public broadcasters in 1992, lodged by the Spanish private channels Telecinco and Antena 3. The private broadcasters of France (1993), Italy (1996) and Portugal (1993 and 1997) had subsequently lodged similar complaints. All these complaints alleged breach of the public aid rules through the use of 'dual' funding systems to finance public broadcasters (that is, the use of commercial revenues and public funding in various forms).

The cases the Commission has been investigating since 1999 are:

- in France, a yearly licence fee amounting to some Euro 879 million and other measures (subsidies, capital increases) of some Euro 333 million;
- in Spain, public subsidies amounting to Euro 595 million between 1993 and 1997 in the case of RTVE as well as authorization of excessive debt, debt write off, delays in payments to public entities and tax exemptions, and also public subsidies to regional channels.
- in Italy, a licence fee of Euro 1.3 billion yearly for RAI, tax exemptions, a capital increase in 1992, as well as measures provided by the law (the so-called Salva law).

For the three cases above, the Commission noted in 1999 both that the governments of these countries had not defined the public service remit as clearly as Portugal (see below), and that the calculation of the extra cost of public service provision was very difficult, in particular because none of the three countries' public broadcasters had implemented a separate accounting system. As a consequence, despite a long investigation, the Commission was not able to take a position on this complex matter. In the meantime, the French and Spanish complainants sued the Commission before the European Court of First Instance (CFI) for failure to act in accordance with its obligations.

The Commission also announced that it expected to receive sufficient information to assess whether the financing scheme of public broadcasters should be considered as pre-dating either the signature of the EC Treaty (France and Italy) or the accession to the EU (Spain). Moreover, the Commission stated that it would not assess the compatibility of the aid with the EC Treaty (that is, the proportionality of funding to the cost of public service obligations), but only its nature (that is, whether or not the schemes constitute existing aid). The compatibility of the aid would be assessed only if the Commission established that the measures could not be considered as existing aid.

However, by mid-2001 the Commission had not taken a final decision with regard to the dual funding of public broadcasters. It had done this only in the case of the Portuguese public broadcaster RTP, after the complaints of the private channel Sociedade Independente de Comunicação (SIC) in 1993 and 1996. SIC's complaints concerned the state grants given to RTP and argued that they were distorting competition. In November 1996 the Commission adopted a decision in which it concluded that the state grants to RTP did not constitute state aid within the meaning of Community law. The Commission considered that the amount of state aid was lower than the extra costs incurred by RTP for the fulfilment of its public service obligations. On 3 March 1997, SIC lodged a new complaint before the CFI for the annulment of the Commission's decision. SIC challenged the classification of the measures complained of, and in particular accused the Commission of infringing the procedure for examining state aid by adopting its decision without gathering the observations of RTP's competitors.

Thus, in May 2000, the CFI annulled the Commission's decision, considering that the Commission should have examined in more detail the state's financing of RTP on the grounds that RTP was present in the advertising market and was, therefore, in direct competition with other television operators and thus could get a financial advantage, within the meaning of Community competition law.

How real are the threats on funding?

Most agree that the future of public broadcasting in Europe will depend on a few factors, one of which is the level of financial support (Brants and Siune 1992: 114). It is likely that the dual funding of public broadcasters will be challenged in the future after strong pressures by private broadcasters. This is also related to the fact that the perception of the EU on what constitutes 'compatibility of aid' seems to be unclear.

On the one hand, the European Commission (CEC 1999c: 21) states that it will scrutinize the digital market in order to ensure that public broadcasters' financial involvement in digital pay-TV platforms is not cross-subsidized by the licence fee. On the other hand, recent decisions silently, although on a transparent basis, favour the digital activities of public broadcasters. For example:

- On 24 February 1999, the Commission approved the financing from public revenues of the two German public interest channels Der Kinderkanal and Phoenix, adopting the position that the transfers were compatible with the EC Treaty, since they allowed for public service remits of their public broadcasting.[3]
- On 29 September 1999, the European Commission approved the financing from public resources of BBC News 24. It found that transfer of sources collected from licence fees were compatible with the EC Treaty because they allowed for public service remits for public broadcasting.[4]
- On 12 May 2000, the Commission adopted a decision that granted an exemption from normal antitrust law to the rules of the European Broadcasting Union (EBU) governing the joint acquisition and sharing of broadcasting rights for sports events in the framework of the Eurovision system. The exemption is valid until 2005.

The above decisions lead us to the conclusion that the future of funding of public channels will probably be dependent on the extent to which the larger European public broadcasters justify their status in their countries. In effect, as in most cases, the fate of public broadcasters in Europe will be decided in the larger European countries. As in the past, the smaller countries will follow. But the future of large public broadcasters is not too safe.

In the UK, the Communications White Paper considers that public service broadcasting will continue to play a key role in the digital future, and perhaps will have a more important role than in the past (White Paper 2000: 47–8). At the same time, it envisages that terrestrial operators, such as the ITV, will remain the main commercial

---

[3] In 1997 private competitors filed a complaint against the creation of two public special interest channels in Germany: 'Kinderkanal' (children) and 'Ereignis und Dokumentationskanal Phoenix' (news, current affairs). Both channels are delivered free of advertising. The complainants alleged that financing these channels by licence fees and giving them preferential access to the cable network constituted illegal public aid (IP/99/132, Brussels, 24 Feb. 1999).
[4] In 1997 BSkyB filed a complaint against BBC News 24. The channel is delivered free of advertising and free of charge to cable or satellite operators. It is financed entirely by the licence fee. BSkyB alleged that financing News 24 by licence fees constituted illegal state aid.

providers of public service, with the BBC the main non-commercial provider (p. 47). Although it does not propose to change the BBC's role and remit (p. 54), it suggests that in the run-up to the Charter Review in 2006, the BBC has to demonstrate not only that it continues to reach the vast majority of the audience, but also that it fulfils its public service remit of delivering high-quality, innovative programmes (p. 56). On the other hand, the UK Government in February 2000 rejected the BBC's request for a supplementary £24 digital licence fee, and instead increased the licence fee from April 2000 by £3 (£104 per year). This was significantly less than the £10–£15 increase that some analysts had predicted. The increase in the licence fee will provide the BBC with an extra £200 million a year, but the Corporation had asked for an extra £700 million. The licence fee will be raised by 1.5 per cent a year above inflation for the period 2000–7, which will make it worth £700 million per annum by 2006–7. This arrangement certainly causes problems for the BBC's digital strategy.

In France, new regulations have decreased the amount of advertising time allowing on public channels in 2000. France 2 and France 3 used to carry up to twelve minutes of commercial breaks per hour. As we have seen, 47 per cent of France 2's annual income comes from advertising. With the new law, the government needs heavily to increase the licence fee. But many wonder how easy it will be to do this on the eve of the digital and PPV television era.

In Italy, in 2000 RAI was planning to undergo a major reform, which would partly privatize its holding company (Cappucio 2000). In fact, in 2000 its licence fee quota was reduced for the fourth consecutive year. Most importantly, this cut in resources came at a time when RAI was required to invest more, especially in content rights in the digitizing and converging television market.

In this respect, the case of Portugal is worth noting. The question of how to finance the public broadcaster RTP is becoming an increasingly difficult issue for the Portuguese Government. In 1999 RTP lost more than five percentage points in audience figures, mainly because of the increased competition from private channels. The downward curve seems unstoppable and it makes the case for the public subsidies to the public broadcaster more difficult to justify. On the other hand, it cannot easily return to the licence fee, which was abolished in 1991, while the pressures by the private broadcasters mean that the government cannot easily revoke the limitations on advertising time imposed on RTP1 and the ban imposed on RTP2 (see Traquina 1995 and 1998).

Spain's RTVE is another example. Since it is not funded by a licence fee, RTVE faces serious financial problems. Despite leading the audience ratings, RTVE is burdened with debts. Financed by a combination of advertising (36 per cent) and state subsidy (64 per cent), the broadcaster declared losses in 1998 of around Pta 700 billion (£2.77 billion) (Del Valle 1999b). In an effort to improve its finances, RTVE sold its 17 per cent share in the Vía Digital platform. The government plans to restructure RTVE, but it seems unlikely that it will introduce a licence fee to finance the public broadcaster. On the contrary, limits on advertising time have been proposed for the public channels and privatization of certain RTVE services is being considered (Del Valle 1999b; Molsky 1999: 119).

The above examples show that, when limitations on the licence fee are imposed, it is extremely difficult to revoke them. Nowadays, it seems much more difficult to increase the licence fee in comparison to the past; it is certainly more difficult in comparison to electricity or telephone bills. On the other hand, the licence fee still plays a pivotal role in the financing of public broadcasting in Western Europe. If this is right, a static or falling licence fee in a highly competitive environment means that public broadcasters have either to cut some of their organizational expenses or even to decrease their production costs (including their quality). A static licence fee income is a problem, because costs of talent and broadcasting rights are rising as competition increases. In other words, public broadcasters may become less competitive to their private rivals and might experience a further decrease in their audiences (Molsky 1999). If public broadcasters continue to lose audience share, the licence fee may come under pressure as the main source of funding. If licence fee funding becomes unjustifiable, then public broadcasters will have to turn to advertising. But if advertising by public broadcasters is disputed now, what will the reactions be if advertising takes on a prominent role in their income, especially when advertising revenue for the majority of European public broadcasters, as a share of total income, remained relatively static over the period 1992–5?

Nevertheless, the abolishment of the licence fee is not easy either. In an era in which politicians feel uncomfortable because of the increased power of the media and their owners, it is unlikely that a government will decide to abolish the licence fee. Politicians and the EU publicly support public broadcasters. But political decisions frequently change. It is also often overlooked that the Protocol on public broadcasting annexed to the Amsterdam Treaty is mainly a political decision and public broadcasters continue to function in a hostile neo-liberal environment (see also Collins 1998b: 371).

On the other hand, it is still the prerogative of the Member States to define public service. In effect, most states have not done so and the prevailing policy is imprecise. For example, in France, Italy, Greece, Portugal and the UK the whole output of public broadcasters is designated as 'public service'. In other words, as in many cases, including the 'Television Directive', there is a major difference between what the Commission says and what happens in individual countries. What worries public broadcasters most in many countries is not the EU but the challenges of the digital era.

Digital threats

While in the 1990s European public broadcasters faced major competition from the private terrestrial broadcasters, at the beginning of the twenty-first century, they have to face stronger competition with the arrival of a plethora of digital, terrestrial, cable or satellite channels. This new television revolution will further fragment the audience and decrease public broadcasters' advertising revenue. Digital channels will provide additional competition, because of their capacity to acquire and derive direct benefit from rights to popular programming such as soccer or films. Analysts also believe that in the new digital environment public broadcasters may witness a further decrease in their audiences, which will certainly pose questions about the legitimacy of their licence fee. Therefore, public broadcasting faces its future in the new media environment with scepticism.

In other words, the real challenge for public broadcasters is to evolve public service broadcasting in a way that will allow them to continue to serve though their traditional transmission infrastructure while taking advantage of opportunities in a new media universe. But even in this scenario their moves are rather limited. According to media analyst Norman Molsky (1999: 19–20), the digital age poses a certain number of threats and challenges to public broadcasters.

- The introduction of digital television means *more costs* in the short and medium term as public broadcasters purchase new equipment and continue to operate older equipment, because of their public service remit, until an eventual analogue switch-off. The numerous services launched by private companies, which do not have similar obligations, will further erode the position of public broadcasters, and hit their audience shares and commercial revenues.
- The *growing cost of programmes* is also adversely affecting the public broadcasters' financial position. This is due to the intense competition from private broadcasters. The latter, both free-to-air and pay-TV operators, have managed to secure rights to popular programmes, such as films and sports. The result is that this

competition has driven up programme prices and has forced public broadcasters either to try to outbid them for the remaining programmes – directly affecting the financing and production of other programmes – or to lose these and see their viewing share and advertising revenue drop even lower.

- Public broadcasters *need to allocate considerable amounts of money to convert to digital* (infrastructure investment), whereas most of their spending has previously gone into programming. Moreover, this needs to be done with what are essentially stagnant revenues.

Additionally, investment in digital adventures has proved to be costly for all operators. The difference for public broadcasters in comparison to private media groups is that their income (especially the licence fee) is not only static, but cannot be easily used for digital ventures. Furthermore, since digitalization offers the prospect of hundreds of new channels vying for viewers while, on the demand size, the amount of time people spend watching television has probably peaked, its is uncertain whether the viewers will turn to digital public channels. As Tim Westcott (1999a: 42) notes, on a standard television set, public service broadcasters are usually 'number one on the dial'. In an EPG, they may be relegated to number 100 or 200. He also gives an example from the UK experience: in the UK, Sky's own services have the main slots on the Sky Digital EPG. Sky is using its EPG very much as a promotion guide. It is unlikely, unless there is a public regulation, that public channels would any longer be number one or two in the digital world.

Despite the above, public broadcasters are responding to challenges. Almost all the public broadcasters of Western Europe have adopted digital strategies. France Télévision has directly invested in the digital satellite platform TPS. Spanish RTVE has launched thematic channels since 1997. The Televisión Española (TVE) Temàtica package consists of Canal 24 Horas, Hispavision, Alucine, Cine Paraiso, Canal Classico, Nostalgia and Teledeporte. Similarly, RAI has launched a number of free and pay-TV digital television channels since 1997. The RAISat package consists of free channels RaiSat1-Cultural e spettacolo, RaiSat2-Raggazzi, RaiSat3-Enciclopedia, Rai Sport, Rai News 24, and pay-TV channels for the Telepiu digital platform were launched in 1999. In Germany, ARD launched a free digital platform in 1998, ARD Digital, via an Astra satellite, and co-produces with ZDF the Phoenix and Kinderkanal channels. ZDF has also launched its own digital platform, ZDF Vision. In Denmark, TV2 launched a channel called Zulu in October 2000, targeting the 15–40-year-old viewers and broadcast on the Canal Digital Platform.

In Finland, YLE will run the country's digital terrestrial television sector via a subsidiary called Digita and has outlined plans for the simulcast (analogue and digital) of its public channels (YLE 1 and YLE 2) as well as a news channel (YLE 24) and a cultural and educational channel. In Norway, Norsk Rikskringkasting (NRK) plans to launch digital sports channels in 2002 in collaboration with private broadcaster TV2. The BBC has launched a number of new digital channels that are licence-fee supported and thus free to air, and are also available by cable. These channels are BBC Choice, BBC News 24, BBC Parliament and BBC Knowledge. The British broadcaster also plans to restructure its digital services and add seven more channels to its package.

Public broadcasters can boast a unique combination of competitive advantages when moving into the digital era. For example, they can join forces with other public institutions, such as schools, libraries or museums, to develop a 'digital commons' that would provide universal access for citizens (Murdock 2000: 55). According to Molsky (1999: 21–2), public broadcasters can also rely on a certain number of significant assets.

- Public broadcasters have been around longer than any other service and have developed a 'brand'. As a result, they have often secured a loyal following. In contrast to their private rivals, which are the targets of takeovers and mergers, or constant adjustments, public broadcasters benefit from a degree of stability.
- They offer a broad choice of programming to the widest possible audience. They also produce quality programmes.
- They are generally popular, often commanding the largest audiences in most countries; audiences are often vital to the success of new digital platforms.
- They generally offer a comprehensive service at a very reasonable cost to viewers (for instance 28 pence a day per UK analogue household).

Although these assets may have a positive result for public broadcasters, it is unclear whether they can benefit from them. This is because any time that public broadcasters try to use their assets, and in effect a part of their licence fee, they have to face the scrutiny of the European Commission, if not the European Court of Justice.

For some, the real competitive advantage of public broadcasters is their rich libraries of programme rights, which can be ripe for exploitation through VOD. This might be an answer concerning their future. Public broadcasters not only have at their disposal rich

programme libraries, but also devote much more income to programming than their private rivals. A similar strategy seems to have
been followed by the management of RTVE, after it had sold its
17 per cent stake at Vía Digital. RTVE aims to become a content
provider, a large library of content able to distribute its programming
through different distribution platforms (cable, satellite, terrestrial)
both on a national and an international scale (Del Valle 1999a: 14).

This approach, to an extent, is reminiscent of the one endorsed in
the UK by the Peacock Committee on Financing the BBC. The
Committee suggested a gradual phasing-out of the BBC, to be replaced by the Public Service Broadcasting Council, which would
award grants to producers, especially to those that could not attract
commercial finance. Blumler and Hoffmann-Riem (1992: 205) re-
mind us that this video-publishing model leads gradually to the
marginalization of public broadcasters. Additionally, it is questionable whether this model caters to the public's habits and expectations. Most importantly, even if public channels become simply
production centres, their future is also questionable, since someone
can dispute whether this is their role and remit. It is much easier to
privatize a public production company, such as the Societé Française
de la Production in France, than a public broadcaster.

The role of public broadcasting in the digital multichannel environment

The future of public broadcasters will depend on whether they justify
their legitimacy and whether the political climate will favour them.
In effect, their role will depend on several important factors: individual countries' media legislation, EU legislation and individual
national policies. The speed of introduction of both digital television and the various interactive services will also be important
determinants. However, as Michael Tracey (1998: 16) has stressed,
'public broadcasting is not about technology. It is about an idea,
which happens to employ technology, of how one creates and feeds
a society and its culture.'

Looking at various studies and reports and papers on the future
of public broadcasters, it is often suggested that, if public broadcasters wish to survive, they need to redefine their role (Burgelman
1986; Blumler 1992a; Weymouth and Lamizet 1996; Collins 1998;
Raboy 1998; Syvertsen 1999: 17–18). This means that the principles
justifying the role of the public service broadcasting are already
passé or 'designed for another age' (Biggam 2000: 21). If this is so,

public broadcasters certainly need to think about their future role in the new media and political ideological environments (Syvertsen 1999: 17–18). But, as Rowland and Tracey (1998: 29) have noted: 'Once sold, the soul of public service broadcasting may never be recovered. In their efforts to survive, many public broadcasters seem all too willing to abandon their public service commitments. These institutions appear to be evolving internally in ways that will not redefine public service ideals but destroy them.' This *convergence hypothesis*, as Siune and Hultén (1998: 29) note, may not be supported by empirical evidence. But neither is the other extreme, the so-called *divergence hypothesis* (that is, that public channels emphasized different content segments, such as programmes not offered by their private rivals), a solution for public broadcasters (see also Pfetsch 1996: 433–6). Achille and Miège (1994: 34) add one more strategy: the strategy of partial confrontation, where one of the public channels moves in the direction of increased commercialization, while the other adopts a strategy of confrontation.

In the convergence case, public broadcasters might increase their audience share but at the same time increase their production costs, and it would barely be possible to differentiate them from their private rivals. Thus, the question arises, what is the reason for their survival if they have become like the commercial channels. As John Keane (1995: 7) has pointed out, 'the combined effect of these corseting effects is to decrease the legitimacy of public service media'.

At the other extreme, the divergence hypothesis, public broadcasters might offer programmes of quality or programmes that their private rivals would not even dare to consider broadcasting because of their apparent low appeal. In this case, their TV market share might even decrease further. As a result, they would face new challenges either to increase or even to justify their licence fee. Achille and Miège (1994: 41) note that these strategies are particularly damaging, because public broadcasters would have distanced themselves from their public service mission, but without improving their position in the market.

By and large, public broadcasters were established to cater for the mass public. On the other hand, the digital era has heralded the end of the mass audience and thus public broadcasters face the most severe challenge in their long and distinguished history. A solution for public broadcasters might be to pay more attention to catering for the neglected minority interests. In this case, however, a major redefinition of their remit would be necessary, which in the long term would not guarantee the universality of the licence fee. Moreover, most of the new channels are expected to cover niche markets or segments of the audience. In other words, the new (or existing) private niche channels would obviously compete with any such new 'approach' of public broadcasters.

In the USA, the major challengers of the public broadcasting system are not the networks but rather the specialized channels on history, documentary, news, sports and entertainment, and even the weather. As Blumler and Hoffmann-Riem (1992: 205) note, 'the USA model of public television of filling whatever gaps are felt untended by private broadcasters, appears a recipe for marginalization and cultivation of an elitist system'. But it is the political climate that will determine their fate, as this was the case of their monopoly status in their beginning. Chalaby and Segell (1999: 364) note that public service broadcasting 'will indeed need all the support it can get from committed civil society, leaders, politicians and academics'. But the political climate of the early twenty-first century is not the same as it was in previous decades. European and national political actors still in principle and rhetorically, as Siune and Hultén (1998: 31) note, support the principles of public broadcasting and the financial status of the public broadcasters – see, for example, the EU resolution of 25 January 1999. But most of their policies indicate the opposite. As a result, public broadcasters have faced increased scrutiny regarding the financing of their operations. In effect, since the mid-1980s, the mainstream policy in Western Europe has been the gradual withdrawal of the public sector from the communications and broadcasting field (see also Garnham 1990).

The EU Green Paper on the *Convergence of the Telecommunications, Media and Information Technology Sectors* notes that traditional public broadcasters need to reappraise their role in the convergent environment and 'the regulatory framework should allow broadcasters to take advantage of these new opportunities' (CEC 1997d: 13). At the same time, it makes clear that, 'if public funds intended to support a public broadcaster in fulfilling its public service mission were used to leverage and cross-subsidize these new activities or the use of new technological platforms, such as the Internet, then such practices should be subject to the Treaty rules on competition and on the freedom to provide services' (CEC 1997d: 29). In their reply to the Green Paper, many public broadcasters stated that their public service mission would continue to require both specific funding mechanisms as well as other regulatory measures to enable them to meet their obligations (CEC 1998b). But the private channels also expressed concerns about the potential distortion of the marketplace resulting from the benefits enjoyed by public broadcasters and called for greater transparency to ensure that their commercial activities were not being unfairly cross-subsidized. Once again it is overlooked, probably on purpose, that, if public broadcasters are restricted to their traditional services without being allowed to devise new outlets for the digital environment, they will be marginalized in the new media landscape.

It becomes clear that in an era of cost effectiveness and the abandonment of the welfare state in which public broadcasting is regarded as an integral part, the future of public broadcasters seems uncertain. If one looks at the various documents, reports, studies and speeches by the EU Commissioners on the information society and convergence, one can see that the main emphasis is not on the survival of the public broadcasters. Instead the emphasis is on the future role of public regulation and the relevant regulatory bodies. In his address to the Spanish parliamentary subcommittee on Spanish public television, Commissioner Oreja noted that 'we must not forget that public service broadcasting activities can be carried out by either public or *private companies*' (emphasis added). On this policy shift, Marc Raboy (1998: 171) points out:

> more and more, public authorities are looking towards the capacity of national broadcasting systems *as a whole* to meet public interests goals and objectives. In a very near future we are going to see a lot more attention being paid to the global ecology of broadcasting as a public service environment . . . in this environment, it is going to be increasingly difficult to distinguish clearly between the conventional categories of 'public' and 'private' broadcasters.

One could also add that stronger regulatory authorities may be a positive step, but the concept of public service broadcasting cannot be left to numbers and regulations. The problem, as with the EU's 'programme quotas', is that, if the authorities require original productions, there are many ways of making such productions cheap in cost and low in quality. This is why, one could argue, a framework of rules for commercial bodies to act as public service broadcasters, as suggests the UK Communications White Paper (2000), will not work. The European experience provides us with a lot of examples. The issue, thus, is not whether private broadcasters can or cannot fulfil their remit. Even if regulatory authorities, in one way or another, forced private broadcasters to behave like their public counterparts and fulfil public service broadcasting obligations, what would be the reason for preserving public broadcasters? The suggested convergence of obligations between private and public broadcasters may weaken further the legitimacy of the latter, since their role could be equally fulfilled by their private counterparts. As Achille and Miège (1994: 45) have noted: 'In the logic of liberal discourse, today well represented in the governments in power, public service has no interest except in relation to a clearly defined public service mission and this mission, it is claimed, can very well be carried out by the private sector.'

Perhaps, the survival of public broadcasters will be associated, as in the past, with the future of Western societies. It is true that public service broadcasting is primarily a European concept (Porter 2000: 34), but, if European society is transformed, as the current trends show, to a highly divided society, public service may need to be devoted to serve the interests of the new underclass (Hobsbawn 1994: 308). There may well be a new underclass, deprived of information that will not be able to afford the new, attractive but subscription services of the 'pay-society' – as is already happening with the PPV sports channels. Such a situation is related, not to the fundamental principles of public service broadcasting and their cultural or even quality dimension, but to the politics and political ideologies of the coming information society. If this society endorses the political ideology of the market forces, as it seems to be doing, the role of the public service will be marginalized in one way or another.

Summary

Public broadcasters face the most difficult challenge in their long history. This chapter has tried to discuss their future in the digital environment and has concluded that it is rather uncertain. This, however, is not the result of the arrival of digital television. It is the outcome of public policies, both at national and at EU levels, which only rhetorically support the real future of public broadcasters. This is because most public policies give preference to the private sector. However, public broadcasters have demonstrated that, if they are left alone, they can react with success. During the 1990s, reductions in budgets and static licence-fee revenue combined with lacklustre performances in advertising revenues drove public broadcasters to initiate cost-cutting exercises, resulting in staff reductions and corporate restructuring. These policies were implemented in order to make public broadcasters more competitive in the sector. As soon as they became more competitive, new pressures started challenging their advertising revenue. In contrast to public telecommunications operators, public broadcasters have not really been allowed to prepare themselves for the digital era.

4

The Funding of Television in the Age of Digitalization

The search for secure and adequate sources of funding is, and will continue to be, the key issue for all television, analogue or digital, systems. Already deregulation, the growing rate of technological change and the irreversible momentum of the digital age have produced a more competitive marketplace. Alliances and joint ventures are on the increase and companies are looking to expand into foreign markets, as digital technology allows them to maximize their programming assets. Moreover, in the age of digitalization, the TV market will fragment; the number of channels offered will increase further, and, to be successful, operators will have to satisfy their customers and convince them of the merits of multichannel digital television.

This chapter tries to explore the changing sources of funding for television and the role these different sources will play in the process of digitalization. The issue of funding public broadcasters is not discussed, as it is explored in detail in chapter 3. This chapter is divided into three sections. The first section looks at the advertising trends in the European television systems and also the EU policies aimed at harmonizing commercial communication across Europe. The second section examines the prospects of subscription television, its types, especially pay-TV, PPV, NVOD and VOD, as well as its current development in Western Europe. The last section examines the evolving model of revenue of television up to the end of the first decade of the twenty-first century and the issues associated with it.

The trends of television advertising in Europe

In contrast to the era of the public broadcasters' monopoly, the West European television systems of the early twenty-first century is experiencing growth in commercial television airtime, both because there are more services to advertise and because competition among television channels has encouraged growth in advertising expenditure. The link between advertising expenditure, competition and deregulation in television has been intensified in many cases. The value of the television industry in Western Europe was $42.8 billion in 1996 and advertising represented 48 per cent of the total (Bunting 1996). Moreover, television advertising expenditure has grown faster than inflation, with a compound annual growth rate of 13.4 per cent over the 1990s. In 1999, European television advertising generated revenues of $27.8 billion (Bunting and Chapman 1996; Singh-Heer 1999). According to Zenith Media (1999), television is expected to consolidate its lead as the main advertising medium between 1998 and 2002, with market share rising from 38 per cent to 41 per cent.

The revenue share collected by television of total advertising differs across countries, with Southern European countries (for example, Italy, Spain, Greece and France), which have high TV consumption levels, averaging a share of 42.5 per cent in 1999 (table 4.1). Levels of television consumption are demonstrably lower in the North European countries of Germany, Sweden, Belgium and the Netherlands, with an average of 25 per cent. In Nordic countries the national press, especially the daily press, is very strong and takes approximately 50 per cent of the advertising market. The United Kingdom is rather balanced, with a 36 per cent share of advertising revenue taken by the daily press, and 33 per cent by television in 1999. Across Europe though, the press has lost advertising share to television since 1993, owing to a combination of factors, including the rise of gross domestic product (GDP) cost, an improvement in television audience measurement. This is also related to the fact that television became the preferred medium for the new advertising spenders – financial, telecommunications and other services.

Germany, France, Italy, Spain and the UK are the largest television markets in Europe, accounting for approximately 70 per cent of European television advertising. Germany has the largest advertising market in Europe, but, since most German advertising expenditure goes to newspapers and magazines, Germany's TV market remains smaller than that of the UK. Mounting private competition for television advertising revenues since the 1980s has raised

Table 4.1 Percentage shares of television in West European advertising expenditure, 1990–1999 (%)

Country	1990	1993	1997	1999
Austria	24	26	25	24
Belgium	24	31	36	40
Denmark	12	18	24	19
Finland	12	19	22	21
France	25	31	34	34
Germany	11	18	23	23
Greece	42	62	49	43
Ireland	38	32	34	26
Italy	49	53	55	53
Netherlands	10	19	17	17
Norway	3	13	34	32
Portugal	n.a.	51	59	58
Spain	31	33	38	41
Sweden	2	15	20	20
UK	26	32	31	33

Notes: The percentages are based on advertising expenditures, which include cinema, posters, etc. n.a. = not available.
Source: Based on data of International Federation of Newspapers Publishers (1991, 1994, 1998) and Zenith Media (1999).

television's share of total advertising spend from 10 per cent in 1985 to 20 per cent in 1995. In France, advertising expenditure has grown, but in real terms it has decreased from 2.5 per cent in 1995 to an estimated 1.3 per cent in 1999.

In short, television fuelled most of the advertising spend growth in the 1990s, and may continue to do so over the first years of the new century. This is due to a combination of several factors: the continued growth of private channels; the expansion of digital television leading to multiplexing; increased local production, which will stimulate viewership and television advertising; improved economic conditions; and cutbacks in advertising on public channels that will lead to more television advertising on private channels in several countries. In fact, the television advertising supply increased in most countries across Europe in the 1990s. This was due to the decrease in the public broadcasters' share (for example, in Germany, the Netherlands, Denmark, Norway and Sweden) and the creation of inspill advertising windows (for example, in Austria, Switzerland and Belgium).

Regardless of the rise of advertising in the 1990s, media pundits argue that, in the television of the future, advertising will play a much smaller role in the funding of television. According to a study by Norcontel (1998) commissioned by the EU, advertising growth is to be largely linked to general economic growth, with some catch-up experienced by developing commercial TV markets. According to Davis (1999), the funding model for television is set to change, as thematic channels will allow advertising to be better aimed at target groups. With viewers able to interact with digital TV advertising and request more information on an advertisement by using control devices, advertisers can look forward to added value. This also means that programmes will become more important as the emphasis switches to evaluation by audience demographics and considerations of profit and cost effectiveness.

However, this will be an incremental procedure. This is because the television industry cannot survive without advertising any more than it can without programming, so it has to find ways to accommodate advertisers even in the form of interactive TV, advertising, split-screen advertising, virtual advertising and t-commerce. But, television advertising is also affected by relevant regulations, since it must comply with EU regulations (the EU is considering revising the regulations for TV advertising in 2002), and, in some countries, with even tougher national limitations. Other forms of funding for television, such as sponsorship, barter and teleshopping, have emerged since the deregulation of television systems. There are numerous problems with all these regulations. The most critical one is whether they will actually work or whether they will merely open the door of an ill-thought-out policy. In the face of the new developments and the problems that new channels (analogue or digital, either terrestrial or satellite) face in their efforts to attract advertising and/or sponsorship, ill-thought-out policies may only exacerbate problems, especially in an era in which advertising will be less and less the main source of funding and competition will be harder.

Advertising

Although television advertising is regulated more extensively in Europe compared to other countries, like the USA, *advertising clutter* (that is, the representation of the total number of advertisements seen by an individual) has increased steadily since the deregulation of European television has stabilized. In several larger countries, TV stations seem to have reached ceilings, owing to demand and legal restrictions on advertising supply. However, there is still considerable variation by country. On the other hand, the EU in the Television Directives of 1989 and 1997 has sought a framework that would permit advertising to be broadcast across national frontiers and impose limits on advertising time. But both could not be implemented easily.

With regard to the harmonization of advertising regulations, national regulatory frameworks still vary considerably. For example, Mediterranean countries tend to take a relaxed attitude towards the consumption and promotion of alcohol, although Italy and Spain place bans on spirit advertising on television. In France, the 1991 law (Loi Evin) strictly prescribes the freedom to advertise alcoholic drink products. It also restricts the televising of sports events featuring alcoholic drink advertisements, not only inside France but throughout the EU. Other countries, such as Sweden and Finland, have limits on alcohol advertising. Pharmaceuticals remain a market where the prospect of a single market in commercial communications is still only a distant prospect. The main problem is related to the fact that each EU Member State has its own definition of what is regarded as an over-the-counter (OTC) product and what should be regarded as a prescription-only medicine (Boyfield 2000: 18). Moreover, comparative advertising is subject to restrictions of varying severity in eight Member States, and four (Belgium, Germany, Italy and Luxembourg) practically prohibit it.

Regarding the regulations on advertising-time, these have remained mostly unchanged. The limit of 20 per cent of any given one-hour period of broadcasting time has been altered to 20 per cent of any given clock hour. Self-promotion is assimilated to advertising and subject to most of the same provisions. Public service messages and charity appeals are not included in calculations (Article 18). But it is questionable whether these rules are applied in all Member States (CEC 1997b).

Sponsorship

Sponsorship has increased its importance in the European television market, as many advertisers see it as a more effective means of reinforcing the strength of their brands by associating them with popular programmes and series. In effect, sponsorship has been a key element within the funding of US broadcasting since the 1930s and from the early days of US television. This is because in most countries there are strict limits on the proportion of airtime that can be devoted to advertising and there are restrictions on the promotion of certain classes of products – for example, alcoholic beverages. Increasing demand can drive up rate card prices and advertising slots are commonly sold well in advance of broadcast.

In recent years sponsorship has grown in popularity. Many leading European programmes have been sponsored – for instance, Kellogg's sponsored *Gladiators* and Wella *Baywatch*. The development of sponsorship varies widely from country to country: options range from bill-boarding – where a sponsor gets a credit at the beginning and end of a programme – to bartering – where an advertiser supplies programming in return for airtime rather than cash. Many broadcasters are suspicious of sponsorship, and see it as the 'thin end' of the wedge. Many advertisers, on the other hand, believe cash-strapped programme-producers have a lot more to gain from sponsorship than they do. Moreover, rules on sponsorship differ markedly within the EU. In effect, there is a growing trend towards outright bans on major commercial sponsors (Boyfield 2000: 19; Havermans 2000).

The 1997 Television Directive states that pharmaceutical companies may in future sponsor broadcasts but will still not be able to promote specific medicines or medical treatments. More precisely, Article 17 states that sponsored television programmes should not be influenced by the sponsor in such a way as to affect their content; they must be clearly identified and not encourage the purchase or rental of the products or services of the sponsor or a third party. The Directive also states that programmes may not be sponsored by undertakings whose principal activities are the manufacture or sale of cigarettes and other tobacco products; and news and current affairs programmes should not be sponsored (CEC 1997b).

Barter and teleshopping

Instead of sponsorship programmes, some advertisers supply programming. This is called barter – the exchange of programmes for commercial airtime gives the advertisers the opportunity to influence the content. Game shows have been the most successful bartering area in Europe. Moreover, multinational advertisers such as Mars, Gillette, Pepsi, Coca-Cola and Procter & Gamble have been keen to develop this practice in Europe. A prominent example was *Riviera*, the European TV series produced by EC Television in the early 1990s and underwritten by Unilever to the tune of $15 million. But *Riviera* 'flopped, proving that no amount of support can guarantee audiences' (Westcott 1992). These initiatives can generate additional revenues, but to some extent they divert revenue away from traditional spot advertising (Bunting and Chapman 1996: 28–9). The 1997 Directive overlooks the case of barter.

On the contrary, the Directive introduced the issue of teleshopping, which is regarded equivalent to advertising. In effect, the one-hour-per-day limit for teleshopping has been abolished. Teleshopping channels are subject to most of the provisions of the Directive. Teleshopping windows on the generalist channels have to last at least fifteen minutes and be clearly identifiable (Article 18). They may not number more than eight per day and their total duration may not exceed three hours per day. Teleshopping must not incite minors to conclude contracts for the purchase of goods or services (CEC 1997b).

Pay-television in Europe

Growth in choice will cause fragmentation of both audiences and advertising expenditure. Neither of these will increase as rapidly as the number of channels competing for consumers' attention and money. As a result, the reliance of subscription television will need to increase in order to support the new services.

The forecasts

Various studies foresee that the strongest growth in television revenues will come through direct consumer expenditures, with rapid expansion of pay-TV and online multimedia services. It is also foreseen that the introduction of digital television will not offer an expansion of free-to-air opportunities, but it will expand the market for subscribed TV services and will extend the sector into a new world of PPV and additional interactive services. For example, Norcontel Ltd (1998) foresees that in 2005 the total market value of the audio-visual sector will be Ecu 58,871 million and its revenue by category will be 39 per cent from advertising, 13 per cent from licence fees and 48 per cent from consumer spend (subscriptions) (figure 4.1).

Baskerville Communications Corporation (1997) forecasts similar trends. According to Baskerville, net European television revenues will double to $62 billion by 2006 and much of the future

Figure 4.1 Audio-visual expenditure by category in Europe, 1995–2005

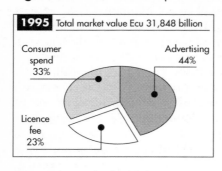
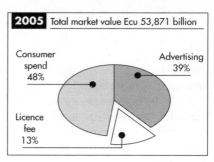

Source: Norcontel Ltd (1998).

growth will come from pay-TV services. The report also forecasts that the five main pay-TV operators (Canal Plus, Premiere, Telepiu, Canalsatelite Digital and BSkyB) will account for 24 per cent of TV revenues by 2006, about double their 1997 share. Pay and PPV's share of TV revenues will eclipse fee income by 2004; advertising will remain TV's main revenue source, but it will contribute 54 per cent of the total by 2006.

Another report by J. P. Morgan in 1998 estimated that the European pay-TV market was set to grow significantly over the next five or ten years. According to its forecasts, it estimates an increase in demand from $6 billion in 1998 (seventeen million households paying an average of $346 per annum or $29 per month) to $26 billion in 2005 (forty-one million households paying an average of $643 per annum or $36 per month – in 1997 prices). This represents an increase in penetration from 12.3 per cent of households to 27.3 per cent (Bertolotti 1998).

Moreover, according to Zenith Media (1999), it is foreseen that pay-TV will have become television's principal source of revenue in Europe by 2002, and be worth $60 billion by 2008. By then, according to Zenith Media, 35 per cent of European homes should be subscribing to cable, and 21 per cent to dish packages. Kagan World Media Ltd also estimates that, in 2005, 65.6 per cent of the income of European channels will come from subscription fees and the remaining 34.8 per cent from advertising. By 2009, the subscription–advertising split will be 71.6 per cent and 28.4 per cent (*Euromedia* 2000).

The reasons for growth

Why do media analysts believe that pay-TV in various forms will increase its profile in the market? The answer is probably linked to television economics and technology exploitation. For example, in terms of cost-per-hour entertainment, traditional television has historically given amazingly good value for money. Licence fees for public television are low, and advertising, an indirect cost to the viewer, has, until recently, funded commercial television. Thus, analysts believe that there is a consumer surplus (that is, the difference between the amount consumers pay for something and the amount it is worth to them) in traditional (as opposed to pay) television, particularly with public service broadcasters. They also consider that consumers are prepared to pay more both to get something that is not offered by traditional broadcasters and because they demand more choice in their viewing, higher programme quality and higher picture resolution (Gollogly and McGarvey 1997: 11; D. Brown 1998c: 5). Since the 1990s, subscription television has begun to exploit that consumer surplus.

The types of pay-TV

As noted in chapter 2, digital technology is considered the optimum mechanism to exploit that surplus value through the various types of subscription television.

- *Traditional pay-TV* covers all television for which viewers pay directly, whether in the form of a subscription or on a pay-per-view basis or a combination of the two. Within pay-TV the 'basic' service is one where the subscriber pays every month for a channel or a package of basic channels. In the history of television, pay-TV is a relative newcomer and it is only recent advances in technology and encryption that have allowed television to be bought by subscription. This includes television provided through cable for a basic subscription but where the channels receive no income from cable operators. This is the case, for example, in Germany and the Benelux countries, where most channels actually pay for cable carriage.
- The next type of subscription is where the viewer pays an extra monthly amount for premium channels, often movie or sports channels, which are regarded as the drivers of pay-TV sales

– that is, the channels that attract subscribers and for which they are prepared to pay. In other words, *pay-per-view* systems enable the consumer to select a single viewing item for purchase. The technique is best suited to one-off viewing events, which have a predetermined time span. In effect, PPV as a means for distributing films emerged in 1996. Prior to that only small-scale experiments had taken place. For example, in France, Multivision was introduced as a trial on the Saint Germain-en-Laye cable network in early 1993 and by TeleSelect in April 1994 (two premium pay-TV channels and five PPV channels). In the UK, BSkyB introduced PPV for the first time in March 1996, when 600,000 subscribers paid around £10 to watch a World Title boxing fight between Frank Bruno and Mike Tyson. PPV has now become established in Italy, France, Spain and Germany covering both film and sport.

• *Near-video-on-demand* (NVOD) is another format of pay-TV and is based on the advantages of digital technology. NVOD, where a film can be watched from staggered start times, is already available on some digital platforms (for example, Premiere, Canalsatellite Numérique). It is also possible to follow Formula One motor racing from several cameras on different channels. Such interactivity with pay-TV channels will be the accepted norm in the digital world for those who are prepared to pay the price (D. Brown 1998c: 11).

• *Video-on-demand* (VOD) is a more advanced format of NVOD. This is a service that allows a subscriber to choose from a menu or library of programming, usually feature films. VOD is still in a relatively early stage of development, mainly because technology has not advanced to a stage that allows it cost effective delivery. Nevertheless, there have been a number of market trials in the USA and in Europe and, from a demand perspective at least, the results have been encouraging.

The picture in the late 1990s

In some countries, such as the UK, the Benelux countries, France and Scandinavia, pay-TV has made considerable progress, while in others such as Spain and Italy it is relatively new, and the sector is small, in terms of both subscriber levels and value. The reasons for the different stages of development are numerous. In Germany and the Benelux countries a majority of television households have paid cable subscriptions for 'free' channels, which receive no revenues from cable operators. The arrival of digital platforms has brought more pay-TV channels. But, as noted in chapter 2, the development of digital television in the major European markets varies and this reflects in the development of pay-TV as well. The largest PPV market in Europe is the UK, followed by France, Spain and Italy (Callard 1999c).

BSkyB is also the largest PPV operator in the world outside the USA, representing revenues of $65 million in 1998. Its PPV platform, Sky Box Office, was launched in December 1997, offering movies every fifteen minutes at a cost of £2.99 ($4.89) each and about fifteen new titles per month. The service has programming deals with Buena Vista, Columbia TriStar, Universal, Warner Bros and MGM, and an exclusive deal with sister company Twentieth Century Fox, and has become the largest PPV movie offering in Europe. In March 1998, the British cable companies Telewest, NTL, Diamond and General Cable launched the analogue cable exclusive PPV service Front Row. Front Row is predominately a movie service, combined with occasional sports events, such as boxing. In November 1998, Channel Four introduced its pay-TV film channel, Film Four, and within a year it attracted 160,000 subscribers.

Pay-TV in France is associated with Canal Plus, the most successful pay-TV terrestrial channel in Europe (4.3 million subscribers). As noted in chapter 2, Canal Plus Numérique and TPS offer a number of PPV services, making France the second-largest pay-TV market in Europe. Canalsatellite Numérique offers movies through Kiosque at a cost of $4.83–5.56 each, and soccer costs $8.33 for a single match. Kiosque subscribers use the PPV service about once a month, with movies proving slightly more popular than sports. It also offers a service called Zapfoot, which allows viewers to switch between seven simultaneous soccer matches with the help of an icon, which appears on the screen. TPS offers a PPV service through Multivision consisting of eight channels, while films and sports cost FFr29 ($4.83) each. Viewers can buy the programming via the purchase of tokens, or by telephone.

In Italy, the development of pay-TV is mainly associated with the development of digital satellite platforms. Stream has two PPV services: Prima Fila Cinema, which offers movies, and Prima Fila Spectacolo, which offers theatre, music, soccer and documentaries. In 1999, both channels were united into one service called Prima Fila. In 1999, the cost of a movie on Prima Fila was L.6,000 ($3.38), while the price of events (music, opera, documentaries) ranged from $1.13 to $5.64. Telepiu offers the PPV service Palco, which includes +Calcio (football), +F1 (Formula One) and D+ (movies).

Soccer matches were available in 1999 for $19.93, the Formula One racing cost $16.93 and movies cost $3.38–5.64. +Calcio broadcasts live Italian championship matches and viewers can buy season home and away matches for $253.41 and just away matches for $163.12.

Spain has operated another terrestrial subscription service, Canal Plus España, since 1990 and has attracted around two million subscribers. As noted in chapter 2, the development of pay-TV is closely associated with the development of digital television, either satellite (Vía, CSD) or terrestrial (Quiero). PPV is again associated with the digital satellite platforms. Vía's subscribers pay Pta 500 ($3.28) per film and $7.85 per soccer event. Viewers can choose between a package of nineteen soccer matches at $118.22 or thirty-eight soccer matches at $210.17. CSD's service offers eleven PPV channels (films at $3.94, Spanish soccer League matches at $7.85 and the Grand Prix Championship at $9.16).

The evolving funding model

As noted above, most market reports have forecast that television subscription will play a major part in the funding of broadcasting in the near future. But, although the balance between advertising income and subscription for television services is shifting in favour of subscription, this does not mean that advertising is in decline. Rather, the total volume of advertising revenues has increased. Zenith Media (1999) points out that, despite pay-TV growth, European television channels are expected to take about $51 billion by 2008, which amounts to 37 per cent growth in real terms. It is also noted that, while very large audiences are becoming rarer, demand from advertisers will continue and will probably intensify, allowing large television channels to increase unit prices. It seems that both advertising and subscription will be the main sources of revenue – the first for the free channels, the second for the 'pay-as-you-see' channels. On the other hand, the conditions that all channels will have to operate under may be extremely different from those of the 1990s.

Conditions and directions for free channels

It is almost certain that advertising will remain television's largest source of funding until 2005, and free-to-air terrestrial television will still get the lion's share of audiences and advertising budgets. But the conditions will differ compared to those of the 1990s. The first reason is that commercial free television has grown faster than the advertising sector average. In other words, more channels, both generalist and niche advertiser-supported channels, have to compete for the same source of revenue. This fragmentation of the advertising market and of audiences imposes a significant threat to the established broadcasters. The direct impact of audience fragmentation – the downward pressure exerted upon the cost of advertising slots – is not, however, the only cause for concern. There is a broader concern among both broadcasters and the advertising agencies that clients regard advertising as an ineffective way of interacting with consumers. Media analyst Charles Brown (1997) notes that one reason for this is that, while competition does exert a downward pressure, the fragmentation of audiences may mean that advertisers have to buy more advertising in order to reach the number of homes that they had been used to accessing in the past. He also notes that fragmentation is not the only reason for the decline in consumer and advertiser enthusiasm for television, since, as recent studies have shown, an increasing proportion of viewers actively seek to avoid advertising messages.

Moreover, the days when advertisers were content simply to reach as big an audience as possible have gone. Nowadays, they are much more selective. Good consumer companies, for example, want to target up-market shoppers. Advertisers may be reluctant to pay the high price of ad-slots that command a large audience when a good proportion of those viewers may not be interested in buying their products.

Analysts Jacques Bughin and Wilfred Griekspoor (1997: 91–2) note that the days when free commercial broadcasters found it easy to make money because they dominated their national markets (the so-called structural advantage) have gone. They point out that, unless a company also has strong operating skills, it will have difficulty protecting itself against new competitors. For free commercial broadcasters, they note, strong operating skills mean the ability to squeeze maximum profits from the cost of programme schedules with the income generated by advertising or programme sponsorship. But these skills have been in short supply among broadcasters accustomed to operating in regulated markets. The result is financial problems for many commercial operators such as La Cinq in France (which ceased operations in 1992), Vlaamse Televisie Maatschappij (VTM; Belgium), Holland Media Groep (HMG; Netherlands), Antenna 3 (Spain) and Vox (Germany).

So, how should European broadcasters improve the way they operate? For the Lehman Brothers, once the advertising television market is mature and a broadcaster's market share starts to decline, diversification can provide a new lease of life for channels. But, while diversification activities are increasingly becoming a key component of mature commercial broadcasters' revenue streams, TV assets continue to represent the biggest portion of their market capitalization. With a relatively stable structure for operating costs (the most unpredictable and significant item being programming costs), top-line advertising revenue growth becomes the main driver of cash flow (Johnson 1998). According to Bughin and Griekspoor (1997: 102), commercial free broadcasters will have to have more than operating excellence in order to sustain their profitability. They will have to adopt a new way of thinking about their business, which will require new skills in areas such as contract negotiation, yield management and programming.

As noted above, general interest channels will continue to be the most efficient medium for advertisers and will get the lion's share of television advertising. But, because of the plethora of new channels, television as a medium, will be forced to derive a larger proportion of its revenue directly from the viewers through pay and pay-per-view services.

Conditions and directions for pay-TV channels

It is estimated that there is a great potential for the development of pay-TV in Europe, especially with the advent of digital television. It is forecast that revenues gained by digital broadcasters will come increasingly from premium services and transactions, rather than from basic all-in-one subscriptions, and that television content will increasingly be demanded on a pay-as-you-see basis. Media analysts Gollogly and McGarvey (1997: 68–9) consider that digital broadcasters cannot base business planning and content budgeting solely on a revenue stream, since it is by its very nature inconsistent. They also believe that, as subscriber numbers continue to grow, it will become possible to increase usage-based pricing. The greater the number of subscribers and the wider the range of population covered by the subscriber base, the greater the possibility of revenue streams becoming consistent. Moreover, they estimate that usage-based pricing is suitable for new media markets and it will help shape the market development (Gollogly and McGarvey 1997: 69). According to this, transaction revenues will be driven by the increasing use of digital television for interactive commercial content. Additionally, quality and exclusive content will continue to be the most important factor in attracting and retaining subscribers. Thus, in the digital market, content costs will be almost half of the service providers' costs. Moreover, digital has changed the economics and dynamics of pay-TV for two main reasons: first, it lowers the cost of entry in the programme-making part of the value chain and, secondly, it lowers the cost of channel distribution because of digital compression.

On the other hand, the downside is that, although pay-TV is the growth sector in broadcasting, it is already very competitive and will become even more so as digitalization brings down the cost of entry into this market. Even if the extra number of channels available leads to viewers watching more television, which is unlikely, there is only a finite number of hours and channels any single viewer can realistically watch.

According to David Brown (1998a: 45), the size of the potential market is particularly important in television, because of the very high fixed costs incurred before a single viewer or subscriber is signed up. This means that small markets are less viable for pay-TV than larger ones. Economies of scale make it difficult for broadcasters in small markets to make money unless they can persuade subscribers to spend much larger sums for their television service than they would normally have to pay in larger markets. This is because smaller European countries would not be able to support DTH pay-TV services. This is due to the fact that the small size of a market generally means that operators cannot benefit from economies of scale to provide substantially different services.

Larger economies mean that competitors can more easily benefit from economies of scope as well as of scale. This allows a product for one market to be reformatted and sold to other markets, thus generating extra revenue. Popular television programmes can be turned into videos, CD-ROMs or published material (such as recipe books), which help to spread production costs.

Brown notes that the wealth of a market is equally important for pay-TV, because subscribers need to have relatively high levels of income before they can afford it. Wealth can be expressed in a number of ways, but a fairly reliable guide is gross domestic product (GDP) per capita. This indicator provides a good guide to the wealth of potential subscribers in different territories, although average net disposable income can vary according to tax levels and costs of living generally. The GDP itself also provides an indicator of the value of the market as a whole, although a large country like Russia may have a high GDP but a low GDP per capita, indicating that, despite its size, it is a difficult market in which to build a large pay-TV subscriber base (David Brown 1998c: 45–6).

David Brown (1998c: 46) also points out that the state of the economy is another factor that has to be taken into account when considering market potential, particularly for a service requiring a relatively high disposable income such as pay-TV. If a country's economy is in recession, its consumers will have less disposable income to spend on relative luxuries like pay-TV. Economic indicators that give a good view of the state of the economy are growth figures for GDP, both current and forecast, inflation and unemployment. If the economy is growing quickly and unemployment is falling, there is likely to be a 'feel-good' factor, which will help to generate sales in subscription television. Moreover, the future of pay-TV in any one territory must depend substantially on the current state of the market in that country. One problem is the maturity of the market, and the other is the competitive state of the market. Countries where pay-TV is relatively new or underdeveloped, such as Spain and Italy, have more potential for growth than the UK, where penetration of pay-TV is much higher. On the other hand, experience in the pay-TV market is an important factor, and this may help to account for the failure of subscriptions to increase in countries such as Italy and Germany.

The impact of the competitive state of the market is more difficult to judge. As David Brown (1998c: 46) notes, in countries where free television has been poor, there has generally been a greater interest in subscription services, although there are exceptions, such as the UK. British terrestrial television is highly regarded, but satellite television has done well and there have been other factors at work. Concerning PPV, media analyst Toby Syfter (1995: 58) notes that it will inevitably compete with other forms of paid-for TV in its claims on the public purse.

Broadly speaking, according to *Screen Digest* (1998), European digital operators implement various marketing strategies trying to encourage their subscribers to buy their services: Pay-TV operators:

- usually include in their package one or two mainstream pay-TV channels, such as sports or films, with less known or attractive channels, intending the strong brand channels to carry the weaker, while the weaker channels boost the perceived value of a package;
- offer a big basic package but keep sport and movie channels in optional premium tiers that can be accessed only after buying the basic package;
- try to create a perception of choice with the use of multiple mini-packages while splitting channels in such a way that the average

subscriber has to buy several packages to get all the most popular channels;
- require subscribers to buy basic packages before giving access to premium channels;
- charge customers who take smaller basic packages more for access to premium channels;
- split off the most popular niche channels with a definite but specific audience into extended basic tiers – that is, at a lower cost than premium;
- package premium channels and basic channels in such a way that they attract different but complementary audiences;
- offer bonus channels with certain combinations of basic in addition to premium channels, in an effort to increase perceived value;
- offer a reduced rate for subscribers taking basic and premium channels;
- offer new subscribers access to all channels (including premium) at a huge reduction for the first few months of service thereby leaving them with the difficult choice of which channels to drop once the offer period has expired;
- offer PPV channels but price multi-channel packages in such a way that they offer much better value;
- offer season tickets for PPV sports.

However, the key, and everlasting, problem for pay-TV operators is to keep subscribers, since in most cases they struggle for subscriber loyalty. Across Europe, subscribers pay their subscription either directly though their bank account or from a credit card.

Summary

Although the main sources of revenue will remain more or less the same, the intensity of the competition for a share of this wealth will increase as the number of players and the rules of the game change. Even though advertising will remain the main source of revenue, subscription funding will also increase considerably in the first decade of the twenty-first century. At least, subscription revenues will not be an unknown quantity, as in the past.

The question remains, however, whether competition for subscribers will have an impact on the overall content of channels. It is almost certain that the fragmentation of audiences will complicate matters further. Another question is whether advertisers will direct their budgets towards mass generalist channels or whether they will be more attracted to the niche pay-TV channels, since they provide them with demographic information, in particular on the purchasing power of their potential customers.

In either case, the basis for digital services will be traditional television content, principally sports and films. In fact, television will become much more expensive for all, operators and viewers. The US experience suggests that most pay-TV cable productions resemble those of the terrestrial networks. As Leo Bogart (1995: 284) points out, 'increasing the number of channels does not mean a commensurate increase in the variety of tastes and interests that are being satisfied, since media entrepreneurs gravitate to the mode where large numbers are clustered.'

5
Media Concentration in the Age of Digital Television

The deregulation of television has led to the creation of larger and fewer dominant groups, since the dynamics of the information industries have encouraged enterprises in the sector to become vertically integrated and to expand horizontally, thereby increasing the levels of concentration (Locksley 1989: 11). In 1992, the European Commission published a Green Paper acknowledging the issue of increasing patterns of concentration and the need to maintain pluralism in the audio-visual field. One of the main obstacles to drafting legislation that deals with the concentration of ownership across the audio-visual landscape is that of determining the market share of any particular media proprietor. With rapid technological change and cross-ownership in abundance, and media entrepreneurs moving into, and out of, sectors very quickly, the picture is in a state of continuous flux.

The issue of media concentration has traditionally been approached vis-à-vis a normative debate. This chapter contributes to the ongoing debate first by highlighting the paradoxical nature of concentration policy and secondly by analysing a number of recent cases in which competition policy has been applied.

The issue of media concentration

Concentration refers to the process by which similar entities are progressively grouped together, while diversification refers to the process by which different entities are brought together under one

Table 5.1 Horizontal integration, 1996–1997

Rationale	Examples
Increasing market power/gaining minimum efficient scale	Vebacom–Urbana Systemtechnik, Cable and Wireless Communications, Demon–Cityscape
High cost of new (digital) technologies	Canal Plus–NetHold
Uncertain demand for new services	Multimediabetriebsgesellschaft (Kirch, Bertelsmann, etc.)
Internationalization	BT–MCI, Global One, UUNet–Unipalm Pipex
Opportunities arising from regulatory reform	MFS/Worldcom, Telenet Flanders, NYNEX/Bell Atlantic

Source: CEC (1997d: 17).

Table 5.2 Vertical integration, 1996–1997

Rationale	Examples
Uncertainty of demand	Hughes Olivetti Telecom (DirectPC), @Home
Market positioning and access to new skills	Bertelsmann–AOL, BBC WorldWide–ICL, STET–IBM
Gaining control of channels from the customer	BT–BSkyB, Disney–ABC–Capital Cities
Moving into higher margin areas of the value chain	Microsoft Network–NBC (MSNBC Internet new channel)
Staving off competition from companies in related markets	US West–Time Warner, Oracle–Sun–Netscape (Network Computer)

Source: CEC (1997d: 17).

central control (see also Collins *et al.* 1988; Dyson and Humphreys 1990; Negrine and Papathanassopoulos 1990; Garnham 1992; Thompson 1995; Murdock and Golding 1999). The former is sometimes referred to as 'consolidation' or 'horizontal integration', whilst the latter is more commonly known as 'vertical integration' (see tables 5.1 and 5.2 for examples in 1996–7). Proponents of vertical integration in the media argue that profits increase as middlemen are eliminated. They also argue that consolidation reduces risk, in that it decreases the possibility of a producer not being able to sell a product. Proponents of horizontal integration argue that it can improve a company's ability (such as a production programming company) to shift unwanted material (such as movies), by packaging it with the hits. It can also improve the terms on which channels buy programmes.

In 1989, a Booz Allen & Hamilton (1989: 11) report on 'mergers and acquisitions' in Europe noted that 'nearly half' of the 130 transactions examined included a process of integration – either 'upstream' or 'downstream' – demonstrating the desire to exert control over large parts of trade in television. The report also identified two other kinds of transactions relevant to the present discussion. In addition to vertical integration, there were also 'strategic acquisitions by non-media external investors' and 'geographical diversification . . . in second or third country markets'. According to the report, 'one third by value of the mergers and acquisitions activity in the survey represent transatlantic deals, while only 10 per cent represent genuine pan-European ventures' (Booz Allen & Hamilton 1989: 16). The dominance of US firms should not come as a surprise if one takes into account the pivotal role played by US media industries – particularly in the production sector – at the international level.

The report also stresses that the 'Darwinian forces' of the international capital markets, unleashed as European countries relax rules excluding foreign investors, mean that company management would be faced with a 'completely new set of variables'. These include the need to handle financial resources in a more cost-effective way, the 'prudent use of debts to ensure high returns to equity stockholders' and the need to 'demonstrate continual diligence in exploiting commercial strengths wherever these may lie' (Booz Allen & Hamilton 1989: 16). Reality has reconfirmed these predictions, since the deregulation of European broadcasting has opened up the markets to new players – in fact, one can observe an ingenuous mosaic of crossovers and partnerships, the growth of mutuality and deals between a small number of players in the field.

These patterns of concentration went on through the 1990s. In effect, new breeds of superconglomerates led by telecommunications and information technology groups tried to replace weaker players through acquisitions and mergers (see also Tabernero et al. 1993; McChesney 1998a, b). For example, the merger between Bertelsmann, Germany's largest media company, and Compagnie Luxembourgeoise de Télédiffusion (CLT) in 1996 created CLT–Ufa, a major player in the increasingly competitive German market. Using Bertelsmann's firm footing in free television, CLT–Ufa was able to exert greater pressure on its main rival, the Kirch Group. CLT–Ufa also has stakes in RTL4 and 5 in the Netherlands, M6 and TMC in France, Premiere in Germany and Channel 5 in Britain.

The beginning of the twenty-first century also witnessed 'merger-mania': the Time Warner and America Online merger ($156 billion) paved the wave for new acquisitions and mergers in Europe. According to analyst Chris Barnes (2000: 32), in the first six months of 2000 a series of large deals spread across the sectors, bringing total media mergers and acquisitions activity to $297.8 billion – nearly double the previous record of $158.2 billion of the same period in 1999. Among the largest deals in this period was Vivendi's $46.7 billion takeover of Seagram's Universal in June 2000 forming Vivendi Universal, followed by France Télécom's $40.1 billion purchase of the British cellular company Orange. Moreover, the number of smaller deals increased massively in 2000. In the first half of 2000, there were 355 disclosed deals, especially in the interactive media sector (Barnes 2000).

In the first half of 2000, merger and acquisitions deals in the television sector amounted to $35.1 billion, presenting a new record. In 1999, the deals amounted to $19.9 billion. This new record is due to the $19.2 billion merger of CLT–Ufa with Pearson TV, which was the fifth largest deal in 2000. Other notable deals in June 2000 were those between rival broadcasters ProSieben and Sat1 in Germany, both owed by the Kirch Group ($5.6 billion), and Telefonica's takeover of the Dutch production company Endemol Entertainment in March 2000 for $4.6 billion. Moreover, in the first six months of 2000, there were thirty-four disclosed deals in the television sector, while in 1999 there were thirty-five deals in the sector (Barnes 2000: 33). It is obvious that the net result of this mergermania will be a consolidation of power that will have effects in the European marketplace. For example, the CLT–Ufa–Pearson merger will put pressure on other players with 'mature' television business such as France's TF1 and Italy's Mediaset. The deal between Vivendi and Seagram brings together a range of entertainment assets, especially content on both sides of the Atlantic. Moreover, with the merger of ProSieben and Sat1, Kirch has officially consolidated his television assets, aiming not only to rationalize his broadcasting holdings and save $100 million annually, but also to compete against his rival Bertelsmann. Needless to say, the German market has been consolidated to these two groups. Consolidation is also witnessed in the UK commercial television market, after the approval of the UK Government in July 2000 of the merger between independent television companies Carlton and United News & Media for the sum of Euro 14.5 billion. Thus, the ITV network has been consolidated from three to two major players.

The reality of concentration

The reasons for which media companies seek alliances and mergers are simple: to maintain and/or gain market strength and supremacy. In attempting to gain these advantages, entrepreneurs and corporations have engaged in mergers and acquisitions, which have given them greater control over specific sectors or combinations of sectors. In effect, they have extended long-running trends in the media industry: first, the long-turn trend towards concentration. Secondly, a tendency towards diversification, which in turn gives conglomerates the advantage to have, if not to control, several stakes of the communication industry (see Locksley 1989).

Moreover, diversification increases the control that individual entrepreneurs or media organizations can wield over a larger part of the whole linkage between content production and distribution. In the media sector, as Armand Mattelart (1994: 210) notes, the gigantic redeployment marked in the field by leveraged acquisitions, transnational alliances and megamergers has been guided by three slogans: 'economics of scale', the 'power of scale' and 'economics of breadth'. In fact, the media enjoy certain tactical advantages, since the legalist and economic character of the EU has played into the hands of the major media lobbying (Tunstal and Palmer 1991: 100). This creates obvious problems in the media sector, since it unleashes pressures for companies to diversify, merge or expand. Size has become an important factor. The trends described above (such as rationalization, expansion, growth, increased competition, larger markets, and so on) may be the unintended consequences of a policy for competition and the process of restructuring the European communications sector. But, as Murdock and Golding (1999: 117–18) argue, two parallel movements were seen in the 1990s in the policies both of the EU and of its major Member States. The first was the ascendancy of *marketization* policies and the second the *convergence* of the communication sector. As they point out: 'Corporate thinking presents the new spaces of private enterprises opened up by convergence as a logical, and therefore, largely incontestable, consequence of digital technologies' (Murdock and Golding 1999: 118). On the same page they consider marketization to be 'all those policy interventions designed to increase the freedom of action of private corporations and to institute corporate goals and organizational procedures'. In fact, many European countries have become less willing to write off the perceived economic opportunity costs associated with restricting domestic media and cross-media ownership (Doyle 1997). For example, in the UK, the White Paper of 2000 suggests new relaxation of current cross-media ownership limits, such as the disqualification of newspapers with a market share of 20 per cent or more from holding an ITV, Channel 5 or radio licence. In Germany, the Broadcasting Treaty of 1996 also relaxed old restrictions on ownership of broadcasting companies (CE 1997: 43). Murdock and Golding (1999: 118–19) provide five basic dimensions to this general process:

- *privatization*: the sale of public communication assets to private investors;
- *liberalization*: the introduction of competition into monopoly markets or its extension into markets with limited competition;
- *corporatization*: encouraging or compelling organizations still within the public sector to pursue market opportunities;
- *a move from licence to auctions*;
- *reorienting the regulatory system*: that is, a reform of the regulatory system, which will increase corporate access to markets and enhance their freedom of action within it.

Murdock and Golding (1999: 120) contend that these moves are not the inherent 'logic' of digital technology, but, through market-ization policies, the ambitions and interests of the 'major corporate players within the communication system'. As they point out (1999: 120): 'They [corporate players] deploy appeals to technological inevitability to provide justifications for continuing and extending marketization to their maximum advantage.'

A short overview of EU regulation

At the EU level, the regulation of concentration is an issue of heated debate. The Council of Europe, after the *Television without Frontiers* Directive, and under Article 10 of the European Convention of Human Rights, which deals with freedom of expression and information, has preoccupied itself with the issue of media ownership and pluralism. Although its powers are rather weak, it has examined the developments and consequences of changes in media structure and ownership within individual countries in relation to the goal of pluralism. The result has been a collection of studies, data and overviews regarding various aspects of the issue of media concentration. Only one regulatory text has been adopted – the 1994 Recommendation on transparency.

The EU does acknowledge and encourage competition, but at the same time it favours large-scale companies competing internationally in a liberal fashion. In effect, as David Coen (1997: 96) points out, large firms in the EU, especially after the Maastricht Treaty, have become integral players in the policy formation process, participating directly as private actors, or collectively through new loose cross-border alliances. He also notes that 'all the indications are that the trend will continue towards an increasing partnership between firms and the Commission at the European level . . . As a result, firms now expect to have direct dealings with the Commission even in relatively "quiet" legislative periods' (Coen 1997: 99).

Since the mid-1980s the European Parliament has been calling on the Commission to take an initiative in order to control, if not impede, the ongoing concentration of ownership in the European media sector. In 1992, the Commission published its Green Paper on *Pluralism and Media Concentrations in the Internal Market* (CEC 1992). This consultative document reviewed existing levels of media concentration in Europe. The Green Paper was heavily influenced by the industrial imperatives and the policy orientations of the DG III (industrial and internal policies) and argued that the European media industry was hindered by extensively different ownership rules in each Member State, whereas media companies were attempting to pursue their activities and investments. The Green Paper suggested three possible policy options:

- no action at the pan-European level;
- action to improve levels of transparency;
- positive intervention, probably through a Directive, to harmonize media ownership rules throughout the Member States.

These proposals were sent to the interested parties for feedback. The European Parliament and the Economic and Social Committee favoured the positive intervention policy option, but were against the main rationale of the Green Paper. On the contrary, the Member States were in favour of the non-action option. Moreover, the media owners were against any EU initiative to harmonize legislation on media ownership at the European level, while some larger ones, such as News Corporation and Fininvest, were against any EU action since it could be regarded as an impediment to investment. In the meantime, within the Commission there was growing debate on the matter. As Alison J. Harcourt (1998) points out, DG III was in favour of creating a strong internal market. DG X (culture/audio-visual) rejected the industrial and internal market argument and favoured harmonization of the media ownership rules at EU level. At the same time, DG X was asking for the cultural dimension (pluralism) of media ownership. On the other hand, DG IV (competition) considered that it is not possible for regulation to keep up with technological change.

Finally, as in the case of the Television Directive of the 1980s, many disputed whether the Commission was competent to pursue policies aimed at safeguarding pluralism (Hitchens 1994). It was argued that the whole issue should be dealt with by the Council of Europe, since pluralism is integral to the principle of freedom of speech (Lange and Van Loon 1991: 26). This was also, to an extent, recognized by the Commission, and this seems to have been the reason for justifying its intervention under the broad frame of securing the proper functioning of the Internal Market rather than the protection of pluralism (CEC 1992: 99). The two main goals, as well as the combination of media ownership and media pluralism, often need different approaches, since some mergers that do not threaten competition might pose a threat to plurality, and vice versa (Doyle 1997).

In 1993, the issue of media ownership became the responsibility of DG XV (internal market). DG XV did not take any action on the issue, such as producing a Draft Directive, which would have been the next reasonable step of its policy making. Instead, in 1994, it published a follow-up to the 1992 Green Paper, in which it presented and evaluated the outcome of the consultation process. The second surprise was that it called for a second round of consultations among the interested parties, in order to have a final answer on whether a Community action was needed. This second round of consultations produced exactly the same results as the first – that is, a lack of consensus concerning any attempt to harmonize media ownership policy at an EU level. After a two-year period of consultations, debates and considerable lobbying from major international and national media groupings, Commissioner Mario Monti was prepared in July 1996 to present a first draft for a Directive on 'Concentrations and Pluralism in the Internal Market' to his colleagues, with the following main proposals.

- There would be a 30 per cent upper limit on 'monomedia' ownership for radio and television broadcasters in their own broadcasting areas. One broadcasting undertaking could not control another (new or existing) if the market share equalled 30 per cent or more in designated market 'zones'.

- A 'multimedia threshold' would be introduced, with an upper limit of 10 per cent for 'multimedia' concentration – that is, ownership for a combination of different media (television, radio and/or newspapers). A venture already in one media could not own a different media (new or existing) if the total audience share of its media equalled 10 per cent or more in the area concerned.
- All market shares would be based on multiple audience measures within the area in question.
- The proposed regulations would allow Member States to exclude public service broadcasters from these upper limits, if they so wished.

Once again these proposals, reasonable and practical for some, raised new controversies. The main one focused on the level of diversity of ownership appropriate for different market sizes (local, regional or national level). The Commission was in favour of the measure of the market share within the specific region for a television or radio station. Some countries (notably the UK and Germany) disputed this, since most of them measure a television station's share of the national market, irrespective of what areas its service is transmitting in.

DG XV's response was to promise a more flexible approach to the upper ceilings suggested in the September 1996 draft, indicating that the 30 per cent threshold could be varied if national circumstances so demanded. But the Commission's negotiating position on upper ceilings was constrained by Parliament's consistent support for robust measures to counteract concentrations. Clearly, the greater the discretionary power left to Member States in setting their own upper limits on media and cross-media ownership, the less effective any new Directive would be, whatever its objectives (Doyle 1997). But at the 4 September 1996 meeting, the Commissioners were not convinced by the proposals and turned the project down, asking for alterations.

DG XV put a new version forth in March 1997. In this new version, the title of the proposed Directive was changed from 'Concentrations and Pluralism in the Internal Market' to 'Media Ownership in the Internal Market'. This signalled a move to deflect the focus away from pluralism (where the Commission's competence would be in question) towards the aim of removing obstacles to the internal market (Doyle 1997).

Secondly, a 'flexibility clause' was added. This meant that the Member States could authorize the overrun of thresholds in certain conditions – for example, when the decision involved local media that would otherwise go out of business, or an independent undertaking whose programming was not profit oriented. This exception would apply if the broadcaster in question was not simultaneously infringing these upper thresholds in more than one Member State.

The proposed Directive would oblige some Member States to reform their legislative approach. They could not introduce stricter rules under the concentration thresholds. In addition, a ten-year transitional period would make it possible to introduce the concentration thresholds gradually, so as to take account of the situation in certain national markets, notably in small countries. During this period, a venture could exceed thresholds in a single Member State, provided that 'appropriate measures' were taken to guarantee pluralism (Doyle 1997). 'Appropriate measures' might include establishing, within any organization that breached the limits, 'windows for independent programme suppliers' or a 'representative programming committee' (CEC 1997a).

It is obvious that DG XV made further compromises in this new version in order to reach consensus. The draft Directive of 1997 differed little from the one of July 1996. What was, however, important was that, with the modification of 'flexibility', it was not securing the issue of pluralism either. As Doyle (1997) points out, it was clear that, in practice, the 'flexibility' clause would allow Member States to maintain whatever upper restrictions on ownership were affordable – either economically or politically – in their own territories. This point makes the fact that the proposed Directive was eventually abandoned more questionable. The fact is that even this proposal, though it enjoyed the support of a number of Commissioners, provoked a storm of protest from media companies, especially the European Publishers Council, which saw it as an obstacle to compete in the 'information society'. Moreover, the EU was already preoccupied with the 1997 Green Paper on the *Convergence of the Telecommunications, Media and Information Technology Sectors, and the Implications for Regulations*. The Green Paper deemed that the trends towards consolidation and diversification in response to new opportunities, opened up by liberalization of EU and world markets and with a view to the opportunities offered by convergence, would go on (CEC 1997d: 6–7). As it points out:

> 'Vertical merger activity is seen as a more significant indicator of a change in industry structures in response to the convergence phenomenon. Underlying that analysis is the reality that few, if any, of today's market players will have the skills or resources to straddle the

whole of the value chain within a converged environment, so that the emergence of major players in the sectors affected by convergence will inevitably rely on partnering to varying degrees. In such a context, the Competition rules will continue to play a key role in assessing new ventures as they emerge.   (CEC 1997d: 7)

It seems clear that any attempt to tackle the issue of media ownership and concentration at a European level is unrealistic. The industrial imperatives of the information society and the new opportunities, stakes and interests of the convergence of the media, telecommunications and information society seem not to allow any attempt to harmonize, let alone to tackle, the issue of concentration. As the European Publishers Council in a letter sent to Commission President Jacques Santer noted, 'to produce final legislation will see such vast changes to European media that the provisions are certain to be out of date' (in *Wall Street Journal Europe* 1997). The European Commission recognizes that regulation of media ownership on a pan-European level is difficult to achieve. As Iosifides (1999: 160) notes, convergence has already revealed the inadequacy of European initiatives to harmonize sectorial ownership regulation. To such inadequacy is added the difficulty of using old methods to measure market concentration – to evaluate who controls what and to measure market influence based on audience measurements.

The European Parliament in its response to the Green Paper on *Convergence* insisted that the Commission should submit a proposal for a Directive on the subject of media ownership and pluralism that took account of all forms of electronic communication (CEC 1999a: 8). But it is highly unlikely that any such action or initiative to promote control or transparency of media ownership will take place in the foreseeable future (see also Cavalin 1998). The same applies to the issue of self-regulation. In the case of self-regulation, as Commissioner Oreja (1999), said 'the public authorities generally lay down a set of objectives to be achieved, but leave it to the operators and other interested parties to establish, implement and sometimes monitor the more detailed rules whereby these objectives are achieved'. It is hardly likely that media conglomerates will self-regulate themselves in order not to hold a dominant position in their market area.

In short, the EU seems powerless to regulate the issue of concentration, apart from scrutinizing the mergers and acquisitions under the competition law. This has been recognized by the Economic and Social Committee, which addressed those questions in its own initiative. On 29 March 2000, the Committee published a statement saying that, in order to prevent the eventual risk of abusive mergers,

EU Member States should consider extending current national media ownership rules (licence schemes, frequency allocation, audience-based thresholds, investments, and so on) to the new digital broadcasting services (terrestrial, satellite and cable). These rules should also be extended to the new sources of audio-visual and written information available on the Internet. Community guidelines could also be drawn up to uphold pluralism and national differences and to complement competition law by focusing on the social dimension and cultural diversity of the media. There should also be coordination at European level, particularly in the event of very strong international growth. On the issue of 'portal sites', which tend to funnel and standardize the information available to the detriment of pluralism, the Committee has proposed extending the powers of Member State regulators, with Commission-level coordination (CES 2000). But nothing had happened by 2001.

Media concentration and the EU

Future market developments will be dealt with in the same way as before – that is, according to competition policy (Papathanassopoulos 1990a); in effect this means under the competition rules and especially Article 81 (previously Article 85) of the EC Treaty, which lays down the basic rules of competition to business firms. Article 81 is concerned with agreements that prevent, restrict or distort competition, while Article 86 prohibits abuse of a dominant position in the market. But, as Goldberg *et al.* (1998: 89) note, 'under certain very specific conditions, the Treaty makes provision for an exception to this principle of prohibition by authorising certain agreements between undertakings'. In general, the rules on competition forbid all restraints on competition or on trade rivalry between enterprises in Member States except where certain agreements are likely to be compatible with the objective of the internal market. These rules effectively ban restrictive practices that distort or prevent competition by the misuse of a dominant trade position.

Subsidies that restrict competition are also forbidden under Articles 92–4. Mergers are dealt with in the 'Merger Regulation' of 1989 (*Official Journal* 1990). The Commission (DG XV) has the power to prevent the creation of monopolies and cartels that would stifle competition in a substantial proportion of the trade in the commodities they produce. In order to put this into practice, the Commission has set out a number of criteria that would permit it to pass judgment on the suitability and appropriateness of mergers.

The Commission, on the one hand, favours mergers, acquisitions and the creation of joint ventures to provide new television (notably pay-TV) services, and, on the other, examines whether these moves can eliminate competition. This is not an easy task, since the one goal contradicts the other. It is obvious that any merger, acquisition or joint merger aims to eliminate competition and at the same time to strengthen its position in the market. As Goldberg et al. (1998: 90) note, 'given the complexity of modern media markets, it is difficult to measure dominance by concentrating on the share of a single market such as television'. Moreover, as Iosifides (1996: 247) points out, the regulation on mergers and acquisitions covers only those that affect competition in the market in question. Consequently, it has allowed many others to proceed simply because they did not meet the high thresholds.

DG XV, the Directorate responsible for competition in the EU, has been called to consider a number of mergers, acquisitions and joint ventures in the television sector (see also Ungerer 1995; Pons 1998; Pons and Lucking 1999). The most well known from the 1990s are summarized below.

MSG Media Services

In 1994 the case of MSG Media Services GmbH (MSG) was regarded under the Merger Regulation as a joint venture that would lead to concentration. This case concerned the German companies Bertelsmann AG, Deutsche Telekom and Taurus Beteiligungs GmbH (Taurus), a company of the Kirch Group. They proposed to form a joint venture called MSG Media Services GmbH (MSG), where each parent would hold one-third of the share-capital and voting rights. The object of MSG was the technical, business and management handling of payment-financed television and other communications services (see chapter 2). The relevant market affected was that for technical and management services for pay-TV and other television services financed through subscription or payment by German viewers. The most interesting element of the case was that Deutsche Telekom, holding a monopoly for telephone network services and owning nearly the totality of TV-cable networks in a Member State, would combine its future activities in the joint venture's market with those of the leading pay-TV suppliers. The Commission considered that this joint venture would create a dominant position, since the involved parties were already important in the pay-TV sector, and it would be almost impossible for a new entrant to enter the field. It therefore declared the venture incompatible with the common market.

Telepiu

In 1994, the Commission accepted the creation of a joint pay-TV venture in Italy, Telepiu, between the Richemont group (Multichoice/NetHold) and the Kirch Group. It concluded that this venture would not pose competition problems in the sector. Moreover, in 1995, the Commission also accepted the merger between Richemont and the French pay-TV operator Canal Plus, including the pay operator's interests in Europe.

Nordic Satellite Distribution

In 1995, it was also considered that the venture Nordic Satellite Distribution (NSD) would lead to concentration. In July 1995, the Commission prohibited the NSD venture to transmit its satellite television programmes. The Commission regarded that NSD would lead to a concentration of the activities of its shareholders,[1] creating a really vertically integrated operation extending from production of television programmes (through operation of satellites and cable networks) to retail distribution services for pay-TV and other encrypted channels. In other words, the Commission viewed the alliance's market position in cable television and pay-TV as a factor that could reinforce its market strengths and programme provision and vice versa. Thus, it would be possible for the involved parties of the alliance to take advantage of their strong position in such a way as to be able to foreclose the Nordic market for satellite television.

Bertelsmann and CLT

In 1997, the Commission examined the merger of Bertelsmann and CLT, under the joint venture CLT–Ufa. This was regarded as

[1]   The partners of the NSD venture were Norsk Telekom A/S (NT), TeleDanmark A/S (TD) and Industriforvaltnings AB Kinnevik (Kinnevik). All were important companies in the Nordic media, especially on cable and satellite sectors.

being compatible with the common market. The interesting thing is that both companies were strong players in the European audio-visual sector, notably in the German phone market. In this case, the Commission considered that the merger in question would not affect their position. By the beginning of the twenty-first century CLT–Ufa was the most powerful private television company within the EU.

British Digital Broadcasting

In 1998, the Commission approved the formation of a digital pay-TV terrestrial TV joint venture, British Digital Broadcasting (which now operates as ITV digital), between Carlton and Granada in the UK. Carlton and Granada each operate regional advertising-funded television channels in the UK and both have interests in pay-TV channels. Granada also has a shareholding in BSkyB and operates a pay-TV joint venture with BSkyB. While some amendments to the notified agreements were required, there was no doubt that the creation of the venture was, in principle, pro-competitive, as it would provide competition to the dominant incumbent operator, BSkyB.

Bertelsmann and Kirch

In 1998, the Commission prohibited the merger of Bertelsmann's and Kirch's pay-TV interests in Germany. The two media groups operated the only pay-TV channels in Germany, Premiere and DF1, and held all-important German-language pay-TV programming rights. The main problem was Bertelsmann's and Kirch's stranglehold over the pay-TV rights, which prevented the emergence of a competitor on the pay-TV market.

Télévision Par Satellite

In March 1999, the European Commission authorized agreements regarding the digital platform Télévision Par Satellite (TPS). The Commission noted the primarily pro-competitive effect of having this new operator created by TF1, M6, France 2, France 3, France Télécom and Suéz Lyonnaise des Eaux. Moreover, TPS would hold certain exclusive rights during its three-year launching phase. The Commission regarded the emergence of this new broadcaster in the

French market as evidence of competition in digital pay-TV and at the same time as favourable to consumers. The decision affected the agreements concluded by the participants to form TPS.

United International Pictures BV

In September 1999, the European Commission renewed the exception under Article 81 (3) of United International Pictures BV (UIP) for five more years. UIP is a joint film distribution company established by Paramount Pictures Corporation, Universal Studios Inc., and Metro-Goldwyn-Mayer Inc. Within the EU, UIP distributes and licenses feature films produced mainly by its partners for screening in cinemas. The Commission first exempted UIP for five years in 1989.

British Interactive Broadcasting Ltd

In September 1999, the Commission authorized British Interactive Broadcasting Ltd (renamed 'Open') for seven years. Open's shareholders were BSkyB, British Telecom, Midland/HSBC Bank and Matsushita Electric Europe. Open provides interactive digital television services in the UK. The Commission viewed the creation of Open as a threat to British Telecom and BSkyB. Thus, it imposed conditions on competition that comes from the cable networks, so that third parties are ensured sufficient access to Open's subsidized set-top boxes and to BSkyB's films and sports channels, and so that set-top boxes other than Open's can be developed in the market. Less than a year after the approval, in July 2000, BSkyB in effect took control of Open, raising its stake from 32.5 per cent to 80.1 per cent after buying out HSBC and Matsushita shares of 20 per cent and 15 per cent respectively. BT, previously a 32.5 per cent shareholder, like BSkyB, will see its holding diluted to 19.9 per cent following BSkyB's agreement to meet future funding requirements.

Microsoft, Liberty and Telewest

In March 2000, the European Commission decided to open a full investigation into the proposed acquisition of joint control by Microsoft Corporation (Microsoft) with Liberty Media Corporation

(Liberty) over Telewest Communications plc (Telewest).[2] The Commission announced that it would make a detailed assessment of the impact of the transaction on competition conditions in various areas of the digital cable industry. In particular, the focus area of the investigation would be the provision of software for digital set-top boxes in the UK and its impact on the choice of British cable subscribers. The Commission raised serious doubts with regard to the compatibility with the EU rules of the proposed acquisition of a joint controlling interest of Microsoft in Telewest because of its impact on competition in the market for software for digital set-top boxes and because of the possibility of it strengthening Telewest's existing dominant position as an exclusive supplier of cable services to consumers within its franchise area.

Kirch and BSkyB

In March 2000, the European Commission cleared the joint venture between the Kirch Group and BSkyB regarding joint control over KirchPayTV GmbH & Co. KGaA (KirchPayTV). Owing to commitments offered by the parties, the Commission concluded – in contrast to previous decisions regarding pay-TV in Germany – that the operation would not lead to the creation or strengthening of a dominant position. In the view of the Commission, BSkyB is not likely to enter the pay-TV market in Germany in the short to medium term. However, it admitted that this new venture would strengthen KirchPayTV's dominant position on the German market. It also admitted that this operation might enable KirchPayTV to enter the digital interactive market more easily, since pay-TV is likely to be an important driving force for digital interactive services. As a consequence, the Kirch 'd-box' may become the standard decoder in Germany for interactive services, as it is already for pay-TV.

This decision is a landmark, because it forces Kirch to allow potential competitors access to the company's customer base, since Kirch will have to allow manufacturers to build set-top boxes that are able to handle its own and other encryption technologies. The

---

[2]   Telewest is a British broadband cable company. It provides a wide range of services to businesses and consumers, including digital television, telephony and high-speed Internet access. Microsoft is a leading PC software company which is also involved in other sectors like telecommunications and multimedia, as well as being engaged in investments in many cable companies in different countries. Liberty, a subsidiary of AT&T, is an international media, entertainment and communications company with interests in several EU states and in the USA.

problem, however, is that there are few premium pay-TV competitors currently on the horizon in Germany.

Canal Plus and Lagardère

In June 2000, the Commission approved the joint takeover of Canalsatellite Numérique by the groups Canal Plus and Lagardère and of the acquisition of Multithématiques by the same companies and Liberty Media. The Commission ruled that these operations would not strengthen a dominant position on the relevant markets (production of thematic channels and interactive television services), and thus did not raise any competition concerns. Canal Plus is, as we have seen, a leading force of European digital pay-TV.

Pearson and CLT–Ufa

In June 2000, the Commission also cleared the acquisition of Pearson TV by CLT–Ufa. It was the Commission's view that, although all the companies involved either directly or indirectly, had interests in the television sector, the deal would not significantly reduce competition. The operation would lead to an addition of market shares in Germany in the markets for independent television production and fiction as well as distribution and would certainly increase vertical integration of the parties, but in the view of the Commission this increase in market shares was limited.

Time Warner America Online

In June 2000, the Commission announced that it would open a full investigation into the merger between America Online and Time Warner and its effects, especially for the emerging business of music distribution over the Internet and on the markets for Internet dial-up access and paid-for-content.

Vivendi and Seagram

In October 2000, the Commission approved the acquisition of Seagram by Vivendi. The Commission was concerned that the deal would have strengthened Vivendi–Canal Plus's dominant position in pay-TV in Europe and created a dominant position in the same market in the Nordic region. The pooling of Seagram's Universal music arm and Vivendi's multi-access Internet portal Vizzavi also raised concerns. But Vivendi offered substantial undertakings to address the competition problems, notably to divest its stake in BSkyB and to give rival pay-TV operators access to Universal's films. Vivendi, according to the Commission, offered a 'package of commitments' that included access for competitors to Universal's film production and co-production. The Commission believed that these undertakings reduced significantly the ability of Canal Plus to influence other major US studios and eliminated the serious doubts as to the strengthening of a dominant position of Canal Plus following its vertical integration with Universal.

A coherent policy?

The above cases leave no doubt that it is extremely difficult for the EU to develop a coherent policy on mergers and concentration of activity, since the measurement of market strength is extremely difficult to assess. Large diversified conglomerates cannot easily be classified under any single category. This is more so with the entry of multimedia companies, which are expanded in various sectors of the communications domain, and the convergence of telecommunications and media sectors, which will alter the structures and the economics in the wider sector. Competition on the new communications environment may be affected by the existence of bottlenecks at each level of the vertical supply chain – the various markets for content, transmission networks and/or technical services – as each of these constitutes an essential input for a pay-TV operator. Competition on the pay-TV market can be affected by leveraging market power from one level to another or through foreclosure effects caused by vertical integration.

The above also proves that in practice the EU seems to favour mergers and acquisitions on a European rather than on a national level. It is well known that the European Commission supports a policy of liberalization of industrial sectors, because it deems that liberalization improves productivity and reduces operating costs and consumer prices. On the other hand, with regard to the application of competition rules, the Commission asks for a new competition policy to follow up the new developments.

This new policy would abandon a narrow approach based on specific rules by category of agreement or by sector of activity and adopt an approach based on apprehension of the economic effects of the vertical restrictions, whatever the sector of activity concerned. This is because, in contrast to the past, mergers and acquisitions have become much larger and more frequent. In other words, it is unlikely that the trends towards concentration in the wider communications environment will stop, since every dominant player will attempt to extend its dominant position into new or neighbouring markets. This, however, does not mean that all transactions are based on sound financial and strategic logic. Frequently, they are based on a largely unproven and risky convergence theory of the so-called benefits of the value chain.

Summary

On the whole, the issue of concentration will remain at the centre of heated debate in the first decades of the twenty-first century. Some governments may wish to pressure the EU to intervene and prevent the creation of more megaconglomerates. Some other governments may take a different view, advocating mergers and acquisitions as an advantage to their home companies in the international markets. Despite the different policies advocated, the current trends of the media convergence show that we may witness a market with new larger groups, or combinations of them and alliances.

These patterns cannot be easily tackled. Past experience has shown that in the era of globalization and convergence of the media neither the European Commission nor the individual Member States seem able to regulate ownership and concentration in the sector, since there are too many risks at stake. The European Parliament could provide a solution, but its influence on European legislation is very limited, since in the EU there are no 'European-wide public controversies, and debates on political issues and policy choices, and we have no European-wide competition for government office that could assume democratic accountability' (Scharpf 1997: 19).

The situation at the beginning of the twenty-first century is that larger media firms will continue to have an advantage over European citizens. This is because the EU and its larger Member States favour the logic of 'economy of scale', 'power of scale' and 'economics of breadth' (Mattelart 1994: 210), resulting in a dominant position being held by the major private enterprises within the communications system.

6

Politics in the Television Age

In the era of the communications revolution, the media are not simply a channel for transmitting messages, but also an autonomous mediator in society, and as a result they follow their own rules, aims, constraints and production logic (Altheide and Snow 1979). Mazzoleni and Schultz (1999: 249) note that the media are not mere passive channels for political communicators and political content: 'Rather, the media are organizations with their own aims and rules that do not necessarily coincide with, and indeed often clash with, those of political communicators.' As Swanson and Mancini (1996: 251) point out, among other consequences, 'media logic' leads to a style of reporting that prefers personalities to ideas, simplicity to complexity, confrontation to compromise and heavy emphasis on the 'horse race' in electoral campaigns.

The television revolution has coincided with a decrease in the status of political parties. Since the 1990s, European politicians have spent an increasing amount of time trying to cope with the new media landscape, and an increasing amount of money publicizing their positions and polishing their public images. This focus on political communication practices has led many to argue that European societies have entered a new era, called 'videocracy' (Mazzoleni 1995), which gives a prominent role to television and results in changes in the political communication process. As a result, this situation leads to a decrease in the power and status of politicians.

This chapter is divided into four subsections. The first one discusses the relationship between television and politics, and argues that the growing indifference of the public towards politics should be attributed to the decline of politics in a new post-Cold War era rather than being considered as the outcome of television's dominance. The second section reviews the role of television in contemporary election campaigning in Europe. The third section attempts to discuss the effects of television on politicians. Finally, the last section of this chapter reviews these developments and argues that the rise of a 'modernized' relationship between the media and politics does not seem to be making a positive contribution to the health of democracy.

Television and politics

In most European countries television has become the dominant medium, not only for entertainment, but also of information. In effect, as the Eurobarometer of 1999 shows, the overwhelming majority of Europeans obtain their daily information from television rather than turning to the press as their main source (table 6.1) (Eurobarometer 1999). With such evidence, it is then hardly surprising that political parties would devote most of their energies to the television medium.

This interest in television is not new. It goes back to the late 1970s, when television was a state monopoly. Political parties in those days had already begun to tailor their conferences and rallies to the needs of television. Nor are media consultants a recent phenomenon. In fact, communication experts were first employed in Europe in the late 1960s. As Blumler and Kavanagh (1999: 212–13) note, since the 1960s, Western society has been faced with a more mobile elec-

Table 6.1 Daily use of the media for information, by country, 1999 (%)

Medium	Belgium	Denmark	Germany	Greece	Spain	France	Ireland	Italy
Television	67	74	70	82	70	59	68	82
Press	30	54	58	16	28	28	43	29
Radio	41	64	55	17	33	37	65	23

Medium	Luxembourg	Netherlands	Austria	Finland	Sweden	UK	Portugal	EU 15
Television	74	75	65	83	67	72	83	**71**
Press	54	59	56	70	60	50	17	**41**
Radio	62	58	67	49	48	46	29	**41**

Note: Fieldwork in March–April 1999.
Source: Eurobarometer (1999: B21–3).

torate and the parties have become increasingly 'professionalized' and adapted their communications to the news values and formats of a limited-channel television environment. As they point out: 'From this development, the core features of the professional model of modern campaigns emerged.'

In effect, this tendency became a 'must' condition in the politics of the 1990s, especially during elections, in most West European countries. In addition, political parties have spent considerable sums of money on television advertisements. By and large, it appears that, in the 1990s, in most European countries, after the deregulation and privatization of their audio-visual landscape, television moved to the centre stage of social and political life. Moreover, television has become a primary factor in the changing nature of electoral communication and other political practices (Blumler 1990; Mazzoleni 1995; Scammel 1995; Swanson and Mancini 1996). At the same time, as the world has become more complex, people have turned to the media, especially television, for an interpretative framework.

The dominance of television on social and political life has also coincided with a decline of traditional political parties, trade unions and political affiliations. In effect, political parties have faced a reduction in the number of their active members as well as great difficulties in communicating their positions to the public effectively without the 'mediatization' of television. In other words, television appears to be the mass medium of greatest importance, because of its strategic position as a dominant source of news and entertainment and its ability to reach a mass audience (Swanson and Mancini 1996: 251).

A longstanding relationship

Can we, therefore, argue that television has changed politics? This is a core question in media studies. In other words, is television a cause or an effect of social change? McQuail (1994: 73–4) has noted that no simple answer can be expected, and different theories offer alternative versions of relationship. At issue, as he points out, are alternative ways of relating three basic elements:

- the technology of communication and the form and the content of the media;
- changes in society (social change and institutional arrangements); and
- the distribution among a population of opinion, beliefs, values and practices.

These three elements are all relevant in the relationship between television and politics. As has already been noted, this relationship is not new (Lang and Lang 1959). Researchers from early communications studies focused on the media's role and on how people choose their leaders (Lazarsfeld *et al.* 1948; Katz and Lazarsfeld 1955; Lang and Lang 1959; Pool 1959). Many of the arguments concerning the impact of television on politics were first expressed when the press was the dominant medium. At that time it was generally believed that the new medium of television would increase political participation (Kraus and Davis 1976: 50–1). Nowadays it is believed to have had quite the opposite effect. It is also argued that people who spend a lot of their time watching television tend to be poorly informed; little television fare is designed to enlighten the electorate and the viewing of news programmes is sometimes not positively correlated with political knowledge (Chaffee and Kaniham 1997: 421–2).

Robinson and Davis (1990) have shown that US TV news shows fail to increase viewers' political knowledge or comprehension. Robinson (1975; 1976) has also shown that watching the news on television often succeeds in making people both confused and cynical, and reinforces the idea that politics corrupts. In other words, the argument is that television fails to inform us about politics and also distorts our understanding of both governance and citizenship (Hart 1995). In fact, the development of television has coincided with a gradual abstention from electoral practices, as well as citizens' growing alienation and cynicism concerning politics and political parties. According to the European Commission (Eurobarometer 1999), the EU is characterized by:

- low levels of satisfaction with the way that democracy works (table 6.2);
- low levels of political interest (table 6.3); and
- low levels of confidence in political institutions (table 6.4).

But even if we accept this picture, can we argue that this is due to television images regarding politics?

Changes in media

Pippa Norris (2000) refers to the modern idea of 'videomalaise', which links reliance upon television journalism with the feelings of political cynicism, social mistrust and lack of political efficacy that

Table 6.2 Satisfaction with national democracy, by country, 1999 (%)
Question: On the whole, are you satisfied, fairly satisfied, not very satisfied or not at all satisfied with the way democracy works in (our country)?

Answers	Belgium	Denmark	Germany	Greece	Spain	France	Ireland	Italy
Very satisfied	9	22	15	9	21	7	21	3
Fairly satisfied	40	59	52	53	51	52	53	32
Not very satisfied	32	15	24	29	24	27	15	41
Not at all satisfied	14	3	6	9	2	10	3	23
Don't know	5	1	4	0	3	4	8	2

Answers	Luxembourg	Netherlands	Austria	Finland	Sweden	UK	Portugal	EU 15
Very satisfied	21	13	17	6	5	12	11	**11**
Fairly satisfied	62	65	47	61	59	52	46	**49**
Not very satisfied	9	17	34	27	25	18	34	**26**
Not at all satisfied	3	3	4	4	7	7	4	**9**
Don't know	6	2	2	2	3	11	5	**4**

Note: Fieldwork in March–April 1999.
Source: Eurobarometer (1999: B6).

Table 6.3 Interest in politics, by country, 1999
Question: When you get together with friends, would you say you discuss political matters frequently, occasionally or never?

Answers	Belgium	Denmark	Germany	Greece	Spain	France	Ireland	Italy
Frequently	9	21	16	25	7	9	11	17
Occasionally	52	62	66	50	43	53	44	56
Never	39	18	15	25	49	37	45	26
Don't know	0	0	2	0	0	1	1	1

Answers	Luxembourg	Netherlands	Austria	Finland	Sweden	UK	Portugal	EU 15
Frequently	16	12	14	13	16	12	8	**13**
Occasionally	60	63	64	68	62	49	45	**56**
Never	24	25	21	19	22	39	47	**30**
Don't know	0	0	1	0	1	0	1	**1**

Note: Fieldwork in March–April 1999.
Source: Eurobarometer (1999: B6).

Table 6.4 Trust in national institutions, by country, 1999

Question: I would like to ask you a question about how much trust you have in certain institutions. For each of the following institutions, please tell me if you tend to trust it or tend not to trust it.

Institutions	Belgium +	Belgium −	Denmark +	Denmark −	Germany +	Germany −	Greece +	Greece −	Spain +	Spain −	France +	France −	Ireland +	Ireland −	Italy +	Italy −
The government	23	71	41	53	43	43	38	57	47	46	36	53	38	49	28	58
Parliament	26	66	54	40	45	42	51	45	45	43	37	48	36	48	30	55
Political parties	17	78	27	63	18	69	20	77	19	72	11	80	21	65	16	71
Civil service	37	55	50	42	43	45	43	53	39	49	44	47	61	21	27	58
The Church	30	59	69	21	43	43	81	17	47	44	37	49	53	36	58	32
The police	42	53	85	13	65	28	55	42	56	39	55	38	72	20	59	32
The army	43	46	73	15	61	25	86	11	57	34	56	33	74	12	57	30
Justice/legal system	22	72	70	25	52	40	55	42	40	52	35	56	49	37	36	53
Trade unions	36	54	50	38	35	49	42	49	32	56	33	55	48	26	28	56

Institutions	Luxembourg +	Luxembourg −	Netherlands +	Netherlands −	Austria +	Austria −	Finland +	Finland −	Sweden +	Sweden −	UK +	UK −	Portugal +	Portugal −	EU 15 +	EU 15 −
The government	64	27	63	37	47	38	53	35	33	56	38	50	55	30	**40**	**49**
Parliament	61	27	62	35	47	35	55	35	42	47	36	48	56	30	**41**	**46**
Political parties	27	56	40	65	22	65	20	70	17	71	16	72	19	70	**18**	**71**
Civil service	51	31	57	24	65	24	43	43	45	35	44	36	40	43	**42**	**46**
The Church	45	43	47	43	39	47	69	23	48	37	56	30	74	47	**50**	**39**
The police	72	22	71	25	67	24	86	10	63	28	67	27	54	36	**62**	**32**
The army	61	24	68	21	59	17	85	10	57	30	74	14	66	17	**63**	**26**
Justice/legal system	59	28	59	35	61	45	61	30	53	36	48	40	42	45	**45**	**46**
Trade unions	44	41	60	27	36	44	54	29	34	52	37	42	37	44	**35**	**49**

Notes: (+) tend to trust, (−) tend not to trust. The difference between '+' and '−' is the percentage of 'don't know' (not shown).
Fieldwork in March–April 1999.

Source: Eurobarometer (1999, B3, B4)

emerged in the political science literature of the 1960s. In the 1990s, with the deregulation and further commercialization of the news media, many analysts believe that the dominance of television in the media landscape has negatively affected the way citizens see the political world. In Europe, this was also associated with the decline of public service television, the rise of commercial television and the merciless competition for ratings, which in turn has given more emphasis to the sensational and negative aspects of the political world. However, as Norris (2000) notes, similar concerns were voiced during the period of 'yellow journalism' in the 1890s. The difference of today is that the coverage of the news media concerning scandals and corruption is more frequent in comparison to previous decades. In effect, since the mid-1980s, in many countries (Greece, Italy, Spain, France, the UK; Germany, and so on), accusations concerning scandals and corruption have been frequent themes in the news media. This coverage is believed to corrode the forms of trust underpinning social relations and political authority. But, as she argues, newer studies in the USA and Europe have found that, contrary to 'videomalaise' and although TV watching was related to some signs of apathy, attention to the news media was associated with positive indicators of civic engagement.

The truth is that nobody can argue convincingly that television is the main cause that mobilizes or demobilizes the public to participate in politics and electoral practices. Besides, television is only one source of information and competes directly with others for citizens' attention. Moreover, one should not forget that television in most West European societies arrived in the late 1950s not in the 1990s. What is in hard contrast to the past is that news television output of today is less directly influenced by the wishes of the political parties or the party in power. The phrase of French President Charles De Gaulle in the 1960s – 'my enemies have the press, I have television' – highlights that television in the state monopoly era was a highly politicized institution following, directly or indirectly, the wishes of the government of the day (see also Kuhn 1995). However, this does not apply to all countries (such as the UK, the Netherlands and Sweden). One can also say that television coverage over politics had 'typically assumed some responsibility for the health of the political process and for the quality of public discourse generated within' (Blumler 1992c: 12). On the other hand, one has to note that public broadcasters were often constrained, owing to their dependence on the governments of the day, by the wishes of the political world. Even the BBC, the most famous public broadcaster for its independence in crucial cases such as Northern Ireland, the

Royal Question, the IRA, and so on, was constrained to prudence. In some countries, such as Greece, Italy, Spain, Portugal or France, the government tightly controlled public television. In some others, such as Germany, the Netherlands, Belgium and Denmark, television was indirectly controlled by the political parties, which used to place their people in senior positions with the public broadcasters (Blumler 1992c: 13).

Additionally, the choice of the average citizen/voter to participate in politics or not is something that can be linked to his or her previous political behaviour and the political situation of a given time (Comstock 1989: 131–3). As David Weaver (1995) notes, contrary to popular belief, media exposure seems to have little relationship to voters' images of candidates; prior political attitudes and educational levels are much stronger predictors of these perceived images. In other words, the way people decide to engage themselves in politics is often complex and unpredictable. Besides, people, if not restricted to formal party participation, have probably never been so active in the post-war years in Europe (Brants 1999: 413). Therefore, if television is not the primary reason, one has to look at the social and political changes that occurred in Europe in the last two decades of the twentieth century.

Changes in society

Jay Blumler (1996: 396–8) points out four interwoven transformations. These are societal; political; changes in the dynamics of inter-communicator relationships; and changes at the level of voter response. Mazzoleni and Schultz (1999: 252–3) note two major trends that have influenced these developments. In Europe one can recognize first the rise of sophisticated citizenry, and, secondly, the crisis of the party system. With regard to citizenry, they point out that Western industrial societies in recent decades have been undergoing, among other things, a change of value orientations and an increase of political skills amongst the population. This is related to the higher levels of education, which has resulted in many people, many more than in the past, developing higher cognitive skills and a higher degree of political sophistication. Thus, a majority of citizens have been emancipated from traditional political institutions and begun to formulate their stance on current issues independently of the positions of the political parties. As Mazzoleni and Schultz (1999: 252) stress: 'Sophisticated citizens have included unconventional modes in their repertoire of political participation and, for instance, may judge referendums as more important than elections and protest as more effective than party support.' In other words, election turnout has become a weak indicator for measuring political participation. Additionally, as Mazzoleni and Schultz (1999: 252) argue: 'the ubiquitous availability of information via the mass media is an important resource that self-mobilized citizens use for developing their political orientation individually and independently of party ideology.'

On the other hand, apart from the 'self-mobilized' citizens, there is a much larger group of people who are poorly informed and express a lack of interest in politics. As Mazzoleni and Schultz (1999: 254) note, in previous times, the majority of this group relied on 'political parties to relieve them of the need for individually deliberated choices. By aligning themselves with social cleavages and prevailing group interests, the parties acquired a profile that served as evidence of political competence for many voters.' With the general trend towards declining party identification in Western democracies, political parties, as noted above, have lost their former orientation function, particularly for apolitical citizens. They argue that, in addition to their weak or non-existent party identification, the 'apoliticals' and the sophisticated have one other thing in common: they turn, heavily or exclusively, to mass media for political orientation and guidance. This has led to a new development: 'in recent years, first public opinion and then electorates have become volatile, more sensitive to current issues, to images of political leaders, and to the changing *zeitgeist*' (Mazzoleni and Schultz (1999: 254)).

Accordingly, Gibbins and Reimer (1999: 104) argue that politics in postmodernity becomes more integrated with other everyday life practices. In the postmodern age, one witnesses a general realignment in politics from 'old' to 'new' politics – that is, a gradual process of societal redirection towards a range of new interests, attachments, alignments, memberships, participation and behaviours. New political activities are not only unconventional, involving protest activities. They are also less structured, allowing more direct involvement from participants. They are less stable in membership and agendas over time. They are less related to economic and social stratification. And they are less about ideology, interest and power. Gibbins and Reimer (1999: 105) do not overlook the crucial role played by the media in political behaviour in relation to these new politics (or social movements). On the contrary, they regard them in many ways as 'media phenomena in the sense that the movements are able to

Table 6.5 Trust in the media, by country, 1999

Question: I would like to ask you a question about how much trust you have in certain institutions. For each of the following institutions, please tell me if you tend to trust it or tend not to trust it.

Medium	Belgium +	−	Denmark +	−	Germany +	−	Greece +	−	Spain +	−	France +	−	Ireland +	−	Italy +	−
The Press	64	31	56	38	48	44	51	43	62	30	60	34	50	43	45	45
Radio	76	20	78	17	67	26	59	34	72	19	68	25	79	16	53	30
Television	79	19	72	23	68	26	61	37	66	31	58	38	77	17	59	34

Medium	Luxembourg +	−	Netherlands +	−	Austria +	−	Finland +	−	Sweden +	−	UK +	−	Portugal +	−	EU 15 +	−
The Press	59	31	73	22	49	38	65	27	53	38	24	68	49	27	**49**	**42**
Radio	71	20	79	12	65	19	81	11	77	16	66	22	65	20	**66**	**24**
Television	74	20	84	12	75	18	79	15	72	21	71	24	75	16	**67**	**28**

Notes: (+) tend to trust, (−) tend not to trust. The difference between '+' and '−', is the percentage of 'don't know' (not shown).
Fieldwork in March–April 1999.
Source: Eurobarometer (1999: B3, B4).

handle the media much better than are traditional political practices' (Gibbins and Reimer 1999: 105).

McQuail (1994: 2) notes that the nature of the relation between the media and society depends on circumstances of time and place. Thus, we can say that the decline of political parties or the lack of interest in traditional politics has more to do with the conditions of modern democracy than with the power of television. In effect, it is the wider political and economic environment that has changed the conditions that traditional political parties have now to work within. It is not a coincidence that, for example, most West European parties face similar problems. Within the EU this is mostly related to the condition imposed by the Maastricht Treaty, the economic globalization and the worldwide integration of markets for capital, goods and services. This has gradually obliged political leadership in most European countries to follow a more managerial policy rather than an interventionist one. And political parties appear not to be able to differentiate their policies. Within the EU more specifically, national governments 'have delegated control over external trade relationships to the Union, and where they have in fact abdicated boundary control over economic transactions within the internal European market' (Scharpf 1997: 18). As Suzan Strange (1998: 101) notes:

> The result has been a widespread and growing structural unemployment in the face of which governments have proved quite unable to keep their electoral promises to bring unemployment down, create new jobs and recover past levels of economic growth. It is against this acute crisis in capitalist societies that we have to ask how globalization and the concomitant imperatives of competition for market shares affects the choice of national and common European policy options.

This new situation has led European citizens to feel that politicians are not in a position to solve either their thorny problems, or the main concerns of their country. This in turn may have led citizens to express their mistrust regarding governments and political parties in comparison to other national institutions (table 6.4). Instead, they tend to trust the media (table 6.5). Television has not caused this, although its news coverage, as in other media, is more critical compared to the past.

Moreover, traditional political parties, instead of innovating their ideological agenda, or even their structures and organization, started using the media, especially television, more and more to address the public, especially during election campaign periods. What has occurred is that traditional political parties have started using the media heavily, and television in particular, in order to become visible and thus to regain their legitimacy in their societies (see also Thompson 1995: 119–48). This development has affected the political process, since 'it is hard to separate out the effects of media change from board changes in society' (McQuail 1994: 371).

Television and election campaigning

Television in the twenty-first century has become the primary domain of European election campaigning, often its arbitrator. When parties started focusing heavily on television, this resulted in party workers, voluntary activists and executive members losing their role, especially during election time. In the past, they used to have more direct contact with the members of the public. But television could do all of these through political advertising, news stories on the main television news bulletins and talk shows. Thus, gradually, the notion and the role of the traditional political campaign changed. More importantly, through the new practices the feelings of a common effort were lost, the feeling of 'political gut' that the parties provided to their followers and friends. As Margaret Scammel (1999: 720) notes: 'By contrast the modern campaign is capital intensive, relying on a much smaller base of volunteers, much tighter central direction of campaign operations, increased reliance on party experts from media and marketing, far less face-to-face communication with voters and increased targeting of floating voters.'

This was certainly the case in the national elections in most countries in Europe during the 1990s. In the 1996 Italian elections, most of the campaign fight was between Freedom Alliance's leader and media magnate Silvio Berlusconi, and Olive Tree Alliance's Romano Prodi, an economics professor and the head of the European Commission at the dawn of the twenty-first century (see also Mazzoleni 1995). He took his Olive Tree Alliance's programme to the people by touring Italy in a bus. Moreover, since their differences on the main issues were very blurred, they understood the importance of using their image to 'sell-themselves'. Prodi was keen to portray himself as serious and trustworthy, and therefore stuck determinedly to his 'down-to-earth' academic image, trying to prove that he was the right character at the right time. This made Berlusconi adopt (or try to adopt) a weightier image by always carrying a pen and a stack of papers, although he was rarely spotted taking notes.

In the 1995 French Presidential elections, some candidates used the experiments of the 1993 legislative elections to adopt more developed styles of political advertising and commercials in tune with generalized multimedia techniques (see Maarek 1997). In the UK, the modern campaign practices have been developing since the late 1950s and by the 1990s parties had become more proactive, coordinated and systemic in their news management (Norris 2000). In effect, a 'permanent campaign' has been developed where the techniques of electioneering and governing have become intertwined (Kavanagh 1995). In the 1998 German elections, the parties competed with each other to see who could attract the most celebrity supporters. In a losing cause, Helmut Kohl attracted support from, among others, the captain of the national soccer team and designer Karl Lagerfeld (Swanson 1998). In the 1994 Dutch election campaign, politicians spent sixty-seven hours on the screen, whereas television spent only twenty hours over the same period on soccer, the most popular sport in the Netherlands (Brants and Neijens 1998: 154).

On the other hand, European political parties, regardless of their *severe crisis of legitimacy* (see table 6.4), have not lost their power in electoral campaigning. They still nominate their candidates and control their election campaigns. Additionally, parties and politicians have increasingly started to adopt the 'modern publicity campaign'. Kavanagh (1995) provides us with the main features of this professional model.

1. *The importance of campaign communications.* This process includes the parties' recruitment of technical experts from the public relations, media and advertising industries to assist with campaign publicity, media presentation, opinion polling and advertisements.
2. *An updating of publicity priorities in campaigning, as the party actors devote more energy and resources to media strategy and tactics.*
3. *The explanation of a party's election victory or defeat in terms of (1) and (2) above, i.e. publicity-related factors.*
4. *The adaptation of the campaign to the presumed format requirements of television.*
5. *The idea of electioneering as political marketing.* Political parties commission public opinion polls to research the mood of voters and the results are used by parties to shape their campaign communications. Opinion polls are also used by the news media to report the parties' performance.
6. *An increase in negative or attack campaigning.* Publicity concentrates at least as much time attacking the defects of opponents as presenting the merits of the sponsoring party.
7. *The dilemma for political journalists in defending a role for themselves in an era of 'saturation' coverage and manipulative politicians and campaign advisers.*

8. *The main gainers from the new political campaigning being the independent experts such as advertising personnel, media advisers and pollsters, most of whom are recruited from outside the parties.*

Moreover, one can also say that the reliance on the 'modern publicity campaign' has not only resulted in a decline, or alienation, of party workers, members and other party groups, but has also transformed their traditional party campaigns into media campaigns (Mazzoleni and Schultz 1999: 257). Furthermore, the importance of television has resulted in a change both in politicians' style of political communication and in the way they contact their supporters. Moreover, the 'images' of political leaders have started to become a major preoccupation of the image-makers (Blumler 1999: 243).

These trends have gradually resulted in a change in the performance of the political scene as well as in a change (in effect, a devaluation) in the role of some party executive members during the campaign period. In effect, the dominance of television has coincided with a kind of downgrading of party discipline. When television is more attracted by 'telegenic' politicians, this attitude affects intra-party politics. Most importantly, political parties had to follow the logic of the media, while on the other hand, due to their intense competition and commercialization, give preference to spectacular and sensationalist coverage of political events and the images of the political leaders rather than to hard issues. This however, is not universal in Europe. Kees Brants (1998: 327) argues that the arrival of commercial television may have resulted in an increase in human interest and sensationalism, but not in political reporting. It is questionable whether commercial news television services have brought better political information.

It was once thought that television would open up the electoral system, encourage politicians to be more honest to voters, increase political participation and eventually help the democratic process. One could say that the multiplication of television outlets has created new opportunities and pitfalls for the public to enter the political world. But this remains a wish. What we have witnessed instead is the emergence of a new era where politics is dominated by images and characterized by an avoidance of tackling the thorny issues of their societies and citizens.

Politicians are constantly under pressure to adapt to new technologies in their attempt to improve their communications strategies but they also tend to overuse any new technology in political rhetoric. In Greece, the chairman of Parliament noted publicly that the sight of Members of Parliament rushing to make statements in front of TV cameras did not fit with the perceived status of politicians. Moreover, the Greek Parliament, a parliament whose sessions at one time used to attract the interest of the Greek nation, has been downgraded for many years now. But the sad picture of the empty seats of ministers and deputies seems to be common in most European parliaments.

Why has this happened? Is it due to television? In his research on the changing relationship between the Parliaments and the media in the UK, Germany and France, Ralph Negrine argues that the nature of parliamentary coverage has been undergoing continual change for well over a century. He notes that one of the contemporary consequences of that change has been the marginalization of parliaments as locations and sources of political news (Negrine 1999: 349–50). He also argues that such a change in practices could not have taken place independently of political changes and that this could be a result of the more commercial approach adopted by the broadcast media, since ordinary images of debates are not enough to attract the public. A second explanation, he notes, for the changes lies in the ever-changing news priorities. A third explanation reflects the adaptation of one medium to another. Journalists interviewed for his project often suggested that, since broadcast media offered a window on parliaments – extracts from speeches in news programmes, countless interviews with politicians, twenty-four-hour news channels and the like – newspapers could perhaps focus more beneficially on explanation and interpretation. Consequently, as Negrine (1999: 350), argues:

> the underlying causes of changes in parliamentary and political coverage reside in a combination of things: a changing media world ('commercialization', 'visualization', 'tabloidization'), a changing parliamentary framework (more powerful executive, absent MPs, other locations of power, etc.), and a changing inter-play between the two continually evolving worlds of the media and politics in which the media are more focused on the search for the newsworthy, the exciting and the visually entertaining. The outcome of all these changes is the current state of political and parliamentary coverage.

Television and politicians

These examples alone demonstrate that a bigger change has happened in terms of political communication. In the past, politicians generally felt that they had clear policy objectives and the means of obtaining them. They had a somewhat 'face-to-face' communication with their constituencies, learning about their problems and concerns. Nowadays, they attempt to do this through electronic means of communication. In other words, European politicians have turned heavily to television for their public communication. This to a certain extent shows that TV is now more efficient in terms of their public communication than their parties. Besides, citizens watching their politicians on the screen sometimes have the feeling that they know them well. This is due to the fact that, as Edelman (1988) has noted, in today's complex industrialized societies, political messages are often presented as simple formulas to the people, and images or myths tend to replace the substantiation of claims. Thus, politicians, by presenting their personality and motivations, may deflect the electorate from judging them by political record (Schutz 1995: 212).

This, in turn, has led politicians to use television more and more. They gradually and unintentionally adopt a role that is more or less equivalent to the television celebrity, perhaps because they have realized that people vote for those who are more 'attractive' on the screen. The result is a further personalization of politics, which in turn is ever more effectively crafted, for television may be a kind of 'virtual politics' filled with attractive but superficial images and slogans that are irresistible to the visual appetites of commercial journalism (Swanson 1998; Swanson and Mancini 1996: 256).

Generally speaking, in the television era, politicians know that we want them to be attractive, interesting, clear and brief in their statements. Having this attitude, of course, we act more as TV viewers than responsible citizens. This happens not only during the campaigning period, but all the time. Mughan (1995: 328) notes that television is better suited for the projection of personalities than the discussion of complex ideas and policy initiatives. One could also say that television is the medium par excellence to evaluate personal qualities of political leaders. In effect, in comparison to old times, in the television era the members of the public have an unprecedented access to their leaders. But, paradoxically, the leaders' authority seems to have declined. Indeed, one of the great paradoxes of our times is that, when politicians decide to enter the TV world and try to acquire a national image and visibility, they tend to suffer from overexposure and consequently lose their political aura (Meyrowitz 1986: 270–1; Thompson 1995: 125–7).

This mostly happens in the course of so-called televised debates between contesting political leaders. As Kathleen Hall Jamieson (1987: 28) notes:

As messages running an hour or longer, debates offer a level of contrast with candidates clearly unmatched in spot ads and news segments. Uninterrupted by advertising, uncontaminated by the devices programmers use to enhance and hold prime-time audiences, the debates offer the most extensive and serious view of candidates available to the electorate.

But, as Jamieson notes, debates have drawbacks as well. They have borne the imprint of television; ideas must be trimmed to fit pre-set time limits (Jamieson 1987: 32). Gradually, debates seem to look more like talk shows than what they are supposed to be. Politicians have prescheduled everything with their advisers before the debate, since they are more concerned about their image than with what they say. An example comes from the French Presidential elections of 1995. Both Jacques Chirac and Lionel Jospin had scheduled all details. Chirac used sparring partners to play the part of Jospin before the day of their debate. The two-hour television debate was a highly orchestrated affair. Each candidate had his own television producer with a third running the programme overall. Both turned down an oval table and ordered a rectangular table to be made specially. A pair of identical chairs was agreed on after three pairs had been turned down. Chirac was seated to the right and Jospin to the left. Seating arrangements had been worked out by flipping a coin. The two appeared in a large studio before a sky-blue backdrop, with guests relegated to a separate room so as not to distract them. Two journalists steered the debate. In such an organized debate, it was no surprise that the two leaders offered nothing but generalities and no precise measures.

The 'anxiety' about TV debates can easily be explained. As Weaver (1995: 42–3) notes, there is no doubt that prospective voters can get a better idea of how a candidate looks, talks and interacts with others from television coverage than from newspapers and other printed media. But, for Neil Postman (1985: 98), what all of this means is that the nature of political discourse is becoming blurred with that of show business. This is also, however, due to the disappearance of ideologies and the lack of differences between political parties (Grigler and Jensen 1991: 189). It remains, however, unclear whether candidate's images are influenced more by media reports than by prior beliefs and attitudes of voters.

By and large, the dominance of television in election campaigning, has contributed to a further personalization of politics. But television is not the primary cause. The end of the cold war, the globalization of the economy, the increase in the profile of the EU, the wider change of international geopolitics and chronic economic problems are some of the major problems that have made governments and politicians unable to provide answers and solutions. As Mancini (1999: 240–1) notes, contemporary politicians' policy making is heavily based upon consultation from individual experts and academic and research organizations, the so-called think tanks. Politicians are judged on their efforts to answer 'to the ever more difficult problem of managing a complex society in which skills are available outside the political world that can be used by those who have responsibility of governing' (Mancini 1999: 241).

Modern television viewers may be regarded as 'couch potatoes', but they still can judge discordant political messages. It is hard to say whether television has turned citizens from being voters to viewers. But they no longer receive their political information entirely through government sources and announcements. This used to give an advantage to governments, which could control the pace of the events and provide answers. With 'live broadcasting' and 'direct broadcast by satellite', citizens receive information almost at the same time as their leaders. This directness of receiving information has often made politicians and political leaders lose control of what they say, when the broadcast media demand immediate answers.

Television and politics in the era of modernization and digitalization

The above discussion illustrates the changes in both media and politics that have often been described as part of a process of 'modernization' (see Mancini and Swanson 1996). Modernization is in its Weberian sense seen as a total process, which implies not only a gradual move from tradition to modernity (Giddens 1990), but also a process towards a functionally integrated national or even supranational political system (Mouzelis 1986). One of the main features of modernization is an increase in social complexity, characterized by the development of 'specialized and competing subsystems', which undermine traditional structures of social inclusion and aggregation – church, political parties, trade unions and so on (Scammel 1999: 721). What we see in Europe, therefore, is not only a move away from traditional forms of election campaigning to more modern ways and means, but also changes within the political system, where the traditional practices are under severe pressure to change in the modern international economy. These individual examples of change can perhaps be treated as symptomatic of the process of 'modernization'.

These developments reflect not only a changing media environment but also changes in the standing of the political parties within the political system as a whole. More importantly, perhaps, these changes reflect a convergence of developments in both institutions. These changes lend support to many of the statements made by Mancini and Swanson (1996), amongst others, regarding the growing similarities in election practices across many countries: there are, it would seem, similarities 'despite great differences in political cultures, histories, and institutions of the countries in which they have occurred'. Such similarities would include the use of political commercials ('pollispots'), candidates being selected in part for the appealing image that they project on television, the employment of technical experts to advise on strategies, the professionalization of campaign communication, and the like. These, and the increased expenditure on strategies aimed at the medium of television, show just how far television has moved to the centre of European elections.

But the European case compromises some, though not all, of the elements that have been identified as comprising 'modernized' or 'media-centred democracy' (Swanson 1993; Mazzoleni 1995; Scammel 1995; Blumler 1996; Negrine 1996; Swanson and Mancini 1996; Mancini 1999). As we have seen, there has been an increased use of 'experts', an increased – and more professional – use of television and media practices, a personalization of politics, a detachment of parties from citizens and more political spectacles, while the media have become more autonomous (Swanson and Mancini 1996). There continue to be dissimilarities, though admittedly mainly with the political communication process in the USA and much less with other democracies – for example, the UK. In most European countries, for example, voters have to choose between different political parties and not between candidates for President as well as other representatives, as in the USA. In most European countries, a candidate for Prime Minister cannot appear out of nowhere and cannot progress far without extensive party political support. In effect, to a lesser or to a larger extent, candidates tend to be known figures before they stand for election. Nevertheless, European politicians of today rely heavily on modern campaign practices.

As in the USA, television in Europe has become central to the conduct of politics. The final result, however, has borrowed new techniques from American political communication (Maarek 1997), such as heavy journalistic use of public opinion polls and extreme simplification of the issues by basing their campaign on the US style, as on the importation of the 'primary system'. In this process of change, political parties and politicians have had to reassess their role in the political system. Thus, although political parties remain important, public support for them is weakening. But their structures and character have changed in the wake of socio-political changes and these have created difficulties for the political parties. For example, political parties – and their leaders – have become 'de-linked' from the stable societal sectors that used to share their interests.

At the same time as these changes have been taking place, the political parties and their leaders have had to confront a media system that increasingly values its independence. This has become a feature of the 'political-media complex' (Swanson 1992), which places the media and politics in a complex, and sometimes antagonistic, relationship. As Swanson (1992: 399) has written, 'within this complex, particular institutional interests often conflict with each other in the battle to control public's perceptions, but mutual co-operation is required for each institution to achieve its aims'. In recent years, European politicians have been ready to criticize the media and to threaten them with a law that would place the media under a more restrictive legal framework. In other words, this is an attempt by European politicians to muzzle the media, though these threats have never been carried out, as chapter 5 has illustrated. Finally, the rise of a 'modernized' relationship between the media and politics is not seen as making a positive contribution to the health of democracy. The European public now regards political institutions as dysfunctional and untrustworthy.

In an era of media expansion, political and social crisis, economic inefficiency and the related insecurity provide the media with what they need. The media focus on contradictions and colour them with drama, since both elements appear to appeal to the public. It is not the media, and television in particular, that have changed politics; it is the whole political arena, which is in a transitional stage – with the media taking advantage of the situation. As Negrine (1996: 180) has noted, politicians and the media claim to be speaking on behalf of the public and the citizen, yet both are pursuing their own 'institutional needs'. 'Both', as Negine points out, 'are part of the problem, of a lack of accountability in democratic systems, of a disillusioned citizenry, and of a host of other ills which critics can reel off'. In fact, in 'media-centred democracies', the 'modern publicity process' and the 'political commercials' continue to treat the public as a mobile and private consumer rather than a real participant in the democratic process.

It is yet to be seen, however, whether the digitalization of television will affect politics. Viewers will have more choices, and the traditional mass audiences will not only be fragmented into smaller groups but will also get their political information from various viewing alternatives. As a consequence, politicians and political parties will have to try harder to 'approach' them, and, at the same time, will be forced to adopt more professional practices. In relation to this and to the growth of the Internet, a serious question is raised concerning the function of democracy in an era in which the citizens of a country will no longer receive common information from the same, major media sources. Looking from this perspective – that is, the 'end of the mass audience', as David Swanson (1998) has noted, 'we may well need to rethink our theories of democracy and communication in the new and more fragmented media environment'. And if in this century we want democracy to be served, then we have to find ways for all new technology to serve our democratic goals (Barber 1999: 589).

Part II

European Television in the Twenty-first Century

7

From the General and National to the Particular and Local

Until the mid-1980s there were only two television channels in most European countries and in some countries there was only one. From the mid-1990s and onwards, European television has been developing into a specialist medium, shaping content to cater for the particular interests of the public. Similarly, the traditional general entertainment family television channel has become an endangered species. In fact, no new channel started in 2000 that aims to follow the traditional general entertainment programme diet.

The new European multichannel environment is constituted by digital platforms, with more than 300 channels transmitted mostly through Astra and Eutelsat satellites. Their arrival has opened up the way for increasing specialization in their content. In fact, digital technology has enabled the analogue thematic channels of the 1990s to proliferate and achieve even more specific levels of segmentation. Nowadays, there are channels specializing in news, music, sports, children, lifestyle, home shopping, animals, wildlife and documentaries, history, science, channels for women and so on.

New technologies, especially digital, and new ways of funding, especially pay-TV and PPV, have allowed the so-called niche channels to survive with far smaller audiences than would have been needed if they were broadcast by more traditional ways and means. Their development has raised questions with regard to the future of the national general entertainment broadcasters.

Thematic channels are a US invention, which, following their success in their domestic market, were adopted by Europe. But, as the market for thematic channels has become more competitive, broadcasters, especially successful international television channels, are being forced both to adapt to the needs of different countries and to market and position themselves in a way that makes them stand out from the crowd. In effect, the new technologies and the internationalization of communication have not eliminated the localized channel. On the contrary, regionalization or localization is clearly something that most channels are going to have to do.

This chapter discusses the rise of the multichannel environment in European television and the rise of thematic channels. It also considers the issue of localization of international thematic channels, so introducing the readers to the following chapters, regarding news, sports, music and children.

The birth of thematic channels in the USA

Home Box Office (HBO), a division of Time Inc., was launched on 8 November 1972 on US cable systems, featuring recent films. Its advent broke the dominant and widespread way of the single television model by offering viewers only one genre of television content rather than the usual mix of programme types. The financial incentive for the development of thematic channels or 'narrowcasting' relates to the traditional economic models of audience programme choice: these assume that, when there is a very limited number of television channels and therefore programme diet, the main bulk of the viewers will be attracted by mass-appeal programming. With a plethora of TV channels in the audio-visual field, however, the average number of viewers available for each channel becomes smaller and smaller, eventually allowing a programmer to maximize audience size with specialized-appeal programming. Therefore, 'with a large range of programme options, it would be economically practicable to provide programmes satisfying numerous minority tastes' (Grant 1994: 53). The success of HBO established a precedent for isolating other strands from the television programme repertoire and marked the beginning of the development of dedicated content channels.

The process of subdividing general content into specific streams has been slow. The categories in the early 1980s were broad and few; the first thematic channels were on news, music and sports. Other dedicated channels followed, covering children, family, lifestyle, fashion or the arts, or dedicated to teenagers or shopping and auctions. These thematic channels were developed in the USA. Market-leading cable operators such as Tele-Communications had a major stake in thematic channels such as CNN, American Movie

Classics, BET, the Discovery Channel and so on. After their home success, they moved into Europe, presenting a new model for European broadcasters.

The arrival of thematic channels in Europe

The first specialist European television service was the Open University in the UK, albeit piggybacked onto the BBC in downtime during the early 1980s. The launch of Canal Plus in 1984, giving preference to films and sports, may be considered Europe's first thematic channel. The advent of thematic channels in Europe can be traced back no further than the tentative moves towards deregulation in West Germany and the UK, as the prospects of cable began to move.

The close affinity between cable systems and channels was evident in the mid-1980s. The early European cable channels tried to imitate the US broadcasting model. Intending their signals to reach cable distributors, they deliberately made their channels near copies of commercial television services, although they were heavily dependent on cheap, imported programming (Woodman 1999: 32). In the UK, apart from Sky Channel, The Entertainment Network (TEN) was launched in March 1984. It closed down a year later and was relaunched as Mirrorvision. The latter was merged with (UK-based) Premiere in April 1986. But the venture was closed in 1989. Meanwhile, Sky Channel, despite News Corporation's involvement, struggled, as did Super Channel, despite some appeal to pan-European cable audiences.

Most channels in the mid-1980s – in most cases satellite to cable – were lured by the concept of featuring a general entertainment channel. Most of them were free to viewers, with low-cost programming, but they attracted low viewership levels and, thus, advertising revenues. They did not provide a suitable package of programmes for cable operators to attract subscribers. Moreover, up to the mid-1990s, the term thematic channel did not really correspond to the services offered, as many thematic channels frequently did not limit themselves to their programme segment. For example, Deutsches SportFernsehen (DFS), a German sports channel, also screened movie films from the archives of its own corporate members, although it was forced to leave the transmission of popular sporting events to the generalist channel ProSieben.

Moreover, the growth of thematic channels is related to the efforts and the heavy investment of leading media companies, such as the

News Corporation or the Kirch Group. But the real incentive for the introduction of thematic channels in Western Europe was the arrival of US-based thematic channels. In fact, in the late-1980s and early 1990s, European television-viewers became very familiar with US thematic channels such as CNN, MTV, Nickelodeon, Discovery and Cartoon Network.

The success of thematic channels in Europe

The success of cable and satellite television in general, and thematic channels in particular, has depended on three key factors.

First, came *the entry of US networks into the European television landscape* in their effort to expand their services to capture the European audience. Although European operators, such as the original Sky Channel, Satellite TV in 1982 or Super Channel in 1987, started their services with a pan-European strategy, they never managed to break through Europe's national and linguistic barriers. This does not mean that US channels were more successful, but rather that their entry worked as an incentive for local operators in Europe to launch similar thematic services to cater for their local audiences.

Secondly, *the availability of technology to reach the targeted audience* was crucial. The number of channels that can be received in cable homes is determined by the technical characteristics of the cable systems. The capacity of the old analogue European cable system was always an impediment for the development of thematic channels. For instance, Germany, one of the largest markets for the development of theme channels, has state cable systems that could not carry more than twenty channels, and the sixteen private channels and the public broadcasters filled most of the slots available. This is why digital compression, as described in chapter 2, is regarded as a saviour of thematic channels.

Thirdly, *the willingness of viewers to subscribe to these channels* was vital. Back in the mid-1980s, most operators regarded 'niche' channels with disdain, preferring mainstream programming. But since then many 'niche' channels have grown to claim a mainstream audience and broadened their advertising appeal. In the late 1990s, the presence of thematic channels in a digital platform offered some indication that an operator was catering to audience tastes and preferences. This is because television audiences, particularly pay-TV audiences, have become increasingly complex and fragmented, demanding greater choice and control over the types of programmes they watch. The content of digital packages is, therefore, generally targeted at much broader audiences whose individual tastes are distinctly different from each other. As thematic channels have increased their market appeal, many digital operators appear to accommodate them in their digital offering (Sutherland 1999a: 52).

A variety of thematic channels

One way in which both the type as well as the number of channels has experienced a stable growth is by dividing existing channels into two or more thematic strands. A number of channels, especially in the UK, have divided the day into theme segments with brand names. For instance, in February 1997, the Family Channel became Challenge TV throughout the afternoon and evening, and Family Late after midnight. Bravo was pitching its daytime schedule at the youth audience under the banner Trouble, reserving the original name for the late evening.

Moreover, names of channels have changed frequently. For example, Super Channel started as Music Box in 1985. In 1993 it was bought by NBC. After combining the two names for a while, NBC dropped the Super Channel part of the name in favour of NBC Europe, reduced on screen simply to NBC. The same happened when CNBC merged with EBN. SBS changed the name of its Swedish service Femman to Kanal 5 in 1995, at around the time Kinnevick launched rival TV6.

The most successful channels, referred to as mainstream thematic channels, have been those on news, sport, music and children. These are examined in detail in the following chapters of this book. In addition, there are an increasing number of thematic channels in the European television universe, with at least eighty-five new thematic channels launched in 2000. Finally, there are the adult channels, whose nature raises important questions with regard to the interplay of niche content and content regulation.

It seems that in this newly established multichannel landscape the concept of generalist television is gradually being replaced by the notion of a generalist digital platform. In fact, it becomes more and more evident that, in the twenty-first century, digital platforms offer their customers what the traditional generalist broadcasters offered to their viewers: a diet of all types of programme genres. The difference compared to the state monopoly era is that the dedicated channels of digital operators seem to have replaced the programming segments of the old generalist broadcasters.

The above is evident in financial strategies as well. As we have noted in chapter 4, digital platforms implement various strategies to attract subscribers, which to an extent are based on the traditional programming scheduling strategies of the terrestrial broadcasters. For example, packaging weaker channels with one or two strong brand-name channels so that strong channels can carry the weaker while the weaker channels boost the perceived value of package is very similar as a concept to the lead-in and lead-out programme strategies of the traditional terrestrial television stations.

This section describes movie channels, home shopping channels, documentary channels, religious channels, ethnic channels and adult channels.

Movie channels

Movie channels were early entrants in thematic television. Demand for film content dates back to the arrival of the video cassette recorder (VCR) in the early 1980s, when video sales and rent on films had a tremendous growth, while cinema attendance was high.

The French terrestrial pay-TV channel Canal Plus, launched in 1984, was the first movie channel in Europe. Filmnet in the Netherlands, launched by Nethold in 1985, was the first film satellite channel in Europe. It was followed by sister channels Filmnet Plus and Filmnet Movies in 1986. Sky Movies was the first British satellite movie channel, launched in 1989, followed by the Movie Channel of British Satellite Broadcasting, launched in 1990. Since then a number of movie channels have been launched such as Ciné Cinéfil and CinéCinémas (in France in 1992), Ciné Classico, Ciné Color and Cinémania (in France in 1995) and Filmnet movie channels (in Greece and Belgium). TV 1000 Cinema was launched in Sweden in 1995 and Premiere in Germany in 1991. A decade later, movies and sports premium content are still considered a driving force for the development of digital television in Europe.

There are two types of film channels. The first is the so-called classic movie channel, such as Turner Classic Movies, which is owned by Turner Broadcasting System and has regional versions in the UK, France, Switzerland, Belgium, Luxembourg, Spain, Poland, Scandinavia and Eastern Europe. Its films range from 1920s to 1980s releases. Another classical movie channel is Cinéclassics, which is owned by Multithématiques, a subsidiary of Canal Plus, which also has twenty-one thematic channels broadcasting in France, Germany, Spain, Poland and Italy. Cinéclassics content is adapted for each regional channel. Further examples include Canal Clásico and Ciné Clásico (in Spain) and Sky Movies Gold (in the UK). Some of these channels are also called 'library channels'. They broadcast old television series and films and are based on the large libraries of their production companies – most of which are also their owners.

The second type is the movie channel that features more recent films, such as CinéCinémas, owned by Multithématiques, which broadcasts recent films, or films three years after their cinema release, to comply with TV rights arrangements. Movie channels such as CinéCinémas or Film 1 in the Netherlands target movie lovers and offer them the opportunity to see films they might have missed when they were on general release at the cinema or simply films they would like to see one more time. These channels also offer their viewers news from the movie industry and interviews with famous directors and actors.

Home shopping channels

Quality Value Convenience (QVC) is probably the most recognized international teleshopping brand. In the USA it shares 90 per cent of the television shopping market with fellow Home Shopping Network (HSN). Home shopping channels have emerged all over Europe since the early 1990s. France was the first country, outside the USA, to embrace the concept of televised home shopping, although home shopping programming has not been very popular. QVC now has regional channels in Germany, the Netherlands and Ireland. It was launched in the UK in October 1993 as a joint venture between QVC and BSkyB. It is a twenty-four-hour themed teleshopping channel carried on the UK cable and satellite networks. Screenshop and Shop are also available in the UK. Screenshop was launched in October 1997 by Flextech Television and is broadcast on Flextech on downtime hours as well as on UK Gold (3 a.m. to 7 a.m.), Challenge TV (5 a.m. until 6 a.m.) and Trouble/Bravo (6 a.m. until 7 a.m.). The home shopping informercial channel Shop! is a joint venture between Granada Media and British retailer Littlewoods – launched on ONdigital in November 1998 and also available on cable systems.

In December 1996, QVC started broadcasting in Germany, and by the end of 1998 it had invested $66.9 million into its infrastructure. By 2001 it was available to twenty-five million German households. HSN also holds interests (41.99 per cent) in another German shopping channel (Hot) as well as in Spain after a joint venture with Uninvision. In June 1998, HSN introduced HSN–SBS Italia, a live teleshopping service in Italy in a joint venture with Scandinavian

Broadcasting System (SBS). HSN–SBS Italia is distributed on the Rete Mia TV broadcast network, reaching around fourteen million of Italy's twenty million television households. In France, Home Shopping service, owned by M6, was launched in May 1998. Club Téléachat, on the TPS platform, is a twenty-four-hour French-language shopping channel and competes with TF1's home shopping channel, Shopping Avenue, which is carried on cable and satellite. In Sweden, TV-Shop was launched in 1992, owned by Modern Times Group (MTG), which is part of the media and telecommunications group Kinnevik. Since March 1999 it has been broadcast on the Eurosport channel. This arrangement gives TV-Shop access late at night and in the early morning to eight-five million households across Europe. It is certain that the arrival of digital television will further extend the market and channel availability for TV home shopping. Moreover, digital television will also encourage interactivity and convergence with the Internet. Already, all of the home shopping channels have moved to the Internet, with their own web pages to improve the promotion of their services and products. As analysts say, new interactive technologies will not only change the face of home shopping in Europe, but will also lead it into the mass e-commerce market (Clover 1993; Margolis 1999; Sutherland 1999b).

Documentary channels

Digital television technology is also reinventing the genre of documentary television. In recent years there have been two types of documentary channels. One type is composed of channels moving towards 'docusoaps' and general factual programming, like UK Horizons, which presents programmes such as the series *Animal Hospital*. The second type includes channels such as National Geographic (launched in 1997) and Discovery (launched in 1989) or the History Channel (launched in 1995), which feature more typical documentaries. In practice, both subcategories feature a mix of traditional-style documentaries and other factual programmes. On the other hand, they define themselves as factual entertainment channels. Either way, documentary channels are welcomed by operators, both cable and satellite. This is both because documentary channels attract upmarket audiences, which are popular with advertisers, and because operators are recognizing their potential as a way of increasing their own customer base (Tobin 1999).

Documentary channels do not only compete directly against each other, but also face competition from the analogue terrestrial broadcasters, especially the public channels, which used to regard this type of programme as their exclusive domain, even in the deregulated television environment. In the UK, there are ten pay-TV documentary channels, amongst them National Geographic, Discovery, Animal Planet, UK Horizons, and the History Channel. In France there are five documentary channels: Encyclopaedia (knowledge and civilization), Animaux (wildlife), Odyssée, Escales (tourism and travel), La Chaîne Histoire (history) and Automobile (motoring); there are also the public channels Arte (arts and culture) and La Cinquième (education and culture). In Germany there are ZDF Doku and Phoenix.

Religious channels

Religious television channels should perhaps be treated as a special case. Their roots in broadcast television were limited in the USA. Their phenomenal growth has been due to their exponents carving out cable and satellite opportunities denied by traditional networks. With the advent of digital television, analysts foresee an important increase in religious television offerings in Europe. At the beginning of the twenty-first century, there are just a few religious channels available in Europe. These are the US-based Eternal Word Television Network (EWTN) – the largest cable television network in the world, founded in 1981; the Christian Channel Europe (CCE) – launched in 1995 and relaunched in 1997, which is available in twenty-four countries; and Muslim Television Ahmadiyyah (MTA) – set up in 1994. All of these transmit religious and non-religious programmes, though secular programmes have to fall within the religious guidelines of the specific denomination. Their general aim is to provide family programming that does not feature sex, drugs and violence (Callard 1999a).

Ethnic channels

As Europe has developed into a multicultural society, it has witnessed the arrival of European cable and satellite television channels such as TVBS, Zee, Chinese News and Entertainment (CNE), Hellenic TV, JSTV, EDTV, MBC, NTV, SET, Arab News Network, and others, as well as the international satellite versions of most European public broadcasters. These channels target specific communities, which live in European countries, mainly the capitals of Europe, where ethnic minorities and immigrants have increased in numbers in terms of both groups and population. For example, the twenty-four-hour Asian entertainment channel Sony Entertainment Television (SET) was launched in March 1998 to target the four million South Asians (Indian, Pakistani, Bangladeshi and Sri Lankans) living in the UK and Europe, and is available in the UK (through operators Telewest, NTL and BSkyB), in Denmark (through cable operator TeleDanmark) and in the Netherlands (through cable system A2000). Rival Zee TV was launched in the UK in 1995 and since 1998 has expanded into Europe. In the UK it is distributed through BSkyB and Telewest. It is also available in Portugal (through TV Cabo), Norway (Telenor), Denmark (TeleDanmark), the Netherlands (Mediacable, A2000, Casema), Germany (Deutsche Telekom) and France and Belgium (Canal Satellite Numérique) (Sutherland 1999d). The USA, a more developed market in thematic television and a much larger multicultural society, not only offers these services through cable and satellite systems, but also has a dedicated television service, the International Channel Networks, which features segments of premium ethnic channels in their languages. Its ethnic service offering consists of ARC (Arabic), CCTV-4 (Chinese), the Filipino Channel (Tagalog and English), TV5 (French), RAI International (Italian), TV Asia (Hindi, Gujarati and English), Zee TV (Hindi and Indian regional languages) and Canales-n (Spanish).

However, the case of the Kurdish satellite Med TV caused a headache for the UK regulatory authorities on 23 April 1999. Med TV was launched as a Kurdish-language channel in 1995, broadcasting an eighteen-hour service of a mix of news, current affairs, religious programmes and entertainment in the Kirmanci, Sorani, Zazaki and Lory dialects, Turkish and occasionally Arabic and Assyrian. Kurdish language teaching and broadcasting are not permitted in Turkey and Med TV was one of the only non-censored forums of cultural information for Europe's Kurdish diaspora. Med TV had its licence revoked by the UK regulatory authority ITC in April 1999, following several formal warnings over its politically biased content. The ITC felt that four of the channel's broadcasts were encouraging acts of violence in Turkey and elsewhere. ITC claimed that the content was 'likely to encourage or incite to crime, or to lead to disorder' (in Callard 1999b). Since its launch, Med TV had been warned several times by ITC over its content, but the suspension of its licence coincided with the arrest of Kurdish leader Abdullah Ocalan in March 1999 and the reactions of the Kurdish people.

Adult channels

'Erotica', whether 'adult' programmes or channels, have become common in European television markets. Their difference from 'classic' porno films is that very often they show programmes produced for television rather than for the video market. Their erotic 'action' fluctuates from 'soft' to 'hard' porn, depending on the time slot in which they are broadcast. These channels constitute proof that the absolute dominance of market forces upon the audio-visual field seems to work in a different way from that envisaged by the proponents of deregulation. 'Adult' programming costs less than other productions and attracts a significant number of, and most importantly loyal, viewers.

In Europe the demand for the 'adult' programme increased tenfold over the 1990s and this demand is escalating. In France in 1992–3, the average viewing of fifty erotica films broadcast by the terrestrial channel Métropole 6 (M6) in a 10.30 p.m. prime-time slot on Saturday nights was 20 per cent, compared to the channel's overall viewing share of 9 per cent. In Italy, following deregulation in 1974, new local channels 'found' that the transmission of late-night porn films consistently boosted their viewing shares (Evans 1992: 39–40). For broadcasters, 'adult' programming offers some 'competitive' advantages or a competitive weapon in their battle for viewers. The fact that porn films attracted viewers during late-night hours gave the stations the incentive to consider the possibilities of broadcasting soft versions of sex programmes that could be scheduled in prime time and attract large audiences. One form of programme was the erotica drama series. A second variation was an alliance with another TV genre: the TV game (Papathanassopoulos 1994).

The new structure of television markets has made these programmes competitive in various aspects. The erotica programmes not only have loyal viewers – although they never state this in the surveys; they also cost less compared to other productions and have a sales value in the international marketplace. For example, in 1992, two French erotica productions, *Venus*, a half-hour magazine programme presented by a naked woman, and *Emotions*, a half-hour compilation of erotic sequences, had a production budget of FF500,000 per episode, of which FF200,000 came from foreign sales. But the demand from television for this genre of programming increased production costs fourfold compared to three years previously (Evans 1992: 40). This is also due to the fact that a programme made for TV standards, purposes and specific demands (that is, censoring limitations) had to have much higher production values than the made-for-video-only, low-budget films (Evans 1992; Papathanassopoulos 1994).

The competitiveness of 'adult' programmes was a strong incentive for some broadcasters, mainly satellite channels, to build a programme strand targeted on this particular theme. Even the UK, where television used to be relatively immune to the advances of erotica, acquired pay-TV services aimed at this market. Transmission of 'adult programming' was first adopted by the French terrestrial pay-TV channel Canal Plus as an attempt to attract subscribers in its early days, when it faced serious problems of survival. For the British, Canal Plus was considered the most daring and risky television format in Europe. Later, other channels followed the Canal Plus way. The Benelux and Scandinavian pay-TV film channel Filmnet used to broadcast a number of hard-core porn movies, as did the rival Scandinavian pay-TV service TV 1000. In both cases, their signals were scrambled and erotic programming proved a natural driver for pay-TV services and a competitive way of attracting subscribers.

Since then, some other channels have been launched in Europe, such as Television X: The Fantasy Channel (UK in 1995), Channel Bizarre (the Netherlands in 1995), Erotica Rendez-Vous (France in 1995), Eurotica (UK in 1995), Eros (UK in 1995). Playboy TV was also launched in October 1995 in the UK as a joint venture of Flextech (51 per cent), Playboy (17 per cent) and BSkyB (32 per cent). Playboy has a distinct style compared to the other channels, mirroring the glossy sheen of the famous US magazine. It is also different from other US networks as regards its international strategy, since, for each international venture, the company owns a minority equity interest in the channel and receives licensing fees for programming and the use of the Playboy brand name (Schreiber 1998).

From international to local

There has been a theoretical debate with regard to the interdependency of the global, regional and local, and in particular to what extent local television serves more than one locality or whether regional and local television content differs significantly from the content delivered by international or global channels (Robertson 1994; Tomlinson 1994; Thompson 1995; Lee 2000; Wang and Servaes 2000; Wang et al. 2000). Such debate is not new. Armand Mattelart (1994: 216) reminds us of the older story of the internationalization of newspapers and magazines, when it was suggested that 'internationalization is a matter of segmentation and asynchronism'. Additionally, Morley and Robins (1995: 1–2) have pointed out that the 'deterritorialization' of audio-visual production, the elaboration of transnational systems of delivery and significant developments towards local production and local distribution complexes have taken place at the same time.

In the competitive environment of twenty-first century European television, broadcasters have realized that regionalization or localization is a strong strategy for survival. In fact, there is no channel with an international strategy that has not tailored its content and schedule in order to cater for local differences. Even a music channel like MTV, as we will see in chapter 10, has had to follow the regionalization path in order to remain competitive.

As John Thompson (1995: 174) points out: 'The globalization of communication has not eliminated the localized channel of (the) appropriation (of media products) but rather has created a new kind of symbolic axis in the modern world . . . the axis of globalized diffusion and localized appropriation. As the globalization of communication becomes more intensive and extensive, the significance of this axis increases.' In effect, the globalization of communication in association with the proliferation of television channels and the development of digital television has produced a multichannel environment, which in turn has led to the globalization of national or local tastes and values. For example, in the late 1980s, Super Channel realized that European viewers were not going to abandon national channels in favour of English-language programming (Burnett 1989). This reverse trend is because 'Global, economic and political factors and communication technologies . . . do serve to compress, but not to eliminate, time and space; and the sense of place, something associated with the essence of local culture, has become a major determinant in the restructuring of the world communications industry' (Wang and Servaes 2000: 6).

There is no uniform model of localization, however, as different markets across Europe tend to have different attitudes to and ideas about which model of localization is acceptable. Often this has as much to do with cultural tastes and values as it has to do with economies of scale (Sutherland 1999a). Broadly speaking, there are four possible ways of localizing output and production.

- *A local language version* (subtitling or dubbing) – as, for example, practised by the National Geographic. In this case the translation has to be factually accurate. There are national differences. In

some countries, such as the Scandinavian countries, viewers prefer subtitles, while in others, such as in Southern Europe, they
prefer the dubbing of programmes (Sutherland 1999a). This also
depends on the type of programme. Some programmes, such as
documentaries and wildlife, travel across frontiers more easily
than others and only the language needs to be changed (David
Brown 1998a: 27).

- *The use of interstitial*. As an example, Nickelodeon achieves this
  by assigning local presenters (kids) with the task of introducing
  its programmes to their local audiences.
- *Programming opt-outs*, or creating an individual local channel.
  Some channels follow this path, since they believe that they cannot have an impact in local markets if they operate their channels
  from their headquarters. For example, the Disney and Fox Kids
  channels prefer fully localized channels, as we shall see in chapter 11.
- The creation of a *regional channel*. This strategy is followed principally by news channels, such as CNNI or CNBC. This is mainly
  due to the nature of their content and the quality of viewers
  attracted and targeted, as we will see in chapter 8.

The cost of localization varies dramatically across countries. For
example, it is far more expensive to localize in Northern Europe
than in Southern and Eastern Europe. Moreover, in France and
Germany the pressure for localization is stronger, because both countries are potentially attractive markets, which can support local channels and production as well as the cost of tailoring the service (David
Brown 1998a: 27). Whichever path a channel pursues, partial or full
scale, localization is still a costly project to implement, and this is
one reason why one sees regional versions of some channels – such
as National Geographic, Nickelodeon, Fox Kids Europe, CNBC,
Disney, MTV, CNNI, Discovery Networks – developing only in key
markets. On the other hand, because of digital technology, the cost
of producing several feeds has decreased (David Brown 1998b).

But, depending on the targeted market, channels follow their localization strategy, which does not always work, as some different
cultures and tastes are more difficult to deal with than others. Humour, for instance, rarely travels across borders, while perceptions
of what is violent, pornographic, offensive or in bad taste differ
considerably from country to country (David Brown 1998b). For
example, the UK is an obvious market for US channels because of
the common language. But most of the children's channels, and

even the music channels, still have to customize their content, language and presenters, to fit British tastes and values.

Localization, however, is not only about altering language versioning and programming. It is also about *marketing, positioning and branding* the channel on a national basis (David Brown 1998b). Most of the thematic channels, in particular those most attractive to subscribers, publicize their thematic character, at the same time as claiming that they provide a programme diet or content that resembles general entertainment programming. This is because they target the whole family. For example, Disney Channel Europe positions itself as a premium channel, unlike its US-backed rivals (Fry 2000: 12). In contradiction to earlier claims, a number of thematic channels claim to be family general entertainment channels, ranging from wildlife or documentary channels, such as Animaux in France or National Geographic Europe, to all-children channels or movie channels, like Film 1. This can be explained in financial terms, as thematic channels cannot simply take the financial risk of excluding potential subscribers.

Summary

The advent of new technologies and especially digital television has accelerated the development of international thematic channels. In the course of such development, international thematic channels have been forced to adapt to the needs of the local markets they are aiming at. In fact, digital technologies have not eliminated the localized channel. On the contrary, localization is something that most channels are going to have to do.

8

More News and More News Channels

One of the most significant developments of television journalism in the 1990s is the rise of round-the-clock news channels, giving the impression that in the era of globalization the entire world wants news. Television news has traditionally been regarded as national in scope, yet, with deregulation, privatization and globalization of television and the arrival of satellite systems, news is now provided not only by local operators but also by international ones. Many believed that all-news channels, especially those international in scope, would change the nature of news dramatically, as local audiences would turn to them to fulfil their increased need for news. This chapter attempts to describe the development of international television news services in Europe and argues that there is more supply than demand for international news channels. It deems that the case of news channels simply demonstrates the (re)-dominance on the international news flow of the large Western operations (agencies and broadcasters), which can, on a permanent basis, restructure, expand and differentiate themselves, and invest heavily in new technologies, new channels and new formats.

International news: from radio to television

The accessibility of foreign television news services is a recent phenomenon, but international news is not new. It emanates from international radio, which, especially after the Second World War, was developed through external broadcasting services, such as the BBC World Service and/or External Services or Germany's Deutsche Welle (DW) or the USA's Voice of America, the Soviet Union's Radio Moscow, China's Radio Beijing, and so on. These services had a common goal – that is, to influence opinion in the interests – political, cultural and financial – of their home states. In effect, even this story is older and can be traced back to the 1930s, when governments started to realize the influence of external broadcasting (see Wallis and Baran 1990: 116–49).

External broadcasting spread rapidly in the 1960s, as did the transistor radio. These cheap, portable radios became widely available in the late 1950s, increasing the number of listeners. Governments encouraged the flood of transistor radios in Eastern Europe, Africa and Asia. In some countries, listening to foreign radio stations became a national pastime or a vital necessity of everyday life (Papathanassopoulos 1999c: 18).

By the end of the 1980s, world broadcasting was no longer just a struggle between West and East. The collapse of communism in Eastern Europe and the disintegration of the Soviet Union changed the landscape of international radio broadcasting as Communist broadcasters, such as Radio Tirana, Radio Prague and Radio Berlin International, went off air. In most cases they changed their agenda, and have since promoted tourism and national culture. Moreover, the deregulation of broadcasting in Eastern Europe following the collapse of Communism resulted in the mass entry of private local, national and regional radio and television stations. In most cases, the main investments came from the West to the international radio stations. In some cases, governments decided to stop, reduce or merge their operations.

But the model of international news broadcasting was there. In the era of television dominance, it was thought that the market from radio would sooner or later turn to television. Satellite television distribution provided the means to reach people around the world.

More news channels

The first all-news TV network, Cable News Network (CNN), was launched in the USA on 1 June 1980. It capitalized on the existence of new technology to make its service viable, first on US cable and then, further down the line, on the international market. Richard Parker, in his study on news (1995a: 48–9), notes that before CNN:

The final supply of nearly all news – no matter what country it was broadcast in – was exclusively a matter of the domestic news broadcaster gathering it, preparing it and distributing it to domestic viewers . . . that every domestic news broadcaster included foreign news along with national and local news as part of the normal news menu. Today, things are different. News broadcasting – considered in an international sense – can . . . itself be seen as having at least four distinct divisions to it.

According to Parker (1995a: 48–9), the first market development is *global* news broadcasting, exemplified by Cable News Network International (CNNI), and, more recently, BBC World. The second is the related *regional news* broadcasting (such as Euronews and the Middle East Broadcast Service). The third market – although decidedly minor economically – is the *retail market*, which is a national television broadcaster that sells a domestic news show, or portions of it, to a foreign market. The fourth is *wholesale* news, in which generally raw news footage is sold to multiple broadcasters in many different nations, for a final processing, scripting, and delivery as part of a domestic news broadcast.

By the mid-1990s, news became central to many broadcasters in the battle for audiences. This is because television is primarily a narrative form (Chris Barker 1997: 74) and news is amongst the most enduring and watched television programmes. For advertisers, news adds unique coverage and is a balance to the downmarket nature of television. In most countries the premium TV news bulletins attract a strong upper-market male audience. Although TV news coverage is expensive, this has not stopped news channels being set up or existing services being expanded. For the established players, as the market expanded and output went up, marginal costs came down, while deregulation brought more competition, with the new entrants prepared to invest money in setting up news operations.

The development of twenty-four-hour news channels was enabled to a large extent by developments in satellite newsgathering (SNG) technology. SISLink, Associated Press Television Network (APTN), Globecast, Northern Europe and BT Broadcast services are just some of the SNG providers. Moreover, digital technology has driven SNG costs down significantly, making satellite links a viable option for many smaller broadcasters (Sutherland 1999e).

The development of news channels means that news no longer constitutes the preserve of public broadcasters. Instead, news markets constitute a key axis in the changing economics of television as they promise to usher in radical changes, with the provision of news being devolved across markets in the 1990s and subcontractors offering services of both a general and a specialist nature. No one can deny that national networks around the world are being challenged. Even for large public broadcasters, such as the BBC and Nippon Hoso Kyokai (NHK) news is becoming an increasingly commercial business. On the commercial side, although the USA is now the main battleground for international all-news networks, it is Europe, Asia and Latin America that increasingly offer the most potential reward (Chakraborty 1998b) – and the most resistance. The paragraphs below describe the most important news ventures, and analyse the news landscape.

CNNI

Europe was CNN International (CNNI)'s first target for distribution in 1985 and it accounts for most of its $106 million annual advertising and subscription revenue, which makes the Time Warner-owned network the only profitable news channel. In 1995, Turner Broadcasting Systems, the parent company of CNN, merged with its long-time shareholder Time Warner, which had substantial programming interests of its own. In 1997–8 CNN had thirteen local bureaux in Europe out of thirty-six worldwide and 800 local news affiliates for major cities all over the world.

By September 1997, acknowledging that it was no longer a monopoly provider in international news, CNNI divided into four separately scheduled channels: CNN International Europe/Middle East/Africa, CNN International Asia Pacific, CNN International Latin America and CNN International US. This regionalization was designed to meet two major challenges. The first was to tailor content to meet regional interests in a highly competitive market at both international and local levels. The second was to meet the challenge of maintaining an audience consistently – that is, in the absence of major world events – and thus to drive viewing. CNN began commissioning documentaries and other feature programmes to supplement its anchor-driven news format. In fact, in the late 1990s CNN allocated $1.5 million to enable the production and commissioning of these programmes from the independent sector, and estimated that 80 per cent of the CNNI Europe was original programming not seen in the USA (Chakraborty 1998b: 3, 11). In Europe, it broadcast on an around-the-clock basis, while up to 4.5 hours of its daily content originated from the London production centre. As part of CNN's regionalization strategy, 3.5 hour slots were broadcast from

Germany. As we will see later, CNN had also begun some local language programming in Germany, which constituted a quarter of its West European audience. CNN Deutschland, a German language window, was available to 7.5 million households in Germany.

BBC World

BBC World was launched in October 1991 and was rebranded on 26 January 1995. In August 1996, the BBC was granted a terrestrial frequency in Berlin–Brandenburg in Germany, as with the case of BBC World's main competitor, CNNI, Germany is regarded as the most important market in Europe. In September 1999, BBC World reorganized its schedule. It dropped the longer feature programmes such as *The World Today* and *Europe Direct*, and structured the schedule around half-hour slots. By 2000 BBC World reached 150 million homes in nearly 200 countries and territories worldwide, and offered separate feeds for European, Asian and Latin American viewers, which contained regional elements. It was available in sixty-three million homes on a twenty-four-hour basis and an additional eighty-seven million homes on a part-time basis (Sutherland 1999e). BBC World's programming comprised hourly news bulletins, plus in-depth regional news programmes at key times of the day. BBC current affairs and documentaries made up the analysis slots, but a spread of lifestyle, fashion, current affairs, interviews, travel and documentary programming also filled the schedules (Chakraborty 1998b: 12).

Euronews

The European news channel broadcasts simultaneously twenty hours a day in six different languages. It was launched in January 1993 by eighteen European public broadcasters, all members of the EBU, including France Télévision, Italy's RAI, Switzerland's SSR and Spain's TVE. The channel's unique feature was that it did not use on-screen presenters, but ran unbroken footage with commentaries in five different languages. But some observers believed that the lack of 'anchors' deprived Euronews of a coherent identity, a perception exacerbated by the channel's apparent reluctance to market itself. Towards the end of 1994, Euronews was apparently in trouble, with accumulated losses of $10 million. After a crisis meeting, the shareholders agreed to seek external funding, eventually persuading

Générale Occidental, a media subsidiary of electronics giant Alcatel Alsthom, to take a 49 per cent stake. In November 1998, the British television company ITN – which supplies news bulletins to the British terrestrial channels ITV, Channel 4 and Channel 5 – acquired the 49 per cent managing stake of Alcatel Alsthom by paying £1.5 million.

Euronews is made up of two companies. The Société Opératrice de la Chaîne Européenne Multilingue d'Information (SOCEMIE) is the operating company responsible for the daily management, in which ITN owns a 49 per cent managing stake. The balance of shares is held by the Société Éditrice de la Chaîne Européenne Multilingue d'Information (SECEMIE) consortium of eighteen public broadcasters, which comprises: France Télévision (France); RAI (Italy); RTVE (Spain); Cyprus Broadcasting Corporation (CyBC – Cyprus); ERT (Greece); Swiss Broadcasting Corporation (SSR–SRG – Switzerland); Egypt Radio Television Union (ERTU – Egypt); Télé Monte-Carlo (TMC – Monaco); RTP (Portugal); Yleisradio Oy (YLE – Finland); Établissement de la Radiodiffusion Télévision Tunisienne (ERTT – Tunisia); RTBF (Belgium); Bulgarian National Television (BNT – Bulgaria); Ceska Televise (CT – Czech Republic); Public Broadcasting Services (PBS – Malta); Television Romania (TVR – Romania); ENTV (Algeria) and RTVSL (Slovenia) (Chakraborty 1998b: 20).

After suffering continued losses of more than FFr220 million up to 1996, Euronews was relaunched presenting a new format, partly to boost audiences, but more importantly to woo advertisers. The revamp featured a package of fixed magazine strands covering everything from sports to the arts. The news hosted had a strong human-interest focus with short news updates supported by in-depth programmes (e.g., political developments and main social, environmental and health issues as well as travel in various European countries). Presenters were still absent. In 1998, Euronews was again redesigned aiming to achieve a more contemporary and more European image, and to make it more 'live' with more regular news updates. This could be done, because, thanks to its partners, Euronews had a tremendous amount of video sources. In November 1999, Euronews expanded its language offering by adding a Portuguese language feed.

Ideally, Euronews represents Europe in its unity: 'through the unity of images and the diversity of languages' (Fichera 1993: 216). Some critics have said that its multilingual approach is one reason why the channel has not attracted viewers. According to this view, the absence of the on-screen presenters is wrong, because having

Table 8.1 International and local news channels in Europe and their broadcasting language, 2000

Network	Language
CNNI	English
CNN +	Spanish
CNN Turk	Turkish
BBC World	English
Euronews	English, French, German, Italian, Spanish, Arabic (peak time), Portuguese
MBC	Arabic
CNBC	English
Sky News	English
n-tv	German
Phoenix	German
Bloomberg Information TV	English, German, French, Spanish
La Chaîne Info	French

on-screen presenters is an essential aspect of television news. Well-known 'anchors' and journalists, it is argued, help give a station its identity. Euronews people, on the other hand, argue that they do not have 'talking heads' for technical reasons, and because the images speak for themselves: viewers want to see what is happening and the role of journalists is to witness the events. But, with no presenters or roving camera crews and only a handful of correspondents covering European events such as summits and elections, surely Euronews is not able to be 'Europe's answer to CNN' (Masters 1994; Tillier 1996; Tungate 1996). One has to note that, thanks to a number of retransmission deals with broadcasters, Euronews is available to seventy million terrestrial homes in addition to thirty-two million on cable and DTH. Moreover, segments of the channel are carried at different times of the day to every home in various countries, including France, Italy, Spain, the Czech Republic and Portugal. The channel is also available in Africa, Asia, North and South America.

More local news channels

Simultaneously, local news has become the lifeblood of broadcast stations and competition at the international and local level has mushroomed. By mid-1998 there were five European news and business channels (CNNI, BBC World, Euronews, CNBC Europe and Bloomberg Information), plus Germany's n-tv and Phoenix, France's La Chaîne Info and the UK-based Sky News.

But local news channels are not a European phenomenon, since there are news channels almost everywhere, such as Globo News, Canal de Noticias, Eco and TeleNoticias in Latin America, Asia Business News and Sky News in Asia as well as Fox News Network and MSNBC in North America. In Europe, in April 1997, Germany's TV networks, ARD and ZDF, launched Phoenix, an information and documentary channel, which blends CNN-style coverage of breaking news with live broadcasts of events such as parliamentary debates in Germany and other European capitals modelled after the C-SPAN channels in the USA. It is free of advertising, while its programme diet also contains sport, music, operas and films.

Sky News was launched in 1989 in the UK and broadcasts on a twenty-four-hour basis mainly for the British audience. Although it is considered a British news channel, it has gradually increased its international news coverage, especially with a partnership with Reuters in 1995. It has bureaux in Belgrade (in 1992), Washington (in 1995), Hong Kong (in 1997), Dublin (in 1995), Australia (in 1996), Moscow, Jerusalem, Johannesburg (in 1994) and The Hague. In 1993, Sky News established a partnership with the US network CBS (Columbia Broadcasting System) News and with Radio Télévision Luxembourgeoise (RTL) in Germany. In Europe and the UK it is available though the Astra ID satellite at 19 degrees east and it is estimated that it is available to thirty million viewers. Despite its poor ratings, Sky News has benefited from coverage on stories like the Gulf War, the handover of Hong Kong, the death of Princess Diana and the Omagh bombing. In the UK it is distributed via DTH in 4.3 million homes and via cable in around two million homes. It also has strong links with its sister US channel, Fox News, as well as programming alliances with European broadcasters including (Vlaamse Televisie Maatschappij (VTM – Belgium), Vox TV and RTL (Germany and the Netherlands) and M6 (France) (Chakraborty 1998b: 27–9).

Until the launch of the BBC news channel, News 24, in November 1997, Sky News had no direct competitor in its home market. Since cable operators started giving preference to News 24, BSkyB applied to the Office of Fair Trading to lower the subscriber fee that cable operators had to pay per month for Sky News from 49 pence per subscriber to 9 pence. At the same time BSkyB was seeking to raise the price of Sky One, the most popular non-premium cable and satellite channel, from 49 pence per subscriber per month to 89 pence (Chakraborty 1998b: 30).

News 24 is the BBC's news channel designed for the digital age and was launched on 10 November 1997. Until digitalization comes of age, News 24 has had to secure distribution via some analogue cable networks – that is, to 1.5 million homes. It is also broadcast across the overnight slots on the terrestrial channel BBC1. Because of its public service remit and the fact that it is funded exclusively by the licence fee, News 24 was offered to cable operators free of charge. Faced with a cost saving of £12 million a year as well as the BBC's standard of news journalism, the cable operators 'miraculously found transponder slots for News 24, and began to take steps to drop Sky News from their schedules' (Chakraborty 1998b: 30). The channel had an annual budget of £27 million in 1998 – that is, around 10 per cent of the BBC's total newsgathering budget – and access to the whole range of BBC newsgathering resources. As noted in chapter 5, in 1999 the European Commission rejected the complaint of Sky News against News 24, since News 24 is free of advertising and free of charge to cable and satellite operators.

N-TV was launched in 1992, mainly as a response to the Anglo-American challenge on news television. Its original shareholder structure included both Time Warner (30.8 per cent) and CNN (32.61 per cent), but, when the two shareholders merged in 1995, German ownership regulations limited them to a single 49.79 per cent stake alongside the newspaper group Handelsblatt. N-tv is distributed across Germany via the Astra 1B satellite and has terrestrial frequencies in Berlin–Brandenburg, Bremen and Heligoland. The channel is available throughout the German cable network, reaching 84 per cent of households. Overall, n-tv reached 27.5 million households in Germany and 42.1 million households in Europe in 1997–8 (Chakraborty 1998b: 61). It is focused on German news, including financial news from the Frankfurt stock market and other international markets, while international news is provided by CNN. There is also some programming covering politics, lifestyles, and so on.

La Chaîne Info broadcasts nineteen hours a day and is owned entirely by the French private broadcaster TF1. It was launched in June 1994, as France's only domestic news channel. At that time, it was distributed as a basic channel throughout the main cable operators, Lyonnaise des Eaux and Général des Eaux. From 1996 La Chaîne Info was also distributed via satellite and the digital satellite packages of the French digital platforms. In 1997–8 its major sources of income were subscription fees (FFr75 million per year) and advertising revenues (FFr25 million a year); the channel had a budget of around FFr200 million from its parent company TF1 (Chakraborty 1998b: 63).

Business news channels

Niche news channels have also emerged. Business news services like the European Business Network (owned by Dow Jones/Flextech), CNBC (owned by NBC – prior to their merger) and Bloomberg Information TV target an even narrower audience (mostly executives). In effect, they target the same sort of audiences as financial newspapers – that is, business professionals with an international cosmopolitan outlook. For example, CNBC's most popular show, *European Money*, is produced by Financial Times Television and draws from the *FT*'s network of journalists across Europe. EBN, backed by Dow Jones and Flextech, was launched in London in February 1995. The channel revamped its programming schedule in autumn 1996 to include more feature-based programming.

In December 1997, EBN merged with CNBC. Their merger was an indication that the market for business news channels was not strong enough to support the two channels. When CNBC entered Europe in March 1996, it was struggling to secure distribution in Europe's key markets – namely, Germany and France. Nowadays, the channel is available in more than fifty-nine million homes in Europe and the Middle East and 140 million homes worldwide. EBN, distributed part-time via Eutelsat across Europe, was bolstered in the UK by its inclusion in the BSkyB's multichannel package, while its cable distribution was patchy.

Thus, both channels decided to merge and develop a global brand under the name 'CNBC: A service of NBC and Dow Jones'. The merger aimed to combine the marketing and promotional investment that CNBC had made into a globally recognizable brand with the strengths of the Dow Jones portfolio of financial content, and at the same time to neutralize competition for the same advertisers. But, post-merger, CNBC appears to have won out (Chakraborty 1998b: 40). The combined channel retains the CNBC name and branding and the stripped and stranded schedule is resolutely similar to the earlier CNBC incarnation. Even so, the new CNBC has to compete with Bloomberg TV, which offers separate, locally tailored channels in five languages.

Bloomberg TV was a latecomer to the European television market. It also struggled to find enough analogue distribution to position itself as a basic channel. In 1995 Michael Bloomberg launched

Bloomberg Information Television in London, soon followed by separate local channels in France, Italy, Spain and Germany. It also broadcasts two channels in Asia (one in Japanese, the other in English), two channels in Latin America (one in Spanish, the other in Portuguese) and one channel in the USA. It has three English language feeds for Europe, the USA and the Asia/Pacific regions. Generally, in these different regions, the channel retains the same look, but with slight modifications. Editorially each market has its own agenda.

Bloomberg TV's rolling programming offers mainly in-depth coverage of financial markets, business and general news, but has expanded to include some sports, lifestyle, travel and weather information. News bulletins run every thirty minutes and include the latest business and international news updates, intercut with financial analysis and feature prices. Moreover, its on-screen presentation is different from that of rival CNBC. Bloomberg TV uses a multi-screen or split-screen format, which is rich in data and information, comprising scrolling ticker, headline flashes and international share prices. In fact, it looks like an Internet page with streaming video and in this respect is ahead of its time (Sutherland 1999e: 28). One has to note that many channels or financial TV programmes around the world use its presidential format. On the other hand, CNBC is more focused on analysis and personality than on providing an over-abundance of data and information.

However, one has also to note that most news channels include business news programming within a broader news format. This is one of the reasons that it will be difficult for both Bloomberg TV and CNBC to have a wider audience, regardless of the new capacities offered by digital technology.

TV news wire agencies

A development is the entry of news wire agencies in the field, since with the advent of news channels 'there is now a greater range of suppliers of "wholesale news"' (Boyd-Barrett 1998: 27). In effect, Reuters' buyout of Visnews, the entry of Associated Press into television and its buyout of WTN, the collaborations among American and European broadcasters and the continued globalization of News Corporation and CNN indicate that the world newsgathering map is being revolutionized. One could argue that nowadays we might speak of a complexity of the landscape, which is illustrated by various sorts of relationships and links. On the other hand, this may not be a surprise. In the media business, parties have long been involved in such kinds of relationships, as in other sectors of the economy (Paterson 2000).

To outsiders, these various sorts of relationships spring from the ambition of newsgathering agencies and broadcasters to achieve the best-quality news coverage at the best possible price. What is not very obvious, however, is whether this board-game approach to news distribution reflects the ongoing flux in the global television industry, or whether it is a one-off radical change that will culminate in some organizations being squeezed out of the equation (Tunstall and Machin 1999: 81–4). From a news agency perspective, there were two main concerns. The first was the increasing number of broadcasters seeking strategic alliances with each other. The second was related to the first: even if broadcasters are not in themselves a serious competition to big organizations, such as APTV and Reuters Television – the two largest operations in Europe – how will the global shifts in broadcaster ownership affect the news agencies?

It appears that, in the era of television's dominance, the traditional big agencies are entering the TV sector and at the same time big broadcasters are entering the newsgathering and information fields. In other words, they have become conscious of the value of news product. A second implication is that the days of large broadcasters supplying pictures without charge are over. In the past, large broadcasters were concerned with strategic expansion potential, but nowadays information is extremely valuable and they have to make judgements whether to exchange it or sell it and make money from it. On the other hand, broadcasters want more news at less cost (Bell 1994).

Moreover, the big agencies believe that the market is not in reduction and their role as newsgatherers is expanding rather than diminishing. APTV's buyout of WTN confirms this. At the same time, it shows an attempt by the large news agencies to redominate the international news circulation (Boyd-Barrett 2000). This is because they are able, on a permanent basis, to restructure, expand and differentiate themselves and to invest heavily in new technologies, as they did in the mid-1970s and in the 1980s. These developments may have changed their character, to the extent that it would be legitimate to ask whether these agencies can still be described as news agencies, but the fact is that they still dominate 'the business of news' in various forms (Alleynet and Wanger 1993; Tunstall and Machin 1999). They have also appeared confident to enter digital technologies since they believe that they will keep them several steps ahead of all the new competition.

Searching for audiences

The appeal of news channels in terms of viewers in the 1990s was paradoxically attributed to the existence of wars rather than to technology. The Gulf War was characterized as a 'good war' for news channels, especially CNNI, in terms of an increase in home and international audience. Eight years later, however, in the course of the Kosovo War, CNNI realized that war coverage was a difficult and costly business. It was difficult because this war had no front line to televise. Furthermore, it was costly because, in addition to the startling $1.1 million worth of equipment that CNNI estimates was destroyed, lost, confiscated or stolen during NATO's bombardment, the news network was spending $150,000 a day on a conflict with no diplomatic end yet in sight (Shakleton 1999; White 1999a). Moreover, CNNI had to face more competitors in comparison to the Gulf War.

It is not clear whether news channels can maintain viewers in the course of long-lasting events. It seems that viewers tend not to watch channels for long periods of time, which in turn makes it difficult to attract advertisers. In Europe, at least, it seems that there was little proof of the public's interest in the latest headlines. In short, in most cases of conflict, news channels deem that there is a market for people who wish to watch news at their own convenience. This is reconfirmed by the level of demand on an international basis, which has not, as was expected, overtaken radio audiences. But, while most of the world's two billion radios can pick up international radio broadcasts, few of its one billion TV households have been reached. Satellite channels thought (and still do) that through satellite broadcasting they would reach individual receiving dishes. But dishes are still expensive, and sometimes restricted by governments. They are still rare in most parts of Africa and Asia, and in countries such as Iran and Iraq.

In the early years of the twenty-first century, it appears that there is more supply than demand for news, since almost all terrestrial broadcasters around Western Europe are producing and scheduling longer news formats. On the other hand, the audiences for news channels are still small, and viewers still prefer to tune into terrestrial news programmes. This is the reason that many news channels refer to an audience as the number of people who, if they turned on their TV sets and tuned to the channel, could watch it. While a small audience share translates into big numbers in a market like the USA, in

Europe a small audience share means only tens of thousands of viewers.

Moreover, international television news can still not go beyond local elites (Tehranian and Tehranian 1997: 159) and reach the broader audiences (Parker 1995b; Hess 1997). For Johnston (1995: 285), success in global news programming 'will depend more on addressing contemporary topics and trends in ways that are understood by global audiences'. But, news is not music or sports and, therefore, demands a different level of localization. It demands new ways of drawing a multinational, multilingual audience and is at the same time produced for domestic national news agendas, but it also demands a good level of foreign language competence. Furthermore, it is well known that domestic audiences turn and give priority to their home news and programmes. Cultural and linguistic boundaries will, it seems, continue to be important determinants of popularity (Negrine and Papathanassopoulos 1990: 159–62; Parker 1995a).

As noted in chapter 7, regionalization and/or localization are clearly something that most channels are going to have to do. For example, CNN began an aggressive regionalization strategy in 1997, investing nearly $10 million, which resulted in the establishment of CNNI's four international feeds (CNNI Europe, CNNI Asia Pacific, CNNI Latin America and CNNI US). Each of these feeds was tailored to a particular market, with its own decentralized programme production, region-specific shows, scheduling, marketing and creative services. Moreover, as part of its regionalization campaign, CNN launched a twenty-four-hour Spanish service – CNN Espagnol – in 1997 and a German-speaking service (CNN Deutschland) in 1998. Around 80 per cent of CNNI's weekday output is generated specifically for CNNI Europe, which broadcasts twenty-four hours a day to thirty-seven countries with 4.5 hours of programming originating from its London production centre (Callard 1998: 68). In short, CNNI's plans for Europe include more regional programmes, more investment in personnel, more local productions and collaboration with local partners.

Moreover, CNN's first such investment was in the German news channel n-tv. Since acquiring Time Warner's stake, CNN is a majority partner in n-tv. CNN, however, declined the opportunity to invest in France's La Chaîne Info when it was launched in 1994 (Westcott 1999b). In 1999 it set up branded channels in Spain and Turkey. CNN+ – a joint venture with Sogecable, a main shareholder of Canal Plus España – was launched in January 1999 and was carried to the Canal Satellite digital platform. CNN Turk was available to seven million terrestrial TV homes from September 1999. The channel is a joint venture with the Dogan Media group. However, CNN emphasizes that the local news channels really are local (Westcott 1999b; White 1999a).

Unlike CNNI, BBC World is keen to maintain its 'one channel strategy'. As BBC World's managing director, Patrick Cross, said: 'We put out global news and the same news goes out everywhere in the world. When people want local news they turn to RAI in Italy or one of the local companies for local news. We are offering a global perspective' (in White 1999b). However, BBC World does have a localization strategy. This involves some dedicated programming for the channel's audiences in Europe, and, in addition, seventy hours per week of Japanese translation. Moreover, Bloomberg Information Television has language feeds in French, Spanish, German and English.

All of these developments clearly show that regionalization is the key to greater distribution. However, it involves enormous costs while the revenues, as we shall see below, are limited or unknown. For example, the amount of investment needed to set up a news channel can be 4–5 billion Euros. And the above noted case of Euronews is indicative. In short, these examples simply indicate that multilingual format is not the only key to attract viewers.

Financial problems

The production and distribution costs of international television news compared to international radio are higher, since it is much more costly to make and to transmit abroad, via expensive satellites. In theory, it seems that behind most expansion plans there is a straightforward economic calculation: companies already in the news business think they can squeeze out more profits with relatively little new cost by expanding to twenty-four hours of TV news. For example, BBC World with an overall news and current affairs programming budget of $408 million and with 250 correspondents around the world, including its domestic operations, can marshal substantial resources in the increasingly fierce news competition. For example, BBC World reduced operating costs by 36 per cent in 1998 and made fifty members of its staff redundant in 1999.

Moreover, while CNN spent massively before its launch, the start-up costs will be relatively modest for the American Broadcasting Corporation (ABC), NBC and Dow Jones, which already have expensive newsgathering operations. None would disagree that the economics of television news are now fundamentally different from those of the past. Indeed, as noted above, the price of news has become less costly, due partly to technology, partly to better management and partly even to the rise of video journalism (one-camera journalist at work). What has remained unclear all these years is whether 'news junkies', on an international or a local level, want all of these alternatives.

In the mid-1990s, the issue of distribution was a major problem for international news networks, especially in Europe. As digital take-up evolved in the late 1990s, many industry observers thought that finding cable outlets would not be a problem and that they would create new revenue streams. But at the beginning of the twenty-first century the financial rewards are still limited. Revenues from subscription and advertising remain low. Around 40 per cent of CNNI's revenues come from cable and DTH subscriptions and 60 per cent from advertising. Despite the stampede of news services, CNNI is the only one of the five players targeting the European region to have turned a profit. As noted above, BBC World lost £15.6 million in 1998, while advertising revenue represents a minority of BBC World's revenues. Euronews's breakeven is expected within 2001, although the channel is still losing money. However, Euronews makes around 40 per cent of its revenues from licensing its output to its members. It also has a substantial co-production contract with the EU, which in the channel's early days provided an annual subsidy. In effect, if one looks at the TV ratings, most of the channels get a tiny portion. Most of the European viewers turn to local channels for their daily information.

In fact, news channels have to fight to attract viewers and advertisers in a market where terrestrial television remains a prime source of television information and where only $259 million was forecast to be spent on television pan-European advertising in 1997. But, the pan-European advertising market remains underdeveloped. Zenith Media estimates that in 1998 pan-European budgets amounted to 1 per cent of total advertising expenditure or about Euro 300 million. The merger of CNBC and EBN refuelled the debate as to how much room in the market there actually is for a news channel.

Probably, the survival of news channels depends not only on a clear strategy, but also on 'deep pockets'. In 2000–1, only Time-Warner, owner of CNNI, and General Electric, owner of CNBC, could provide some security to their news ventures. We may witness a new wave of mergers of news channels by 2005. The reality, however, at least in Europe, is that the continental market seems to be oversupplied, and other niche markets such as music and children's programmes may soon experience the kind of consolidation that the business news market is experiencing.

Implications of the development of news channels

A number of implications are associated with the development of news channels. These include geopolitical implications and implications related with television journalism as well as the relations between developed and less developed nations.

Geopolitical implications

International news channels transmit their material across political boundaries, unprohibited by national political considerations. At the same time, the produced content originates from different cultural and national environments. Their interpretations of news events may, therefore, differ considerably from those of the domestic news television services. This means that local viewers will have a variety of news sources and will be informed by news with foreign values. This was supposed to be a novel situation, which would undoubtedly have an impact on governmental practices and their policies. In this new media environment, governments were supposed to find it increasingly difficult to ensure that their own judgements of current political events dominated.

This, however, does not entirely correspond to reality. In effect, it has to do with the size of the market that the international news channels aim to attract and the power of their governments in the international political arena. The case of the Chinese authorities preventing the reception of the BBC World Service in the Star TV package is indicative. Rupert Murdoch, in his speech in London in September 1994 regarding the issue, said: 'We certainly intend to do everything we can to resolve certain difficulties with the government of China' (in Westcott 1994: 30). In reality, Rupert Murdoch considered China as a key market in order to get the so-called first mover advantage in the media wars of the new millennium (Atkinson 1998).

The dilemma of reporting the news while remaining on good terms with the authorities is not confined to the authorities where press freedom is frowned on. When, in 1994, Larry King's interview with Sinn Fein spokesman Gerry Adams was broadcast on the European feed of CNNI, Adams' voice was dubbed in lip synch by an actor to comply with the UK Government ban on interviews with Adams' organization. CNNI, which is licensed in the UK, obeyed the ban, no doubt to the bemusement of the more numerous viewers outside the UK. During the Gulf War, Israeli authorities warned the network not to report on the location of Scud missiles. Moreover, CNNI has reciprocal agreements with over 200 broadcasters world-wide enabling them to exchange footage. Furthermore, since these channels are – as the news wire agencies were in the past – mostly watched by government officials and diplomats, their journalists appear to have close relationships with them, yet, regardless of that, officials sometimes express their displeasure with their reporting. In other words, this means that depending on the region and the com-mercial implications that a region or country has, international news channels sometimes appear to be careful with their reporting and to use double standards. For example, channels have been careful to avoid offending the Chinese authorities and being banned from China's 1.2 billion potential viewers.

In other cases, they follow a different stance. In the case of the war in Kosovo, Yugoslavia news channels were criticized for regurgitating NATO's script. In a News World Conference, held in Barcelona in 1999, for example, BBC World Affairs editor and senior corres-pondent John Simpson, accused by the UK Government of being pro-Serb, commented that he was 'more censored than any other journalist at Belgrade' (in White 1999a: 9). He also said that he came under political fire because what he was saying was uncom-fortable for the UK Government, and did not fall in with the NATO, Washington or Downing Street lines. Simpson also raised the issue of relationships between governments and the media and claimed that the difference between the reporting stances of the BBC and CNN was that 'we [the BBC] prefer not to get too close to the governments we're reporting on' (in White 1999a: 9). As is well known, CNN denied that it had made journalistic compromises to gain access. But, 'it appears that CNN played a role, in shaping, as opposed to just reporting' (White 1999: 9). Perhaps the two tele-vised wars in the 1990s (Gulf and Kosovo) indicate that, in order to get a competitive advantage news channels may become subject to manipulation and at the same time may take an active hand in shaping events.

This seems to be a recent trend, but in fact it is an old one. Although governments still rely on the press, in the age of television's dominance they also appear to consider that television will gradually have a larger impact on international news. As with the case of international radio, many governments consider that international channels can also promote their interests abroad. The US Government finances World Net, which distributes television programmes to 'enhance United States diplomacy abroad'. DW armed with government money, has since 1992 launched its international television service. The French government pays for Canal (or Télévision) France International and TV5 (joint venture with other francophone state broadcasting bodies) to provide free programmes in French aimed at viewers in Europe, Asia and Africa (Dutheil 1995). Cross-border television is used increasingly as a tool of foreign policy. Turkey's national broadcasting corporation beams Turkish television by satellite through an International Turkiye Radyo Televizyon channel to Turkish-speaking Azerbaijan, Turkmenistan, Uzbekistan, Kighizia and Kazakstan to promote its interests (Sahin and Aksoy 1993). Moreover, the European channel Euronews, and its predecessors Eurikon experiment and Europa TV, started as a joint venture by European public broadcasters and co-financed by the EU in order to be the European answer to CNN (Papathanassopoulos 1990b; Collins 1998b; Machill 1998). But even Euronews has been coloured by Euro-politics since key members of the EBU (BBC (UK), ARD and ZDF (Germany)) declined to participate because they wanted to create their own news channels and also because they regarded the European news channel as too much influenced by the French.

Implications for television journalism

The production of news holds a strategic position in debates about television for its presumed, and often feared, influence on public life, a concern that has been heightened by the emergence of global cross-border television (Chris Barker 1997: 96). A relevant concern focuses on the extent to which current domestic standards of fairness and impartiality will apply to international news services. The growing availability of international television news from privately owned services such as CNNI or Sky News may also be reinforcing the idea that national and international media ought to be neutral. Carla Brooks Johnston (1995: 305–6), in her global news study, points out that:

> Global TV news must provide for the globe in the twenty-first century the common denominator that the three [US] networks provided for the whole of the United States in the twentieth century. It must simultaneously set a standard for common self-interest that does not

slight any race, any nationality, any religion, any gender, any political viewpoint. And it must learn to offer programming with this tone in formats that transmit truthful information in ways that are as compelling to the psyche as are drama, sports and special events.

On the other hand, international news channels provide models to local journalists and a means for them to understand other cultures, sensitivities, particularities and laws. Many argue that, as news coverage becomes instantaneous, it also seems to become less meaningful or lacking in comment and explanation. With the advent of news channels, television journalists have been compelled to wonder what their function is; whether new technologies provide opportunities for improving news or whether 'the news' as we know it is about to disappear. It remains unclear, however, whether instantaneous international and live television journalism will contribute to a democratic society, create a new universal model of professional journalism or even lead to a new homogenization of reporting, editing and presenting the news. Live broadcasts, TV windows and continuous coverage appeared around the world during the 1990s, especially after the expansion of CNNI and the coverage of the Gulf War. Within this context, international television news has spread American news values around the globe. Barbie Zelizer (1992: 78) notes that CNN's role in the Gulf War

has generated suggestions that its mode of news gathering signals an end to recognized journalistic practice and the beginning of a new era of journalism . . . CNN does not offer 'new' journalism, but faster, more continuous, less polished and less edited journalism. Journalists continue to engage in generally the same activities of news gathering, although they may emphasize and reveal different aspects of the process for public viewing.

Implications for smaller countries

It has become clear that technology (in our case satellite technology) is not the only necessary condition regarding the development of new media (in our case news channels). As noted above, after years of international adventure, regionalization is a new expansion of news channels into various versions. But it is questionable to what extent this expansion will affect their economics. Technology does not in and of itself create a push towards market solutions; 'rather it has been used by vested political and industrial interests to justify such a move' (Chris Barker 1997: 56). The question is whether these players can come from poor or less developed countries. As Tomlinson (1997: 188) has noted, 'the globalization process is essentially a "decentred" one, producing new patterns of advantage and disadvantage that we are only just beginning to recognise and which do not map neatly on the familiar geographies of domination that the discourses of cultural imperialism assumes.'

These developments, in the final analysis, reinforce the dominance of the large operations (agencies and broadcasters) on the international news flow. As Boyd-Barrett (2000: 12) has noted: 'What I see is the overwhelming Euro-American dominance of global news flow: initiatives come either from established players or from the USA.' The ambitions of CNN, News Corporation, Reuters, AP and the BBC to build global news networks are within their vision to 'occupy the strategic heights of global news and information flows' (Chris Barker 1997: 57). They are the only ones that can, on a permanent basis, restructure, expand and differentiate themselves and invest heavily in new technologies, new channels and new formats (see Mowlana 1996: 207; Ginneken 1998: 41–64). Moreover, many small, developing countries and their broadcasters will continue to rely on them for international news and news models. That means the big commercial or public agencies and broadcasters will continue to be the dominant players in the world news domain. As Herbert Schiller (1991: 15) has pointed out: 'The role of television in the global arena of cultural domination has not diminished in the 1990s. Reinforced by new delivery systems – communication satellites and cable networks – the image flow is heavier than ever. Its source of origin also has not changed that much in the last quarter of the century.'

The Western news system has reinforced its position and the less developed countries are forced to follow in order to close the gap, which always remains wide. Of course, the implications are more complex. The fact is that, after the end of the cold war and the advent of the Internet and the information society, the development of new media came from the West or the more advanced societies. The rest have been obliged to follow them either to keep in touch with developments or even to increase their relative (or virtual) power in their regions. There may be new struggles that take place at the regional, local and international levels, but it seem that Western big media have simply devised new ways and perhaps more efficient means of control. It is not a coincidence, as Tunstall and Machin (1999: 90) note, that, regardless of the emergence of regional and local news channels, 'it seems safe to predict that the "truly international all-news channels" will be predominately American or British'.

Going online

Media pundits consider that the expansion of the Internet with its interactivity will question the survival of news channels, at least in their current mode of distribution. In effect, the Internet's significance as a medium for news has been growing steadily. Microsoft NBC (MSNBC), for example, is designed for a hybrid TV/PC platform, where stories are updated first on the Web and then in edited TV packages and the viewer can track news across both platforms for the latest news. In other words, interactive news will be very different from television news, offering consumers total control of the type of news that they want delivered to their home and enabling them to 'log on' without getting up out of their armchairs to switch on their PCs.

In practice, all news channels operate web versions. These web versions do not merely function as brand extensions, but are increasingly being developed as additional distribution platforms that enable channels to reach international audiences in countries where they have been unable to gain carriage (Sutherland 1999e). For example, CNN recognized the importance of the Internet and invested a considerable amount of money to tap into this new distribution platform. CNN Interactive comprises a network of around eleven web sites that provide up-to-the-minute news and information. These include: CNN.com, cnnfn.com, ALLPolitics.com, CNN Custom News, CNNSI.com, and local language web sites: CNNItalia.com, Svenska CNN, CNN Norge, CNN Denmark, CNNenEspagnol.com and CNNemPortugues.com. CNNtext, the channel's teletext service, combines the Internet and television provision and is available over cable, satellite and in selected hotels. The channel, which records nearly twenty million unique users per month, saw a staggering 450 per cent increase in traffic between 1997 and 1999 and gets 600 million page impressions per month. On most CNN sites there are at least two broadcast programmes where users can watch streaming video.

BBC World likewise has a heavy online presence and draws on the in-house expertise of BBC Online. Sky News also has a key online service and is launching enhanced news services on its digital platform. Euronews began experimenting with video on the Web, having launched a multilingual web site (www.euronews.net) site in 1998. Bloomberg is offering interactive tailored content.

In fact, major news stories over 1998 helped bring traffic to Internet sites, culminating in the release of Kenneth Starr's report on President Clinton's indiscretions, which was first released on the Internet rather than on the traditional news outlets. News channels' executives believe that analysis of news through the Internet is going to become more and more important. But another incentive has been the need of news channels to approach the younger audience, which has turned away from the TV set and has switched on the PCs in the search for news and information. By and large, new technologies offer the viewers the opportunity to customize their own news and news agencies the opportunity to bypass news channels by going straight to the Internet. In Europe, the British ITN online has launched personalized desktop news, providing computer-users with e-mail text, pictures and video news reports when they want it.

Summary

One of the effects of the worldwide deregulation of television systems and the advent of satellite broadcasting has been the proliferation of news channels. Competition at the international, regional and local level has increased considerably and news output has expanded dramatically. In fact, TV news is provided not only by local operators but also by international ones. Many believed that all-news channels, especially those that are international in scope, would dramatically change the nature of news and that local audiences would turn to them to fulfil their increased need for news. But the financial rewards are still limited. Revenues from subscription and advertising remain low. The advent of the Internet has also raised questions about the future of news channels.

We do not know whether news channels will become a kind of Internet news portal, neither can we predict the format of television news in the future. It seems, however, that, because of the exponential growth of the Internet, especially in Europe, and the convergence of media technologies and ownership, news can be either on TV, the Internet or PC, or even through mobile delivery. Probably, if there is a breaking news story, most people may prefer the Internet to get quick updates. Equally, they may stay with their TV sets, since television is still the faster medium, especially for breaking news. The case of the unprecedented terrorist attack on the World Trade Center in New York and the Pentagon in Washington DC on

11 September 2001 – if anything like this could ever be reduced to such a term as breaking news – illustrates, not only the role of TV news, but also the evolution and the global role of the Internet as a news provider.

Perhaps, TV news will continue to be the preferred medium for news, but no one still knows in which format. The reality is that all news channels still have to find ways to keep their viewers watching their programmes longer and, most importantly, to show that there is money in the pan-European advertising market.

9

More Sports Channels
The Advent of Sports Channels in Europe

Sport has had a symbiotic relationship with broadcast media ever since the days of radio. The arrival of digital television and pay-TV in Europe complicated the relationship between sports and television. Since sports events, along with movies, are considered one of the highest audience attractions, there has been a sudden increase of sports games on television, an increase of sports dedicated channels, and, of course, increased competition for sports rights. In fact, Europe is becoming one of the most competitive sports markets in the world. The massive investment in sports channels is a direct result of the deregulation of European television allied to the commercialization of the sports market.

About a handful of private media companies have used their power to buy exclusive sports broadcasting rights and to charge additional fees to the viewers who may want to watch a 'live' game. The fear is that, in the long run, global media interests could undermine free broadcasting, with people being forced to link up to satellites and cables to buy extra equipment and to pay additional fees, if they can afford it. Moreover, popular soccer clubs and sports federations have realized the importance of television as a source of direct revenue, through TV rights and indirect income, since televised games attract sponsors. As the European Commission notes (CEC 1999b: 2): 'Television has replaced ticket sales as the prime source of finance for professional sport . . . (And) sports organisations have pocketed this easy money from television without further thought.'

This chapter describes the inflation of TV sports rights and the association of PPV channels to sport. It also discusses their effects on both soccer and television, especially the efforts to regulate the issue, the subordination of sports to television and the effects on viewers and TV viewing.

The arrival of sports channels

Traditionally, sport – and especially soccer – was broadcast almost exclusively on public broadcasters. With the entry of private channels, sport became the most wanted television content. Commercial channels aiming to increase their advertising market share started to pay more money than their public counterparts in order to get television sporting rights. Very quickly, they 'captured' the television rights of the main sporting events in most European countries. This was an additional loss for the public broadcasters, which had monopolized TV sports in the past. Private channels paid a lot of attention and money to sports, especially soccer and motor racing, that had broad appeal. Although there are major differences across Europe, soccer was and still is the most wanted sport for commercial free-to-air channels and later pay-TV channels (Kilbride 1999; Lewis 1999; see also Mediametrié 1996–9).

Thus, it is no surprise that new sports-dedicated channels arrived to explore this market. In fact, since the mid-1990s, there has been an explosion of sports channels in Europe. In 1995 there were only three sports channels in operation: Eurosport, a pan-European sports channel, Sky Sports in the UK and Deutsches SportFernsehen (DFS) in Germany. In 2000, there were approximately sixty sports channels around the Continent (Koranteng 2000: 16).

According to many media analysts, sports have been the driving force for the development of both commercial and pay-TV channels, analogue or digital. In contrast to other thematic channels, there are only two pan-regional sports channels in Europe. One, and the oldest sports channel, is Eurosport; the second is the Extreme Sports channel. Eurosport was launched in 1989 and Extreme Sports was launched ten years later, in May 1999. A recent major development in the area is the concept of channels owned by individual sports clubs. The first to launch in the UK was Boro TV, targeted at fans of Middlesbrough Football Club. MUTV, jointly owned by Manchester United football club, BSkyB and Granada Media, followed a little later. In January 1999, Olympique de Marseille, the French football club, launched OMTV, in Spain there is the Real Madrid TV, and in Italy Inter and Milan channels. The format of these niche channels is a mixture of an electronic fan club brochure, behind-the-scenes interviews, archive footage and a home-shopping service for club merchandise. Soccer team channels, on the whole, are losing money because of their lack of rights to live games, but analysts believe that the future of soccer TV lies with club-owned networks.

Eurosport

Eurosport was originally set up by the EBU and News Corporation's Sky Television (see Collins 1998a: 658–60). In 1991 it entered a legal dispute with another sports-channel, Screensport. The latter took Eurosport to the European Court, claiming its partnership with the EBU was anti-competitive. Eurosport was led into a new ownership scheme in 1991. TF1 bought Sky's stake (50 per cent), and maintained a link with the EBU with a ten-year rights licensing agreement. In 1993, Eurosport was merged with the European Sports Network, which was owned by Canal Plus, and the Disney Entertainment and Sports Network (ESPN). In May 2000, ESPN withdrew from the ownership, and TF1 and Canal Plus bought up ESPN's share at about $155 million. Thus in 2001 the new ownership scheme of Eurosport was TF1 (50.5 per cent) and Canal Plus (49.5 per cent).

The channel generates two services, the pan-European Eurosport available in twelve languages and a French version, TV France (Eurosport France). It operates from TF1's headquarters in Paris. In September 2000, it added a new service, Eurosport News (sports news).

Eurosport is available in eighty-five million cable and satellite households in Europe, it broadcasts in seventeen languages, it is still the only European sports service and it is dependent on advertising revenue and sponsorship. It broke even in the financial year 1996, posting a $2.1 million net profit on a $61.1 million turnover. The second localized version is British Eurosport, which started in January 1999 as a joint venture with Premium TV and NTL. Its presenters and programme schedule are tailored to a British audience. If this format becomes profitable, Eurosport plans to introduce more localized editions in other major European markets and to start a news sports channel. The channel features top international sporting events, including grand slam tennis, motorcycling, football world championship, the Rugby World Cup, the Tour de France, the World Cup final qualifying rounds and the UEFA Champions League, as well as risky or minority sports. There is live coverage of several tennis tournaments, the Indoor Athletics World Championships and European soccer matches among the top teams (Koranteng, 1998a: 10). During the Sydney Olympics, it claimed an average daily reach of thirty million viewers.

Extreme Sports

The Extreme Sports channel is a joint venture of United Pan–Europe Communications (UPC) and the British programme distributor Extreme Group International. Its sports programme diet consists of risk-taking sporting events, such as snowboarding, surfing, skateboarding and mountain biking. It targets mainly young viewers between 14 to 24 years old, and aims to be available all over Europe by 2003 (Koranteng 1999: 34). By mid-2000 it was already available in twelve European markets and five million homes (Koranteng 2000: 13).

Sports channels in the larger European countries

In the larger European countries – the UK, France, Spain, Germany and Italy – most sports channels are local and are targeted at their national markets (table 9.1), since sport remains national in its appeal and perception, and national myth-making, though sport is common everywhere (Rowe *et al.* 1998; Maguire 1999).

The United Kingdom

The UK is the largest sports market in Europe. BSkyB's sports channels dominate the British sports market. They offer more than 30,000 hours of TV sports per year, 350 hours of sport every week. Thanks to digital technology, BSkyB's three sports channels, Sky 1, 2 and 3 – launched in 1991 – broadcast live sports, covering all major sporting events, even those taking place at the same time. Sky Sport was launched on analogue in April 1991 (Plunket 1999), and, with the launch of its digital platform, it also offers a twenty-four-hour news channel, Sky Sports.com (previously SkySport News) and Sky Sports Extra (interactive programming). Apart from soccer, Sky channels offer golf's Ryder Cup and European boxing tournaments, especially with Mike Tyson. There are also the Racing

Table 9.1 Major sports channels in Western Europe, 2000–2001

Sports channel	Region/country	Operator/platform	Ownership
Eurosport, British Eurosport, Eurosport France	Pan-European	Eurosport	EBU, TF1, Canal Plus
DFS	Germany	Premiere World	Kirch Group
DFS Plus	Germany	Premiere World	Kirch Group
DFS Golf	Germany	Premiere World	Kirch Group
DFS Action	Germany	Premiere World	Kirch Group
Seasons	Germany	Premiere World	Canal Plus
Premiere Sport 1	Germany	Premiere World	Kirch Group,
Premiere Sport 2	Germany	Premiere World	Mediaset, Telecinco
Sky Sports 1	UK	BSkyB	News Corp., Vivendi,
Sky Sports 2	UK	BSkyB	Kirch Group,
Sky Sports 3	UK	BSkyB	Standard Life,
Sky Sports.com	UK	BSkyB	Capital Group
ONrequest	UK	ONdigital	Carlton/Granada Media Group
Plus Calcio Full	Italy	D Plus	Telepiu/Canal Plus
Plus Calcio Gold	Italy	D Plus	Telepiu/Canal Plus
Plus Calcio Away	Italy	D Plus	Telepiu/Canal Plus
Formula Uno	Italy	D Plus	Telepiu/Canal Plus
Calcio Stream	Italy	Stream	Stream/News Corp.
Sport Stream	Italy	Stream	Stream/News Corp.
Kiosque	France	Canalsatellite Numérique	Canal Plus
Supersignal	France	Canalsatellite Numérique	Canal Plus
Equidia	France	Canalsatellite Numérique	Canal Plus/Amaury
Seasons	France	Canalsatellite Numérique	Canal Plus
France Course	France	Canalsatellite Numérique	Canal Plus
Superfoot	France	TPS	TPS
AB Moteur	France	CS Numérique, AB Sat and TPS	Groupe AB
Liga de Futbol, Liga ACB+,	Spain	Canalsatélite Digital	Sogecable
F1 2000	Spain		
Futbol Mundial, Sportania		Canalsatélite Digital	Sogecable

Table 9.1 (cont'd)

Sports channel	Region/country	Operator/platform	Ownership
Futbol Activo, Teledeporte, Multifotbol	Spain	Vía Digital	Telefonica Group
Supersport	Turkey	NTV Plus	Most Bank
Supersport 1 & 2	Greece	Nova	Multichoice Hellas

Sources: Koranteng (1998a: 33–4); TV International (2000d); Cable and Satellite Europe 2001.

Channel, for horse-racing fans, British Eurosport and the Manchester United channel, the MUTV. Nearly, all BSkyB's subscribers – about seven million – have access to the three Sky Sports channels. The terrestrial digital platform ONdigital broadcasts BSkyB's sports channels as well as British Eurosport. It has also developed its own original sports services and started to acquire exclusive sports rights, among them the UEFA Champions League and eighty-eight live games of the Worthington Cup Tournament.

France

In France, Canal Plus spreads its live sports coverage over a multiplex service that includes the weekends on its analogue service. Also available on its digital platform are the PPV channel Kiosque and L'Équipe TV, a sports news channel. Kiosque subscribers pay extra for multichannel (in fact six channels) coverage of all Formula One Grand Prix races and the games of the First Soccer Division. Second Division is covered by another channel, D2 Max. There are also six more sports services: Pathé Sport, which was originally launched on the AB Sat platform in July 1996 but is also broadcast on the Canalsatellite Numérique platform; OMTV, the channel of the Olympique de Marseille soccer team; AB Moteur (motor racing); Equidia, a horse-racing channel, and Eurosport and Eurosport France. However, from the 1999–2000 season, CSN, for the first time, had to share the exclusive rights to Ligue National de Football sporting events with its rival TPS. Thus, TPS broadcasts one soccer game a week live in a pay window and has launched a new premium offering (Superfoot) with a season ticket for all PPV games or a subscription for a one-day-a-week channel carrying the exclusive pay-TV game (*TV International* 2000d).

Spain

In Spain, the rival satellite platforms CSD and Vía were transmitting the same soccer games and claiming exclusive coverage prices. In June 1999, the two competitors agreed to share pay-TV and PPV rights to the UEFA Champions League, the Primera Division (Liga) games and the Copa (Del Rey) matches from the 1999–2000 season to the 2008–9 seasons. The two rivals formed a joint venture called Audiovisual Sport II to handle the rights, which was notified to the Commission on 30 September 1999. It developed and extended the Audiovisual Sport agreement of 1997. In the Audiovisual Sport agreement, Sogecable (through Gestsport), Antena 3 (through Gestora de Medios Audiovisuales del Fútbol (GMAF)) – acquired later by Telefónica Media – and Television de Cataluña set up the joint venture Audiovisual Sport SL to exploit the broadcasting rights to the Spanish Liga and Copa during the seasons from 1998–9 to 2002–3. By means of the 1999 agreement, the parties reaffirmed their commitment to exploit the above-mentioned broadcasting rights via Audiovisual Sport SL and to assign to it their respective rights of pre-emption and first refusal in individual contracts with Spanish soccer clubs. The parties also agreed to assign to Audiovisual Sport SL any resulting contracts with the soccer clubs possibly concluded for the 2003–4 to 2008–9 seasons. In addition, CSD authorized Audiovisual Sport SL to broadcast the matches in PPV, on equal terms and without exclusivity, through Vía, up to the 2008–9 season. Sogecable also granted a licence to broadcast the matches in PPV to the cable operators controlled by Telefónica Media.

For its part, Vía granted Sogecable an option to acquire a nonexclusive licence in respect of the pay-TV and PPV rights to Champions League matches for the 2000–1 to 2002–3 seasons. The agreement also provided for the sharing among the parties of the broadcasting rights to the main Spanish soccer clubs. The European Commission received various formal complaints, both from competitors in the pay-TV market and from a Spanish soccer club. After a preliminary analysis, the Commission, in its decision of 12 April 2000, announced that the notified agreement might represent an infringement of EU competition rules – the object and effect of the infringement being price fixing as well as the sharing, among the parties, of the relevant markets. In particular, the Commission considered that competition in the market for the acquisition of rights to the broadcasting of soccer events would be seriously restricted.

The sports-dedicated Spanish channels are Sportmania (featuring Spanish soccer games and other sports) and Futbol Mundial (soccer other than Spanish soccer). However, CSD covers most sports from athletics and basketball to handball and horse racing, as well as the Spanish rights to the UEFA Champions League. Its PPV service Taquilla is complemented by the Spanish version of Eurosport, a sports magazine channel Sportmania and the soccer club, Real Madrid TV.

Germany

In Germany, DFS, part of the Kirch Group, faced problems at its launch, since it did not have the popular soccer games of the Bundesliga, the German soccer league. It was introduced in 1993 and used to broadcast on the DF1 platform. In 1996, it launched its new sports channels on DF1, DFS Plus (general sports), DFS Action (wrestling) and DFS Golf. With the merger of DF1 and Premiere to make Premiere World, Sports World, its programming arm, featured more than 1,000 events a year on the two sports services: Premiere Sport 1 and 2. More digital sports channels are planned to transmit live major sporting events. Games by the Bundesliga will be among the exclusive events.

Italy

In Italy, Telepiu offers the matches of eleven soccer teams in Serie A, B and C through the three Calcio channels (full, away and home), and Stream offers the matches of seven teams of Serie A through Calcio Stream. Live matches are available through the season ticket concept. This is targeted at loyal supporters of the Lega Calcio, who are accustomed to purchasing one ticket to attend a whole season of soccer matches. However, the split of the games between Plus Calcio and Stream means that fans wanting to see all their clubs away games have to buy smart cards from both digital operators.

Sports channels in smaller European countries

In the Netherlands and Denmark sports channels have faced many problems. In the Netherlands, Sport 7 was a joint venture by KNVB (the-Royal Dutch Soccer Federation), the Dutch electronics multi-national company Philips, the newspaper publishing company Telegraaf Holding, the investment bank ING, the telecommunications group the Royal KPV and executives from Endemol Entertainment, the television production company (Koranteng 1998a: 74). Sport 7 started in August 1996 and paid $450 million to acquire the TV rights of the Dutch soccer division. But cable operators were reluctant to take the service. Even though subscribers and advertisers showed a little interest, EU and national law forced Sport 7 to give up its exclusive TV sports rights. Moreover, Holland's biggest soccer teams, such as Ajax and Feyernood, disputed the KNVB's authority to sell broadcasting rights to their home matches. Within less than a year, Sport 7 ceased operating. Canal Plus took over the sports rights left by Sport 7 (Koranteng 1998b: 28).

In Denmark, the public broadcaster Danmarks Radio, the national telecommunications operator TeleDanmark and the Danish Football league used to own TV Sport (TVS), a sports-dedicated channel. The channel closed down at the end of 1997. When TVS management went public in September 1997, it was forecast that it would have 60,000 subscribers by the end of the first quarter of 1998 and 200,000 two years after its launch. When it closed down it had attracted approximately 11,500 subscribers. Generally speaking, Scandinavia has seen the most sports channel failures, with Sportkanalen (Modern Times Group), Supersport (NetHold) and TVS (Dodd 1998). The main provider of sports on television in Scandinavian countries, Belgium and the Netherlands is Canal Plus, which, after acquiring NetHold in 1996, relaunched its services as TV channels partly dedicated to sports.

Other countries with sports channels include Portugal, where Portugal Telecom, the Portuguese telecommunications operator, transmits Sport TV on the TV Cabo platform. In Russia there is NTV Sport – owned by Media Post, a unit of the Russian conglomerate Most Bank. In Turkey, there is Supersport – owned by the Multicanal pay-TV service, which belongs to Avrupa America Holding. The channel was launched in October 1997. In Greece there are Supersport 1 and 2 – owned by Multichoice/NetMed Hellas – which were launched in 1996 and 1999 respectively.

The most valuable programme

Popular sports associations are constantly being tempted to enter into new, more economically rewarding contracts with television interests. With the deregulation of television in Europe, as noted above, private television stations started bidding for popular sporting events. Some thought that the success of Canal Plus in France, which featured predominately sports and films, provided the model of how to become successful in the new competitive television era. And, since popular sports have been crucial in attracting subscribers to pay packages, media moguls are willing to buy everything.

Sport has proved to be the strongest force in building pay-TV subscriptions, more so than films. Sport also attracts the affluent male viewer, whether on pay-TV or free terrestrial television. It is significant to note that in 2000–1 no digital pay-TV scheme was being launched without owning the league soccer broadcast rights. From state-monopoly television, to private television and then to pay-TV and PPV channels, one sees steps that have led to the considerable increase of TV sports rights and the live broadcasting of sporting events. In effect, between 1990 and 1999, European soccer rights were subject to approximately 800 per cent inflation. Moreover, TV rights to games of leading soccer clubs in England, Germany, Spain and Italy increased by nearly 200 per cent to $694 million in the 1997–8 season from $240 million in the 1994–5 season (Koranteng 1998a: 3) (see table 9.2). Rupert Murdoch, when he spoke to shareholders at the annual meeting of News Corporation in Adelaide (15 October 1996), said:

> Sport absolutely overpowers film and everything else in the entertainment genre . . . We have long-term rights in most countries to major sporting events . . . that is [we] use sports as a 'battering ram' and a lead offering in all our pay television operations . . . Sports will remain very important and we will be investing and acquiring long term rights and becoming part of the world sports establishment. (Reuters 1996).

All seemed simpler when the EBU was the sole rights broker (see Barnett 1995). By snapping up rights to most of the major sports competitions in Europe, the EBU used to ensure its public service broadcasters had sports rights at a relatively low cost. But it had also been widely accused (and not just by Europe's private channels) of sitting on rights. It has been said that the public stations did not compete for the sports rights, but rather agreed on prices between

Table 9.2 Sports rights expenditure and growth, 1992–1998

Country	Expenditure		Growth
	1992 ($m)	1998 ($m)	1992–1998 (%)
Austria	21.01	35.40	68.5
Belgium	23.06	46.24	100.5
Denmark	16.42	43.17	162.9
Finland	17.05	35.31	107.1
France	224.75	451.05	84.3
Germany	318.83	841.09	163.8
Greece	6.95	28.00	302.9
Ireland	9.32	17.89	91.9
Italy	233.21	500.18	114.5
Netherlands	52.21	108.79	108.4
Norway	14.04	25.06	78.5
Portugal	15.04	28.94	92.4
Spain	108.77	260.82	139.8
Sweden	22.57	55.65	146.6
Switzerland	25.01	33.77	35.0
UK	350.34	793.09	126.4
TOTAL	1,478.58	3,304.46	123.5
AVERAGE	92.41	206.53	123.5

Sources: Molsky (1999: 20); *Euromedia* (1999).

them. In the following pages we shall try to describe the inflation of TV sports rights in some European Countries.

Inflation of TV sports rights

In Germany, in 1988 the RTL Plus caused a furore when it successfully bid for rights to German Bundesliga soccer. ARD and ZDF were later cut into the deal for complementary rights after the German public (or at least those in cabled areas or in states where RTL Plus was not available over the air) reacted angrily. But the precedent had been set. In 1990, the exclusive rights to the Bundesliga went up to more than five times the price paid in 1988. In 1995–6, the Bundesliga appointed the sports broker company International Sports Rights (ISRR), owned by the Kirch Group, to negotiate on its behalf for free-to-air and pay-TV rights in two five-year deals.

The expenses of CLT/Bertelsmann rose from DM25 million in 1991 to DM65 million in 1996, and RTL sports programming costs increased from DM3,500 per minute in 1991 to DM21,900 per minute in 1997 (Godard 1997: 108). The free TV rights of the Bundesliga live games went to the private channel Sat 2, for DM450 million for the period 1998–2000. The pay-TV rights went to Premiere, to broadcast three live games a week on Pay-TV and six games a week on PPV for DM600 million for the period 1998–2000.

In the United Kingdom, in 1986, the BBC and ITV paid £6.2 million for a two-year contract for the live broadcast of fourteen league games and the League Cup. In 1988, ITV paid £44 million for a four-year contract (1988–92) for twenty-one live games and the League Cup. In 1992, BSkyB paid £191.5 million for a five-year contract for the exclusive right to broadcast sixty games live. In 1996, BSkyB paid £670 million over four years (1996–2000) for the exclusive right to broadcast sixty games. In 2000, BSkyB paid £1.1 billion for four years to broadcast sixty-six matches on Sundays and Mondays (that is, a 66 per cent increase compared to the previous deal). These figures contrast with the £3,250 paid by the BBC for the UK's FA Cup in 1949 and the £5.2 million for a two-year contract paid by the BBC and ITV for ten live league games in the early 1980s.

In France, TV soccer rights increased considerably after the bid submitted by TPS in July 1999. It offered FFr2 billion ($311 million) to the Ligue National de Football per year for rights from 2001 until 2004, meaning a rise of 300 per cent compared to 1996–2000, when Canal Plus paid FFr470 million to the Ligue. Canal Plus reacted quickly. The two rivals agreed to share rights in an overall deal worth $1.3 million over five years. Canal Plus and the commercial free-to-air channel TF1 share the rights for Champions League matches until 2003. TF1, which originally wanted to split the rights with part-owned TPS, paid $89 million for its share, with Canal Plus likely to have contributed a similar amount.

In Italy, Telepiu's contract with the Lega Calcio went up from L45 billion ($21 million) to L112 billion ($51 million) per year between 1996 and 1999. The issue of who is entitled to sell TV rights, whether individual soccer clubs or their representative body, the Lega Calcio, was at the heart of the debate, after the government introduced a 60 per cent cap on Serie A pay-TV rights. Moreover, the clubs negotiate their own rights. The eleven clubs on Plus Calcio (including Juventus, Inter and AC Milan) receive between $39 million and $49 million per season. In February 1999 Telepiu gained the TV rights of the European Champions League for four

Table 9.3 The evolution of Olympics TV rights for European broadcasters, 1980–2000

Place and year	TV rights ($m)
Moscow 1980	5.7
Los Angeles 1984	19.8
Seoul 1988	28.0
Barcelona 1992	90.0
Atlanta 1996	255.0
Sydney 2000	350.0

Source: Papathanassopoulos (1998b: 22).

years at the amount of L700 billion ($318 million). RAI won exclusive coverage of the national side's games until 2002 for $121 million in February 1999.

In the Netherlands, after their dispute with KNVB in 1997, the leading division clubs formed the Eredivise in order to negotiate their own deal centrally. The clubs decided to contract their new television partner Canal Plus on an individual basis, although the resultant $14.6 million deal was collective.

In Greece, NetMed Hellas holds collective rights for $9 million for 1996–2001. The Greek League aims to negotiate the current deal on a new basis.

In effect, the TV-rights business has had an increasingly high profile worldwide since the 1980s. The cost of screening the Olympic Games is a further example (see table 9.3 for European broadcasters). In total, broadcasters worldwide paid $107 million for the rights to screen the 1980 Moscow Games. This jumped to $278 million for the 1984 Los Angeles Games. The Seoul rights in 1988 leapt another 40 per cent. The global cost of screening the 1996 Atlanta Games went to $1.2 billion, double that of the Barcelona Games in 1992. That figure increased to $1.3 billion for the Sydney Games in 2000. Moreover, the EBU paid Euro 128 million for the rights of the soccer World Cup of 1998. The TV rights for the World Cups of 2002 and 2006 were sold to ISL/Prisma for the sum of Euro 1.75 billion. The cost of the European Football Cup grew rapidly from £1.3 million in 1980 to £32 million in 1996.

In short, with the proliferation of new channels and especially with the spread of pay-TV and PPV services, the market has boomed, and prices have increased rapidly. As a result, terrestrial channels are looking to televise smaller events and less mainstream sports, such as volleyball, American football, sumo or amateur soccer games. But pay and PPV operators want to avoid a head-to-head competition and would like to allow the leagues, mainly soccer leagues, and clubs to deal individually over their TV rights. On the other hand, the bankruptcy in May 2001 of the rights agency ISL illustrates the problem of the inflation of TV sports rights.

Is sport the driver for the growth of PPV?

Sport differs from other programming and its value is in live coverage or in delayed highlights. Sport, however, has followed a convergent path with other types of programming. As with films, sporting events were originally produced primarily for live audiences. The diversification of film distribution methods witnessed in the 1980s, through pay-TV, video and increased free TV revenue, was experienced by sports in the 1990s. But whereas film producers still have a variety of distribution outlets to work with, major sporting organizations are evolving rapidly to become suppliers of a single media, television (Godard 1997).

Not only has sports coverage moved towards other forms of TV entertainment, but the value of rights has also made it one of the most expensive categories. Sports rights have been affected in recent years by two sets of trends, which have reshaped the European television industry: economics and technology. *Economics* has been important because, in most countries, commercial channels have faced problems financing the exploding costs of sports through advertising – although European advertisers are prepared to pay inflated rates in order to target football's key audience. *Digital technology* has been relevant because it allows more channels to broadcast. Moreover, as noted in chapter 4, pay-TV would revolutionize the economics of television and television companies would raise revenues directly from the viewers.

The combination of these factors has brought a further increase in TV buying power. In most of Europe, the biggest buyers of TV sports rights are now pay-TV and PPV channels. So soccer appears to be in the vanguard of the PPV revolution or, as Murdoch has said, 'Football of all sports is number one.' In effect, pay-TV channels in most European countries are already offering football. Moreover, many soccer federations have already sold or committed PPV rights (table 9.4).

But PPV sport has, like many of the anticipated highlights of the digital television era, made a false start. The take-up of what is effectively a new electronics product for consumers failed – in most

Table 9.4 European football: Pay-TV deals, 2000–2001

League	Provider	Current status	No. of matches
Championnat de France D1	Canalsatellite and TPS	Exclusive five-year pay-TV/PPV deal until 2000–1; from 1999–2000 it is shared with TPS	340 (325 PPV)
English Premier League	1. BSkyB 2. NTL	1. Four-year pay-TV deal 2001–5 2. Four-year deal 2001–5	1. 66 games a season broadcast on Sundays and Mondays 2. 40 games a season broadcast on Sundays *One club cannot be featured more than 8 times in a season*
Deutsche Bundesliga	Kirch Group/ Premiere Sport	Exclusive five-year deal for live broadcast and PPV	3 games a week on pay-TV and 6 games on PPV
Liga	Vía Digital	Barcelona for five years	Home games
Liga	Canalsatélite	Audiovisual Sport (Sogecable and Vía Digital/ Telefonica) has seven-year deal with league until 2003–4; disputed by the EU	Not available
Serie A (Italy)	Plus Calcio	Telepiu has exclusive three-year deal with 11 Italian soccer clubs	306 games a season
Serie A (Italy)	Stream	Stream has exclusive deal with 7 Italian soccer clubs	

Table 9.4 (cont'd)

League	Provider	Current status	No. of matches
Dutch First Division	Canal Plus	Clubs on individual basis	2 premier games a week
Greek First Division	Supersport	NetMed Hellas acquired the exclusive soccer rights for the Greek championship until 2001	3 games a week
Belgian First Division	Canal Plus	Pay-TV deal runs from 1997–8 until 2001–2; includes PPV	35 games a season
Scottish Premier League	BSkyB	In negotiation	17 games a season

Source: Papathanassopoulos (1998b).

cases – to meet expectations (Westcott 1997: 1; Koranteng 1999: 38). In Germany, for example, it is estimated that the pay-TV rights for Bundesliga games paid by Premiere in 2000 had increased about four times compared to the 1997–8 season. But three years after that agreement, Premiere World does not plan to offer PPV until the service attracts 3.5 million subscribers.

On the other hand, in the UK, BSkyB had some success with four live boxing matches. The first was the heavyweight fight between Frank Bruno and Mike Tyson in March 1996. Over 660,000 subscribers paid a fee of £9.99 to watch the bout – 15 per cent of BSkyB's subscriber base. In France, CSN launched the first full-scale digital PPV service in September 1996, but it still seems fair to characterize PPV sports as an idea whose time has yet to come. The same applies for the TPS PPV soccer service. In Spain, both digital platforms, Vía and CSD, have made PPV a strategic part of their business model. In Italy, D+ is based on a PPV format, with fans being offered the option to subscribe to all the games of one team, all the away games or every Division Serie A and B game (Westcott 1997; Koranteng 1999: 38).

European PPV revenues from domestic league soccer are going to increase considerably by 2009. According to Baskerville Communications forecasts, PPV soccer revenues in 2009 will increase to $276 million in France, $1,464 million in Germany, $635 million in Italy, $260 million in the Netherlands, $388 million in Spain and $754 million in the UK. But, as we will see later, the issue of PPV for sports is a bone of contention in Europe. On the other hand, pay-TV and PPV channels faced with an uncertain future have been attempting to secure the source of the value by buying stakes in soccer clubs. As will be discussed later, this move has a twofold advantage: it keeps them on the inside track over how rights are distributed, and it provides an insurance policy for at least some football, should a rival snatch the league rights – or that at least, was the theory.

The effects of sports television

Pay-TV and PPV channels broadcast a growing number of major sporting events. This trend has already sparked controversy, as viewers face the choice of either doing without their favourite sport or having to pay for it at what is effectively an electronic turnstile. The deregulation of European television, the decline of the public sector, the welfarist TV system in Europe, as described in chapters 1 and 3, and the advent of pay-TV and PPV channels, allied with the corporatization of sporting teams and organizations in soccer, are the causes for the big changes in the field (see also Hoehn and Szymanski 1999). In other words, a policy change towards deregulation, allied with the regeneration of sports teams as profit centres rather than as parts of a not-for-profit civil society, has produced a number of side effects.

Efforts to regulate the issue

This situation provoked the scepticism of the European Parliament, resulting in the regulation of the 1997 *Television without Frontiers* Directive. In May 1996 members of the European Parliament questioned the European Commission on measures such as whether the EU would guarantee all its citizens the possibility of watching television broadcasts of major sporting events. They also pointed out that it is vital to keep major sporting events from being broadcast exclusively by channels not accessible to all citizens and referred to three articles of the Treaty, namely Article 85 on competition, Article 86 on abuse of dominant position and Article 90 on the notion of the 'service'. The European Commission recognized the importance of all citizens having access to information on events (not just sporting events), which could constitute 'great common experiences' of shared social and cultural values. The 1997 Television Directive foresees that major events, such as sports, must be broadcast unencrypted, even if pay-TV stations have bought the exclusive rights. Each EU country has been asked to draw up a list of national or international protected events, such as the Olympic Games, the World Cup or the European Football Championship, to which the public should be guaranteed free access.

The above concern echoed similar scepticism expressed in the USA, Australia, New Zealand, Canada and South Africa relating to the development of pay-sport channels. Similar views were expressed in the UK, France and Germany. In the UK, the Broadcasting Act of 1996 lists eight events for free-to-air channels: the FA Cup Final, the Scottish FA Cup Final, the FIFA World Cup (soccer); the Derby and the Grand National (horse racing); the Wimbledon Championship (tennis), and cricket matches involving the English national team. In France, the regulatory authority Conseil Supérieure de l'Audiovisuel has listed the Olympic (Winter and Summer) Games, the Tour de France, the World and European Cup tournaments, the French Football Cup Final and the Five Nations Rugby games, involving France.

However, this does not mean that the problem has been resolved. The PPV channels argue that with this new legislation the future of sport could be seriously damaged and that the customer take-up of newly developing digital services could be seriously retarded with restrictive legislation. Sports organizations have also opposed the Directive, claiming it will harm sport by depriving it of additional financial sources. In effect, there is no assurance as to how the EU's Member States will tackle the issue, since each list is optional and not compulsory, and it will be a product of negotiations and pressures at both international and national levels. In effect, the European Parliament was in favour of a single EU list, but this proposal was regarded as not realistic. What was approved instead was a compromise with no certain implementation.

Denmark has provided a legislative model with a law 'on the use of TV rights to events of major importance to society'. This law is in accordance with the Television Directive. According to the law, the following events are regarded as being of major importance for society (*OJEC* 1999a):

- Olympic, Summer and Winter Games: the Games in their entirety;
- World and European soccer championships (men): all matches with Danish participation together with semi-finals and finals;
- World and European handball championships (men and women): all matches with Danish participation together with semi-finals and finals;
- Denmark's world and European championship qualifying matches in soccer (men);
- Denmark's world and European championship qualifying matches in handball (women).

Moreover, regarding the use of TV rights, it is stated that a substantial proportion of the population is regarded as being prevented from following an event on free television, save in cases where:

- the events are broadcast on a channel or channels that can be received by at least 90 per cent of the population without any extra cost for acquiring technical installations – for example, a satellite receiver or cable connection to a communal aerial installation; and
- the receiving of the event does not cost the viewer more than DKK 25 per month, apart from the TV licence and the subscription payment towards a communal aerial installation.

Later, Italy and Germany also passed laws following these lines. Major events, that should be broadcast on free-to-air channels are (*OJEC* 1999b, 2000):

- the Summer and Winter Olympic Games;
- the soccer World Cup final and all matches involving the Italian and German national teams;
- the European Football Championship final and all matches involving the Italian and German national teams;
- all matches involving the Italian and German national football teams, at home and away;
- the final and the semi-finals of the Champions League and the Union of European Football Associations (UEFA) Cup where an Italian team was involved – in the German case only the final.

Moreover, for Italy, major events also included: the Tour of Italy (Giro d'Italia) cycling competition, the Formula One Italian Grand Prix and the San Remo Italian music festival.

The paradox of owners of sports rights

Meanwhile, the owners of sports rights face a paradox. Events such as the Olympics and golf and tennis tournaments became valuable precisely because they picked up a mass global audience who could watch them for free. Restricting the audience could spell a slow decline in interest – and therefore a decline in the value of events. On the other hand, we may see a return to the basic economic philosophy of sports. As Rowe (1996: 569) notes:

> The economics of sports were founded on the principle of persuading large numbers of people to leave their homes, to travel to enclosed sporting events and to pay for entry in order to view professional performers engaged in various forms of structured, physical competition. Long before the arrival of cable, satellite and microwave, this was pay-per-view sport . . . It is not difficult to see why sports that relied on crowd attendance were nervous about television.

In other words, in the future, we may witness a new development in European sports – stadiums empty of spectators but with plenty of TV cameras visible – since, on the one hand, this would be economically viable for the clubs, and, on the other, it would offer a better view of the game for spectators at home. There is little evidence to suggest that this will happen. It is undeniable that, on a permanent basis, live sports broadcasts have led to a decrease in the number of attendances. But, if this trend were to go on, it would bring a striking contrast to the way sports used to be: a public event that required an instant interaction between the players, the teams and the spectators. The crowd atmosphere of sports would be lost, as has happened elsewhere, for example, public libraries, which have tended to be replaced by information centres and the virtual libraries of web sites in cyberspace.

It is exactly what Schiller was pointing out some years ago, when he was speaking on the commercialization of the public sector (Schiller 1989: 69–86). There is also a danger for television on this. To watch a game, a viewer also wants to 'feel' the crowd atmosphere, and sport can never work as a studio event. If few people are sitting around the stand, the game may be unattractive for viewers to watch, especially if they are paying for this. This danger, however, alerted UEFA, which in July 2000 decided that from the 2000–1 season its national soccer associations could block the broadcasting on television of soccer during $2\frac{1}{2}$ hours either on Saturday or Sunday to protect stadium attendance. In April 2001 the Commission decided that this rule falls outside the scope of EU competition rules, but, in practice, only ten out of twenty-one national soccer associations chose to have blocked hours in the 2000–1 season.

The new sports viewer-fan

Moreover, the new television sports viewers will be divided according to their purchasable power. In Italy, for instance, Plus Calcio's price structure is based closely on the cost of actually attending matches. In effect, subscribers are classified to Serie A and Serie B. Subscribers of Serie A get thirty-four matches of their choice live (a kind of season ticket). They can only subscribe to the full package – for a team's home and away matches – if they live outside the city of the team in question. In the UK, financial analysis by UBS Global Research, which assessed the potential level of revenue of UK soccer, concluded that soccer could attract from television and especially from PPV by classifying the potential viewers in four categories/prices. These are: *Bronze*, which means the viewer will have to pay £100 per game and will have a PPV service; *Silver*: £14.99 per month/£9.50 per game, a kind of away season ticket; *Gold*: £19.99 per month/£6.31 per game, a kind of full season ticket for an individual club; and *Platinum*, £24.99 per month/£0.39 per game, for complete coverage (in *Television Business International* 1997).

The subordination of sports to television and media companies

Television, and especially pay-TV and PPV, are regarded as the saviour of modern sports, since money in sports has increased tremendously. In the longer term television has become its principal paymaster, dictating what and when a broadcast takes place. Joseph Maguire (1999: 149) notes that the 'global media-sport complex' is made up of three key groups: sports organizations, media/marketing organizations and personnel, and trans-multinational companies. Maguire points out that the nature of interdependency between them has varied over time and within and between the continents. But he also concludes that:

> Sports have a largely dependent role in this media-sport complex. That is organizations have little or no control over the nature and form in which 'their' sport is televised, reported or covered . . . This dependency on the media has grown over time and is arguably

connected to sport organizations' increasing reliance on revenue from sponsorship and marketing.   (Maguire 1999: 150)

In other words, rights owners, especially with regard to soccer, have become dependent on television companies to whom they have sold pay-TV rights. A more recent, and perhaps more important, development is for media companies to buy stakes in soccer clubs. In 1998 BSkyB offered approximately $1 billion (£623 million) for Manchester United Football Club to buy its stakes (this was eventually rejected by the British Authorities on anti-competitive grounds). But, since then, BSkyB has acquired minority stakes in various English Premiere League clubs: Manchester United (9.9 per cent); Leeds (9.9 per cent); Sunderland (5 per cent) and Chelsea (9.9 per cent). Behind these moves was BSkyB's attempt to secure its negotiating position regarding the new rights for the Premiere League by having a stake in as many clubs as possible (Paul Barker 2000), and eventually it won the new TV rights. Other broadcasters and distributors have followed the same route and invested in clubs. NTL has a 6.3 per cent stake in Newcastle United and in Aston Villa (NTL was also awarded the new TV rights), and in 1999 media group Granada bought a 9.9 per cent stake in Liverpool.

A similar 'relationship' has been evident in other European countries as well. Ufa Sport, the sports rights division of German media group Bertelsmann, holds an equity investment in the Italian clubs Sampdoria and Genoa. Since 1989, AC Milan has belonged to Silvio Berlusconi, owner of Fininvest. Vittorio Cecchi Cori, owner of TV stations TMC 1 and 2, owns Fiorentina Football Club. Since 1991, Canal Plus has owned Paris Saint Germain in France and Sevette of Geneva in Switzerland. Moreover, M6 and CLT–UFA have owned Girondins de Bordeaux since 1999. In Greece, NetMed NV, owner of Supersport channel, owns the football club AEK Athens, and the owner of terrestrial channel Seven owns PAOK (Thessaloniki). Both clubs are leading teams in the Greek first soccer division. In Scotland, Scottish Media has owned the soccer club Hearts since September 1999. However, it should be remembered that other companies from the industrial sector are owners of soccer clubs, such as PSV Einhoven, Juventus (Fiat), Sochaux (Peugeot), Bayer Leverkusen (Bayer) and Gothenburg (Volvo) (Hoehn and Szymanski 1999: 207). As the European Commission notes: 'Audiovisual groups would like to have exclusive rights to teams in order to ensure their broadcasting rights should competition authorities prevent collective selling . . . The question is whether the principles of sporting ethics are compatible with this interpenetration' (CEC 1999b: 4).

But while media companies are trying to enter the soccer field to secure and develop their business, there are also trends moving in the opposite direction. One is the aforementioned launch of TV team channels. A second trend is that of teams trying to form alliances in order to negotiate their rights on a national basis, as in the Netherlands, or on a regional basis. The latter was behind the attempt in August 1999 to organize a European league consisting of top European soccer teams (see Hoehn and Szymanski 1999). This was organized by sports media organization Media Partners, which was formed in 1998, threatening UEFA's Champions League's existence. But a similar European League, the Euroleague, was formed in basketball by twenty-four European teams. This was organized by Telefónica and threatened FIBA's Suproleague. A third is the formation of soccer media companies. Società Diriti Sportivi, which is formed by soccer clubs Roma, Lazio, Fiorentina and Parma, is one of the shareholders of the Stream platform (chapter 2).

The above examples indicate that, with PPV, the biggest and most successful clubs stand to make the most money, while the smaller clubs, which provide their opposition, stand to make less. In practice, big clubs could destroy smaller ones if they rush into deals to show matches on PPV. In Britain, larger clubs want to go ahead, following the examples of other clubs in Holland, Spain and Portugal, signing separate deals with PPV channels and, in effect, breaking up the collective PPV rights dealt by the federation. But there is also a danger. By investing money into certain clubs, broadcasters may diminish the thrill and surprise of soccer that made it so attractive in the first place. There is also a professional media ethics question. To what extent would a sports-journalist have the freedom to express his or her opinion, if his or her channel owned a sports club?

In a longer term, this development simply indicates a deeper transformation of some main aspects of the public sphere, at least, in Europe. Both television, as a public service, and soccer, as a field of public expression that was not for profit, used to be regarded as expressions of civil society, but nowadays, with the deregulation and commercialization of television, globalization and technological diffusion have started to become the main profit tools of large corporations.

The metamorphosis of sports TV events

Finally, the sports issue is related not just to sports but to the future of television in general, in that it also changes the way we watch television, especially in respect to live sporting events (Papathanassopoulos 1998b). The fact is that, in more than fifty years of analogue television, the coverage of sport experienced remarkably little change, other than the introduction of slow-motion displays. In fact, the viewer of the 1950s watched a soccer game in much the same way as a viewer in the 1990s – for an hour and a half a viewer sat in front of a TV set looking at the pictures and listening to the commentary. With the advent of digital television technology applications, as in the case of the digital channels Sky Sports Extra or the Zapfoot and Notepad of Canal Plus, the viewer will have more active involvement when watching the game. The viewer can choose a different camera angle, switching to an alternative view of action while keeping the main match coverage in a box in the corner of the screen. The viewer can also call up highlights of the game, as it is going on. Digital services can also offer replays on demand or statistics. By and large, the viewer can have at his or her disposal the tools that producers and directors have while covering a game (Harverson 1999).

The fact is that, with the new interactive applications, the viewer will watch not only football but any game much more easily and with more comfort than in the past. However, there are doubts over exactly how much demand there will be for interactive sports coverage. Watching television is an inherently passive experience, and viewers may like it that way. A similar danger is related to the hyperinflation of live sports matches. An implication of this is that the live game as a television event – that is, as an interruption of the schedule, intervening in the normal flow of broadcasting (Dayan and Katz 1992) – has become routine in the modern television landscape. On the other hand, because of the proliferation of TV channels in general and the subsequent fragmentation of the audience, live sports might remain the last frontier of the mass television audience.

Sports on the Internet

Sports have also become an area of intense competition on the Internet, with a number of sites offering news and live coverage spanning time zones and cultures. This is because sport on the Internet is becoming an attractive alternative to television. Web sports sites are growing because they satisfy a need to employ journalists, not aggregators, they can market themselves, they have no traditional competition and they have unique content/rights. But their development is also related to the fact that a number of advertisers bought banner ads around web sites devoted to the World Cup in 1998. Sports TV operations such as Sky Sports, CSD and Vía have launched complementary web sites. This move highlights the desire for media companies to control both content and distribution, since small Internet sports content providers have been successful and, to an extent, become new competitors to the sports channels.

The Internet is considered the perfect medium for the average sports fan. It is also seen as ideal for expatriates to keep up with home sports news and for fans to exchange information, to delve as deeply as they like in one sport, and at the same time get an instant, comprehensive overview of all the others. Sports web sites can attract large audiences. According to research conducted by *Screen Digest*, traffic to the official Wimbledon tennis championships web site has grown up to 700 per cent year after year. The soccer World Cup web site france98.com received more than thirteen million visitors from more than 170 countries and generated seventy-four million page impressions and over one billion hits in the lifetime of the site (Church 2000).

Sport on the Internet is influenced by a growing base of computers in the home and at work, cheaper, faster and more convenient Internet access and increased public awareness of new web technologies, including Wireless Application Protocol (WAP), which will allow access from mobile phones and interactive TV. Thus, Internet sports sites are developing global strategies.

Summary

The advent of digital television and pay-TV in Europe has complicated the relationship between sports and television. Sports events are considered one of the highest audience attractions, resulting in a tremendous increase of sports games on television, the arrival of sports-dedicated channels, and the rapid inflation for TV sports rights. Large media companies, which own the sports pay-TV and PPV channels, have invested huge sums to buy exclusive sports broadcasting rights and charge additional fees to the viewers who may want to watch a 'live' game, especially football. However, the arrival of sports channels is only one side effect of the deregulation of European television. The problem is deeper and is related to the transformation of television and sports in Europe. Sports-dedicated channels offer more money to the sports organizations. But it is

questionable whether this revenue compensates for the lack of accessibility for watching the sports and sporting events that are shown
only on pay-TV or PPV channels. At the same time, the EU and
sports federations are increasingly anxious about the growing infil-
tration of sports clubs by large media companies.

10

More Music Television Channels
Europe Dances to a New Rhythm

Although radio has a longer history of association with music and the music industry, it is television that has become the dominant medium for the dissemination and promotion of music and its artists. Television is naturally thought of as a visual medium, but music is everywhere on TV. While initially music was an element in programming, nowadays music has become an autonomous part of TV programming. In effect, music plays an important role in setting the mood and tone of programming. Music is a programme's signature. Music helps define characters, it cues the attention and creates anticipation, and it underscores words, touches the emotions, heightens the impact of images and lingers in the memory long after the images are gone. Music programmes have been present since the earliest days of television.

The universal language of classical music has been marketed in all territories. Rock music is a bond joining young people throughout the world, as highlighted by live concerts starting with Live Aid. In effect, as Real (1996: 5) notes 'music is central to the cultural practices of all societies and can overcome the limits of time and space'.

Music television channels want to benefit from this, and indeed a number of music channels have emerged across Europe. In fact, after the USA, Europe is the most mature music TV market, and for some a market that is overcrowded. A large number of the major countries have four or more services in operation or scheduled to be launched. Because most are on subscription, their survival will be based on viewers' choice. Music channels principally target young viewers (aged 16–34), who traditionally treat television more and more like radio, using their zappers to switch channels for a better programme the way they spin the radio dial to find a better song. The wide variety of music radio stations illustrates the potential audience for a wide spectrum of music television channels.

Music television is a hybrid of two opposing forms of revenue generators: content provision (rights owners, such as the record companies, performers and composers) and distribution (the operators who want to use music to enhance the quality and variety of programmes but are reluctant to pay the royalties demanded) (Koranteng 1997). This chapter looks at the development of music channels and the intense competition in music television in Europe. It also looks at the strategies adopted by the music channels for localization and their entry into the Internet age.

MTV and the rise of music television

Music Television, the well-known MTV, initiated the revolution of music television in the USA in the early 1980s. Warner Communications launched MTV on 21 August 1981 in the USA (Aufderheide 1986; Jhally 1990; Banks 1996). Media giant Viacom purchased it in 1985 (Campbell 1998: 69). Cheap programming was the original *raison d'être* behind the music channel. The product – variously called pop videos, music videos and music clips – was originally regarded simply as a promotional vehicle to help sell records. The fortunes of the record industry reached their nadir in the period 1979–82, at the very time when the music video was coming into its own. The music video therefore became a device whereby record companies attempted to retain their share of a diminishing market. Thus it was that the US cable music service MTV, which began with a relatively modest budget and an even more modest viewer base, was allowed to develop and eventually to prosper on the back of a record industry willing to supply it with premium products free of charge.

MTV is still a front runner in a number of countries across Europe. MTV and its international offspring – including MTV Europe (MTVE), MTV Brazil, MTV Japan and MTV Latino – reach nearly 300 million households worldwide and it is considered as one of the vehicles of the Anglo-American cultural influence globally, since MTV's programmes play mostly American and British artists or local acts that mimic US music styles (Banks 1997).

A decade earlier, music and variety shows had just about reached their demise on American television. Though television's earliest offerings had been variety programmes, music shows simply did not appeal to mass audiences any more; even popular performers could not muster the kind of ratings necessary to survive on the networks. Unlike network television, cable did not have to appeal to a mass audience and MTV honed in on a demographic that could guarantee those numbers: the 'rock 'n' roll' generation. This model of television was gradually transferred to Europe in the mid-1980s and now MTV has to compete with local rivals and new technologies as well. The channel's success can, to a large extent, be attributed to the fact that it was the first off the block in broadcasting what is essentially a very cheap form of TV entertainment – readymade pop videos. These days MTV offers original programming, such as special events and documentaries, but the pop video is still at the heart of its programme schedule. In fact, MTV is unlikely to move away from its video format, but the new technological developments indicate that the future of music television in Europe will be digital as well as online.

The development of music television in Europe

MTV soon realized that it was onto a good thing. It began to dictate taste by its demand for a particular form of programming in which previously key areas of recorded music, notably black music, played little part. It was no surprise that record companies, blinded by promotional arguments, should fall over themselves to give products away. After all, they had supplied TV companies in many countries with material for years. Gradually, there was considerable doubt as to whether broadcasters could ever be persuaded to cough up for what they had long been getting free of charge. At the same time, quite apart from escalating production quotas, record companies were actually paying out money to artists under an agreement with British Musicians Union, negotiated originally in 1976 and substantially revised in 1982.

Since then things have changed considerably. When in the autumn of 1986 MTV announced its intention to start a European satellite operation, it expected UK companies to react as their US counterparts had done five years earlier. A great deal of effort was expended in trying to persuade UK record executives of the benefits of free supply in terms of the promotion that would accrue. The ploy failed. Learning from the past, the record industry realized the importance of pop videos not just to itself but to the various media – notably the dedicated channels – that it had spawned.

The resolve was principally a response to the original growth of MTV. When Sky Channel and Music Box announced their proposed European services in 1983–4, the response of the British record industry was to set up Video Performance Limited (VPL) to act as the central licensing authority. After a period of negotiations, agreements were reached that attempted to reconcile two elements: the intrinsic programming value of music videos and the profitability of the new satellite services.

One of the arguments encountered in those days was that satellite and cable channels could not expect to make profits in their early days of operation. Huge percentages of their budgets were allocated to the acquisition of hardware and other technical areas, leaving little for the acquisition of programming or 'rights' as they are usually called.

Running and distribution costs were a factor in 1987, but the principle of payment for programme material was accepted, based upon a realistic guaranteed annual licence fee. A share in the net advertising revenue generated by the programmes provided topped this up. In the UK, Sky Channel and Music Box (then part of Super Channel) concluded new agreements with VPL to cover the European footprint of their operations. In the years separating the two sets of negotiations, the record industry succeeded in creating an international negotiating body coordinated by Producers of Phonograms and Videograms (IFPI) and VPL, which could guarantee a clearance of rights across the entire pan-European footprint, local autonomy having bowed to international solidarity. Thus it was a matter for the record industry as to how income generated by these services was distributed.

When MTV entered European television in 1987, it was embroiled in conflict with record companies over the above 'pay-and-play' principle. Moreover, in the same year the Italian music channel Video Music had a run-in with the Italian collection society Società Italiana degli Autori et Editioni (SIAE) over payment for the use of videos. Video Music argued that it did not see why it should have to pay certain prices to do promotion for the record companies. While the battle was going on, the channel continued to show the videos, but without showing the artists' names or song titles on the screen. Video Music won the argument and the names reappeared.

MTVE objected to the collective licensing system used in Europe and in 1993 it sued VPL, arguing that this system was monopolistic, forcing it to pay very high fees for videos, and that it should be abolished, letting MTV negotiate video rights individually with each record company (Banks 1997: 46). The record companies opposed this move, because it was considered that it would lead to much lower licence fees. Sony Music reached a separate accommodation with MTV in November 1994 by signing a global licensing agreement that provided MTV with rights to Sony music clips on all of its services (Banks 1997: 28).

But the most serious challenge facing MTV was the news that record companies were to join forces to set up music channels in key European markets. One of them was Viva, founded in Germany in 1993. About 40 per cent of the music and videos featured by Viva were to be German in an attempt to boost the sales of recordings by domestic artists. Four multinational record companies – Warner Music, Sony, EMI and Polygram – founded the group Viva Fernsehen. Its ownership structure – which was considered as an outlet for the record companies – prompted MTV to file a complaint in the European Court accusing Viva of anti-competitive practices. It claimed that Viva would receive licensing deals from the four record company shareholders, which also happened to supply a majority of the videos seen on MTV. It alleged that the German station was breaching Articles 85 and 86 of the EU's Treaty of Rome, which deal with price fixing and abuse of market dominance.

In those days European broadcasters had started launching domestic national channels to balance the dominance of the Anglo-American repertoire on MTV. These included Italy's Videomusic, France's MCM, S-Plus in Switzerland, Z-TV in Sweden, Music Factory in the Netherlands and Viva in Germany. In the mid-1990s, MTV was feeling the pressure in Europe for the first time.

The need to localize music channels

Music is supposedly a medium that crosses borders around the world. But broadcasters know that there are untapped revenue streams to be found from regionalizing their services to cater for local cultural tastes. Indeed, in the mid-1990s, MTV realized that American pop culture had its limits as an export product. Some said: 'MTV has lost its way, failing to react to the changes in the youth markets' (Elliot 1998). On the other hand, other music channels such as BET On Jazz International – a music channel designed to cater for an audience with diverse musical tastes, while focusing predominately on jazz-related music genres – do not consider localization, especially language localization, as an effective strategy. For some others, localization is too little and too late.

This, of course, does not diminish the impact of MTV. The power of branding can be very valuable for international broadcasters with an established reputation, such as MTV. Herbert Schiller (1992) has argued that globally circulating media images promote a similar ideology, regardless of their national origin. In fact, all music channels, at least in Europe, have mimicked its way and style of doing music television. Needless to say, music charts around the world are dominated by Anglo-American music (Roe and De Meyer 2000: 151–5). MTV in Europe is still dominated by Anglo-American artists, and even more by the use of English in songs, even though there is more diversity in the languages in which the programmes are hosted. In effect, the influence of MTV is not limited only to its content and messages. MTV and its mimics have tapped the heart of Western teenagers with a message format that is purely commercial and is derived from the accumulation of capitalism (Jhally 1990: 102).

MTV Europe

MTV Networks Europe (MTVNE), the European operation of MTV networks and subsidiary of US media and entertainment giant Viacom, controls the most sophisticated music TV network outside the USA. In effect, Viacom gained complete ownership of MTVE by 1991 after British Telecom (25 per cent) and the Maxwell Communications Corporation (50 per cent) had sold their shares (Banks 1997: 45). In 1992 MTVE had a turnover of nearly $70 million, while in 1999 revenues were estimated at $2.25 billion.

In the beginning MTV's strategy was to combine a global presence and a single global brand with a product designed for separate regional markets. Thus, in the mid-1990s MTV's approach was to transform MTVE from a one-for-all formula of American tunes and trends into a regionalized operation with more local music, live events and national news (Rohwedder 1994). Thus, in 1996, MTVE, based in London, expanded its scope to pull in more advertisers with the creation of four separate services – MTV in the UK and Ireland, MTV Central (Austria, Germany and Switzerland), MTVE (thirty-five territories including Belgium, France, Greece, Israel, Romania and others) and MTV Southern (Italy). A fifth dedicated service, MTV Nordic, was launched in June 1998 for the Nordic territories Sweden, Denmark, Norway and Finland.

There was further regionalization, including the Netherlands, France, Spain and parts of Eastern Europe. For example, in April 2000, MTV Network Europe and UPCtv, the programming arm of United Pan-Europe Communications, jointly produced and distributed two twenty-four-hour music television channels – MTV Polska and VH1 Polska – produced in Polish and specifically targeted at the Polish marketplace. In the UK, MTV has dominated the sector since its entry on 1 August 1987. Previously, Super Channel, Sky Channel and KMP had large chunks of their schedules devoted to pop and rock videos. At that time, non-stop pop videos, while popular with young people, were far from the biggest lure for audiences and, consequently, advertisers. The chequered history of Music Box, which finally found its salvation as part of Super Channel, confirms that a pop video diet was no recipe for satellite success. Ten years later, in July 1997, MTVNE launched MTV UK, a British-only edition, which became available to BSkyB's subscribers.

The regionalization was due not only to the fact that more channels were spreading across Europe, but also to the fact that record companies would like to see a more differentiated approach to Europe's fragmented market. Moreover, a more regionalized structure of MTV would allow it to offer music companies more targeted promotions of their products. Additionally, by taking a more local repertoire, MTV could also test new local artists that music companies might be interested in or even 'sell them' outside their local market. Moreover, music tastes differ across Europe. For example, the UK chart is very fast moving, but the rest of Europe is completely different. In Germany, for example, it can take several weeks for a single to grow, whereas in the UK it can enter the charts one week and drop out the next (Schreiber 1997).

This regionalization approach became evident when in July 1995 MTVE suffered a serious setback. It lost ten million households in Europe after it had decided to encode its signal in an effort to earn subscription fees on top of advertising revenues. In effect, reports suggested that MTVE had lost up to two million cable viewers and eight million satellite viewers who were unable to afford the $200 decoder to receive the channel. MTV later countered this, saying it had lost nearer six million DTH homes and no cable homes (Watson 1996). Van der Rijt et al. (2000), in their research on young people and music television in the Netherlands, have shown that the Dutch local music channel TMF competes successfully with MTV and it seems to be better able to fulfil the music needs of Dutch teenage viewers.

On the other hand, things in Europe are not the same as they were when MTV started. This is because gradually local channels have started transmitting local MTV versions to their viewers. When pop idol Elton John introduced MTVE in its debut show from the Roxy Club in Amsterdam in 1987, the first music video to be shown was 'Money for Nothing' by Dire Straits. At the time, the European version of US MTV reached 1.6 million European households. In 1994–5 MTVE was reaching sixty-one million households in thirty-seven countries and in 1999 it was available in thirty-eight European countries and eighty-five million European households.

The fact is that, although MTVE's audience accounts for almost a quarter of MTV's audience worldwide, MTV Network's reach on a country-by-country basis is uneven. In terms of penetration, youth-oriented MTVE is very strong in leading markets such as Germany, the Netherlands, the UK and Italy, but needs to strengthen its presence in France and Spain. It remains a major player in smaller but lucrative markets such as the Benelux and the Nordic countries. Moreover, it has always found it difficult to attract advertising. When MTV entered the European television landscape, it was believed that international commercials would have the same appeal across Europe. But, as is well known, most advertising is still dominated by domestic brands, which want to reach a specific audience, and it has been this advertising that most satellite stations are after. The regionalization of MTV means that the music channel also targets local advertisers. As Brent Hansen, chief executive of MTV, has said: 'we want to build relationships with local advertisers. Today's local client is tomorrow's pan-European client' (in Elliot 1998). The channel claims that advertising revenue doubled between 1996 and 1999. For example, in 1996 only 20 per cent of its advertising revenue came from local windows. It is estimated that the figure in 1999 was closer to 60 per cent. In addition, the growth has mainly been represented by local advertising, with pan-European advertising revenue remaining static (Alonzi and Burrows 1999). It should be noted that, in the USA, about 65 per cent of MTV's revenues derive from advertising, while the figure in Europe is about 90 per cent.

MTVE's position as a twenty-four-hour pan-European music television service has been threatened by competitors offering national music programming dedicated to local audiences. In response, MTVNE, including M2 (launched in October 1998), MTV Extra, MTV Base (July 1999) and VH1 Classic, is constantly evolving its corporate, programming and advertising structure to challenge both emerging and established rivals at the national level. The competition has been most intense, or is becoming so, in Germany, the UK, the Netherlands and France.

Since 2000 MTV has been working out the next strategy for regionalization. The regionalization strategy is to make MTV more flexible with regard to the programmes offered to its international audience. In 2000, MTV channels featured about 60 per cent localized programming and 40 per cent international English-language programmes.

MTV has also launched a local version in Spain and has similar plans for the Netherlands, France, Belgium and Switzerland.

Viva

MTVE's achievements prompted other European music and broadcast entrepreneurs to enter the niche music television channels, transmitted mostly via cable and/or satellite systems. Some television services used terrestrial systems where spare frequencies were available. The national music television channels that have made an impact on the local music markets include Germany's Viva, MCM in France, Benelux and Eastern Europe, Videomusic and TCM 2 in Italy and Sweden's ZTV.

The fact is that more and more countries possess 'their own popular music' and that the days of international superstars have peaked. There are more than twenty domestic music television services in Europe and several more are scheduled to be launched, especially within the rapidly growing digital terrestrial and satellite TV sector. Apart from the lucrative Viva, it is difficult to assess which are making profit.

Germany has five major music TV channels: Viva, Viva Zwei (Viva 2), Onyx Music Television, Classica and MTV Central Europe. Launched in late 1993, the Viva network consists of two channels: cable-delivered Viva is targeted at young viewers (12–29 years old) and is the region's leading music service, which offers 40 per cent German music, while Viva Zwei – launched in 1995 – is aimed at the older segment of the population. Both channels belong to the group Viva Fernsehen, which also owns 44 per cent of Swiss Music TV. Viva and Viva Zwei screen music clips for 65–70 per cent of airtime, relying heavily on a magazine-style format, with V(ideo)J(okey)s introducing the musical material in programmes whose strength depends on that of their presenter. Like MTV, Viva is tentatively diversifying its programme offering with teen music and drama, such as *S Club 7*.

Viva is the major competitor of MTV in Germany. In fact, it is decidedly German and rejects MTV's vision of Europe with one musical taste and one common language. Since 1993 it has grabbed the lead among high-school students and young adults who have not gone to college (Levinson 1995). As noted above, most of its shares are owned by four of the biggest names in music: EMI, Universal, Sony-Warner Bros. and German company Edel Music. In 1993 Viva was mainly a response by Sony-Warner Bros. to the predominance of Viacom's MTV and it attacked MTV for its lack of local music coverage. It soon generated more than twice the advertising revenues it had expected for the first year and quickly reached profitability. Its success was helped by the decision by MTV to encrypt its signals in 1993 when it joined the BSkyB package (*TV International* 2000c). In June 1997, Viva was available to 22.7 million of Germany's 28.2 million cable and satellite TV homes. This gave Viva a 69 per cent penetration of the country's total TV homes. It was available in 95 per cent of Austria's 1.1 million cable homes, and 80 per cent of Switzerland's 2.4 million cable homes. By the end of 1995, Viva was profitable. It reported revenues of about $39 million in 1996, up from $37 million in 1995. Profits in 1996 reportedly reached $5 million.

However, since 1997 Viva has once again had to face the strong competition of MTV, through the latter's dedicated service MTV Central Europe – targeting Austria, Switzerland and Germany. In February 2000, MTV Central Europe reaped $17.6 million in advertising revenues, while the two Viva channels got about $11 million combined (*TV International* 2000c). On the other hand, in terms of viewership Viva was still ahead in 2000. The other music channels in Germany are Onyx and VH1 – owned by Viacom. But they do not pose much of a threat to Viva and MTV. It is estimated that the total revenues of Viva Fernsehen in 1999 were DM 90 million ($45 million) and breakeven was reached in 1998 (*TV International* 2000c). Viva has been profitable since 1995, while Viva Zwei is reported to be losing about DM 10 million annually (*TV International* 2000c). In Spain, Viva Fernsehen reached an agreement with the local authors' and publishers' society Sociedad General de Autores y Editores (SGAE) and a twenty-four-hour channel was planned for the Spanish market for the beginning of 2001. It is also considering launching local Viva channels in Poland, Hungary and Italy. It entered the Internet and the 'Neuver Markt' stock-trading market in 2000.

MCM/Euromusique

In France, there are three contemporary rock and pop channels aimed at a young audience – MTVE, MCM/Euromusique and Fun TV – and one classical one – Muzzik. The market leader is MCM/ Euromusique, which was launched in 1989 by a consortium including Canal Plus, the radio network NRJ (pronounced 'énergie'), the cable operator Général d'Images, the state savings bank Caisse des Dépots, the TV station Radio Monte Carlo, and the music companies PolyGram and Sony Music.

MCM's unique selling point was that 50 per cent of the total repertoire played was devoted to French music. Through subsidiary MCM International – created in 1993 – MCM's programmes and the channel itself are sold overseas. The service is distributed by cable operators in Spain, the UK, Switzerland, Belgium, Portugal and Scandinavia, and by terrestrial channels in Eastern Europe, Greece and Italy. In 1996 MCM International launched two new channels: MCM Africa, which focuses on African and world music, and Muzzik channel, which features mostly classical music, jazz and world music. The MCM channels were created to provide viewers with an alternative to the US-influenced style of music TV provided by the likes of MTV and VH1. MCM International distributes all three channels across Europe (and around the world) and is aiming to increase its distribution and brand image. MCM Africa is already available in France (Canalsatellite Numérique), Spain, Portugal and the Netherlands. In effect, MCM Africa reaches about two million households in Europe and five million households in Africa. MCM seems to follow a similar strategy to MTV, since it aims to provide the European audience with local-language services. For example, in April 2000 its Muzzik channel was available in twenty-two countries in Europe and had around 4.2 million subscribers.

Music on digital and online

At the moment it is hard to foresee what effect broadband technology will have on music television, but it has already opened up the market for audio distribution and it is likely to do the same for video. The increase in digital technology has enabled niche music channels to enter markets that would otherwise have been very difficult. Digital satellite platforms have offered extra space and allowed music channels to reach new markets and to offer competitive prices. For example, MTV's digital services on digital platforms BSkyB and ONdigital in the UK have five strands offering a choice of programming. In June 1999, MTV launched two British digital channels, MTV Base (R&B, Dance) and MTV Extra (targeting 16–24-year-old males).

The future of music television, however, will probably be interactive. Moreover, digital technology lends itself to audio broadcasting and the future points to the TV becoming a central entertainment point, on which one can watch TV as well as listen to high-quality music broadcasting. For example, Music Choice Europe was designed for this purpose. It is a twenty-four-hour digital audio provider with more than 1.5 subscribers across sixteen European countries and the Middle East, and delivers around fifty genre-specific channels of commercial free music programming to cable, satellite and online distributors.

The online revolution that is turning music distribution on its head at the beginning of the twenty-first century will soon be sweeping through the TV industry. In the first years of the decade streaming video is not yet widespread enough for producers to use the Internet for the direct distribution of video, but this is set to change with the rollout of broadband and superfast Internet access. The number of broadband consumers is also relatively small, but the numbers are expected to increase rapidly in the short term.

MTVNE, following its US parent, is already investing heavily in online ventures and also has a regionalized web service in Europe with five points of entry into the following European territories: Germany, Italy, the UK, Ireland and the rest of Europe. In 2001 Viva was planning to enter the Internet creating a portal. In a related deal, in 1999 MTV Networks Online and RioPort, a wholly owned subsidiary of Diamond Multimedia Systems, announced an exclusive, five-year agreement to deliver digitally downloaded audio content, and Viacom earmarked $300 million for the network's online operation. As part of the agreement, MTV Networks Online provides content and promotional support and receives an equity share in RioPort and a share in revenues from the sales of digitally distributed music. Moreover, in April 2000, in a bid to bring faster downloads of its online video and music, MTVi Group announced a broad alliance with Excite@Home, the leading broadband company. For MTV, a presence on Excite means better Internet traffic and probably new sales.

Summary

While music television channels are morphing into another form, pure music video is already finding a life outside conventional TV on digital platforms and the Internet. Internet channels in the USA such as The Box Music Network and Entertainment Boulevard are already showcasing interactive music videos and other entertainment events through streaming-media technology. But young adults expect to get their music, whether live or on video, through the Internet, just as they already download audio-only from the Internet using

Napster, and just as they still listen to the radio or watch television. In other words, just as music videos certainly did not kill radio nor put an end to 'concert-going', neither are Internet music videos becoming a 'death knell' for music in other formats. As the media history has shown, every new medium that comes along, whether it is radio, television or a music channel in the USA in the early 1980s and in Europe in the late 1980s, simply provides another medium for music distribution. Every new medium or technology that emerges in fact gives a boost to the music industry overall. Perhaps the Internet will bring to videos another outlet and opportunity to increase the diversity of music.

11

More Children's Channels
The Fastest Growing Television
Market in Europe

Undoubtedly the arrival of digital TV has led to an exponential growth in the number of channels targeting children, increasing choice for children as well as competition between channels. In contrast to the past, where children's programming was limited to a few hours every afternoon on terrestrial channels, kids across Europe can now enjoy the services of a large number of dedicated channels on cable and on satellite. At the beginning of the twenty-first century there are more than ninety channels devoted specifically to children (fifty of them were launched between 1996 and 1999) and broadcasters spent an estimated $2.1 billion on producing, commissioning and acquiring children's programmes in 1999. Moreover, the popularity of these channels seems to be increasing.

This is a tremendous change compared to the past when children-dedicated programmes used to start at four o'clock and ended by the early evening news. How children as an audience are perceived has also changed, ending the notion that children constitute a uniform viewing segment with similar tastes who can be satisfied by a range of limited programming. Children can now choose from a varied and significantly developed content portfolio, across narrow age ranges and national boundaries (Chakraborty 1997). There are children's channels for pre-schoolers, children and teenagers with specific tastes and preferences, which differ from market to market, and at the same time reconfirm the 'central role that television plays in a multimedia environment for children' (Murray 1993: 9).

This chapter attempts to describe and discuss the development of children's channels in Europe. It looks at the entry of US-originated children's channels in the European television landscape, their strategies to localize their output, and the reaction of local channels. Moreover, it discusses the increased volume of co-productions, especially animation production, and the issues concerning the programming and content aspects of children's channels. Finally, it looks at their entry on the Internet and how they use it as a promotional tool regarding their activities in general.

Key players in the European children's channels market

As with other thematic channels, the USA, which saw the launch of the first children's channel, Nickelodeon, in 1979, has been the home of new channels, and has provided the main funding model. In 2000 Nickelodeon reached more than 100 million homes worldwide through four specially created Nickelodeon channels. As with music channels, Nickelodeon has spread quickly across Europe, as did other children's channels such as Fox Kids, Disney and the Cartoon Network. In fact, all major US children's channels have launched European versions of their original services since the mid-1990s.

In the UK, Nickelodeon was launched in September 1993 in partnership (50:50 per cent basis) with BSkyB, and in effect its audience tripled within its first three years in operation. The channel offers a mix of animation, live action and pre-school shows. Some 60 per cent of its programming is home produced, mainly in the USA. The remaining 40 per cent is acquired from Europe, Canada and Australia. In Germany, the channel was launched in July 1995 in partnership with Ravensburger Film und TV (10 per cent) and used to be the country's first channel exclusively for children. There are also joint ventures in Spain and Turkey, and in September 1999 it launched Nick Jr. in the UK, a channel targeting the pre-school market.

Another key player, the Disney Channel, began rolling out its channels in April 1995 with the launch of the CLT–Disney joint venture Super RTL in Germany and the Disney Channel in Britain, which started broadcasting in October 1995. Like most other US channels, Disney's programming strategy is aimed at turning the family entertainment channel into a localized service by producing and acquiring locally produced material as well as using tailor-made graphics. Animated and live-action shows from the Disney library are at the top of the ratings charts.

The TNT/Cartoon Network was principally programmed from Turner's vast animation library of more than 8,500 hours of cartoons produced under the MGM, Warner Bros. and Hanna-Barbera banners. It was launched in Europe in September 1993 and was available in about thirty million homes in Europe in 2000. The service broadcasts in seven languages – English, French, Dutch, Spanish, Finnish and Czech – throughout Europe via cable and satellite.

The Fox Kids Network, which had the advantage of being part of Rupert Murdoch's News Corporation international group, was launched in Europe in October 1996. Before that, in October 1995 Fox had formed a worldwide programming alliance with Saban Entertainment. With 3,400 hours of episodes, Saban has one of the world's largest libraries of children's animated programming. With the addition of the Paris-based C&D catalogue (1,200 episodes of family fare), which Saban acquired in 1996, its library was up to around 5,300 episodes of children's programmes (Callard 2000).

A US model?

North America accounts for 40 per cent of the total children's television market, followed by Western Europe (33 per cent) and Asia (22 per cent). The USA, Japan, the UK, France and Germany account for over 80 per cent of spending by broadcasters on children's programming (Westcott 1999c).

The funding model for children's TV channels originates in the USA too. Although services like Nickelodeon (owned by the Viacom company MTV Networks) now make most of their revenue from advertising, subscription revenue is another very significant element of their funding. Nickelodeon captured around 45 per cent of the $750 million children's advertising market in the 1999–2000 season. But several channels are challenging Nickelodeon's dominance of the US marketplace. Nickelodeon's main threat is Cartoon Network, owned by Turner Networks, part of Time Warner. Fox Family Worldwide, owned by Fox Broadcasting and Saban Entertainment, and the Disney Channel, owned by the Walt Disney Company, are also competing for the 2–11-year-old audience.

Independent producers and distributors have also emerged as the pivotal players in the worldwide children's television industry. Their role will become even more important as funding from public broadcasters stagnates. Children's television producers have led the way to the financial markets: children's television companies like Canada's Cinar and Nelvana, the UK's Britt Allcroft Company and Hit Entertainment and Germany's EM.TV have invested heavily in children's programming.

The opportunities for companies involved in supplying children's programming to television broadcasters are great. Television continues to be the most effective platform for launching children's properties with the potential to open up new revenue streams from home video, licensing and merchandising and new media. The UK experience proves this, since in the British multichannel environment the most viewed category of cable and satellite channels (apart from the non-specific 'light entertainment' category) is children's channels, which in 1999 accounted for 6 per cent of total viewing.

Despite this, the European market for children's television compared to the US one is still underdeveloped and it is difficult to predict whether US channels will dominate. This is because US children's channels have to localize their output if they want to be successful.

Localization and strong competition

For the big US-originated international children's channels looking to expand their operations beyond the UK, owning content that will travel across Europe was important. The channel operators soon realized that, in order to be successful in continental Europe, it was vital that they co-produced and consulted with local television companies in the regions they wanted to move into, to draw upon their expertise and local knowledge, and, most importantly, to comply with the European programme quotas. Thus all the major US networks had to approach each market remaining sensitive to its local needs. Packaging and localization became key elements for success. The 'trick' for these channels has been to remain true to their all-American roots, while remaining sensitive to local markets (Cairns 1999: 31). In other words, they had to maintain an exclusive identity despite the localization constraints.

Nickelodeon

Nickelodeon was, perhaps, the first to learn the lessons of tailoring for local viewers, helped by links with its sister company, the MTV Network. In effect, with its launch in 1993 it became apparent that a schedule based solely upon its US properties was a mistake. Since June 1994, Nickelodeon has started to localize its programme output. In July 1995, it launched a dedicated channel initially sharing satellite capacity with Arte. Later it switched to the Astra 1B transponder after losing its original slot to Der Kinderkanal. After being voted into the programme packages by individual states, it secured distribution in over 60 per cent of Germany's homes in 1997. This was because it made a special German version of its programming, although some of the content originated in the USA. Nickelodeon, however, was forced to close its channel in May 1998, despite being distributed to twenty million homes in the territory. Nickelodeon attributed its German failure to the structure of the German TV industry and a poor advertising market across children's channels, rather than to a lack of popularity (Price 1998).

In February 1997, Nickelodeon launched a daily service for the Nordic region, and another in 1998 in Turkey. It also featured a branded block on the Icelandic children's channel Banavasin, which is distributed via Icelandic Telecom's cable system.

Fox Kids

Fox Kids hired local programmers from the very beginning. This was to ensure that 50 per cent of its output was made in Europe, according to the *Television without Frontiers* Directive. It started to run the Fox Kids station in the UK and Holland on 2 August 1997 as an eleven-hour, branded block on TV10, since its philosophy was to customize its brand image to each local market (Atkinson 1997). Spurred on by the Fox Kids launch, TV 10 was rebranded in 1998 as a Fox Channel and doubled its weekly market share in just over a year. Fox Kids France was launched in November 1997 as part of Canal Satellite's digital DTH platform with success. In April 1998, it launched Fox Kids Polska via Wizja digital satellite and cable platform, again with success. On 4 April 1998 it launched a new service in Scandinavia. Fox Kids Spain, a joint initiative with Sogeacable subsidiary CITSA, was relaunched on 5 December 1998. Fox also launched channels in Belgium – on 15 January 1999 on the digital platform Le Bouquet – and in Central and Eastern Europe.

In effect, since the first Fox Kids European channel was launched in October 1996, Fox Kids has expanded significantly, operating twenty-four channels across Europe in eleven languages. In April 2000 it was transmitted in Italy through Stream (part of News Corp. Europe). In Germany it airs on Premiere World. In mid-2000, the total Fox Kids Network distribution network was composed of twenty million homes in thirty-four markets. The biggest markets are Holland via 5.8 million cable homes and the UK via 4.9 million BSkyB and cable homes (Fry 2000).

Cartoon Networks

As part of its European strategy, Cartoon Networks made conces-
sions to local European markets by dubbing channels into Swedish,
Danish, French, Spanish, Italian and Dutch. Using the sales and
distribution infrastructure of its sister, CNNI, to launch itself quickly
into new markets (Barker 1993), it relied heavily on cartoons as a
universal language for children. According to its executives, 'cartoons
travel well . . . they have a universal language' (in Chakraborty 1997:
28). In 1997, it entered the Dutch market (July), the Italian market
(October) and Scandinavia (November), in 1998, France and Spain
(April) and Poland (September).

Disney

Disney followed a similar strategy. Between 1996 and 1998 it opened
three European channels: Disney Channel France on the Canal
Numérique digital platform in March 1997; Disney Channel Spain
on the Canal Satellite digital package in April 1998, and Disney
Channel Italy on the Telepiu digital package in October 1998. Before them, it had launched its channel in the UK on BSkyB in 1995,
and, in September 2000, Toon Disney and Playhouse. In Germany,
Disney Channel's service is aired on the Premiere World platform.
Walt Disney TV International also sells programmes into the terres-
trial channels. The next phase of its expansion is to take place in
Scandinavia.

The Disney Channel in Europe insists on working with platforms
that have an aggressive approach towards increasing the children's and
family audience. For example, in the UK, France, Italy, Germany and
Spain it positions itself as a premium channel, unlike the other US-
originated children's channels. It has also insisted on retaining 100 per
cent control over its channels, rather than sharing equity with local
platform partners (Fry 2000). The only territories where Walt Disney
TV International takes a non-branded approach are Benelux and
Eastern Europe, where it is a partner in premium channels.

The success of localization

In contrast to other US-originated international channels, children's
networks have performed better in Europe. They not only build

successful children's channels, but also build a distinct local children's brand. In effect, each aims to be the first choice for children overall. Most of the content, especially cartoons, is US made by their parent US production companies, which, in contrast to European channels, have the 'know-how' as well as the resources to support their ventures. This is obvious in the UK and less obvious in continental Europe. Some, however, doubt whether US channels can tailor for markets and invest in local production and acquisition. Some others point out that children's channels are another version of the American challenge in Europe, arguing that, for the US major channels, 'going local' does not necessarily mean making programmes locally.

United Kingdom

In the UK, the arrival of the four US networks put The Children's Channel (TCC), out of business. The British TCC was launched in 1984. In fact it was the first children's channel in the UK and was targeting pre-schoolers, children and teenagers. TCC also had a separate service for Scandinavia (subtitled in four languages). The channel invested £13 million ($19.5 million) in programming for 1995 and 1996, ranging from dramas, comedies and game shows to pre-school programmes. But it had to struggle against a background of poor ratings (Westcott 1997). The situation was not helped when the parent company Flextech hived its teenage shows off to a new channel, Trouble, and, with UK Living created another channel, Tiny Living. In January 1996, however, TCC Nordic was launched, broadcasting to Scandinavia. It reported a 25 per cent growth in subscribers when it began to programme to the Nordic region (Atkinson 1997).

There was a similar case with Carlton Kids. Carlton Kids was launched on the UK's digital terrestrial platform ONdigital in November 1998. Carlton's mission was to offer typically British children's programming and a less violent alternative to other available channels. It hoped to appeal particularly to parents who were worried by the level of on-screen violence to which their children were exposed (Price 1998). But the channel folded in January 2000, after falling to gain ratings and, therefore, advertising. ONdigital replaced Carlton Kids with two new channels from Discovery Networks Europe – Discovery Kids (children oriented) and Discovery Wings (about all things aviational).

In fact, the British market for children's channels is comprised solely of US spin-off channels, which have varying commitments to local production. British channels found themselves squeezed by the four US major players, since they were not linked to a voluminous library. For example, Cartoon Networks' ambitions and successful entry were helped by its vast library (including Hanna Barbera, New Line and MGM). This meant that short-term losses could be offset against potential future earnings from other areas such as merchandising. Additionally, Fox Kids had the huge Saban library, that allowed the network to join the international race of children's channels late.

On the other hand, the BBC always had a strong commitment to children's programming and rumours of a plan for a BBC-backed children's channel have been around since 1999. One of the aims of the BBC is to create branded blocks, often with successful programmes, such as *Teletubbies* and *Tweenies*, as the anchor programmes of such blocks (Callard 2000). It seems that the BBC, with its huge library resources and global recognition, is the only British broadcaster to compete against the US networks (see table 11.1).

Germany

Germany was always a difficult territory for US-originated channels. Moreover, children's fare and cartoons formed an important part of programming on the public networks and private broadcasters. As above noted, Super RTL was launched on 28 April 1995 by Walt Disney and CLT. Nickelodeon, on the other hand, faced many problems.

In July 1996, DF1, the digital satellite package, launched two channels – Junior (pre-schooler) and Clubhouse (6–13 years old) – plus a cartoon channel K-Toon. Moreover, at that time ARD's eleven regional channels had their own children's programming, which used to air on weekends from 6 a.m. to 12 noon, plus two hours on weekdays. ZDF aired children's programmes for $1\frac{1}{2}$ hours a day during the week and from 7 a.m. to 10 a.m. on Saturdays. On Sundays it aired its most popular pre-school shows *Siebenstein* and *Lowenzahn*.

In January 1997 ARD and ZDF launched Kinderkanal, backing it with $67 million for its start-up operation costs (Kindred 1996). The success of Kinderkanal (rebranded Kika in 2000) prompted ZDF to reduce its animation slots and focus only on weekends. Pro-Sieben, a private general entertainment channel, stopped its children's co-production activities when its advertising revenue fell. TV 4, another private general entertainment channel, reduced the volume of its children's broadcasts to two hours per week for similar reasons in 1999.

A recent German contender in the market is EM.TV & Merchandising, which in December 1998 signed an agreement with the Kirch's TaurusFilm to form a 50:50 joint venture called Junior TV. The deal was made in order to exploit approximately 28,500 half-hour episodes of children's and family programmes. As part of the deal EM.TV has the exclusive unlimited free-TV, pay-TV and ancillary distribution rights in all media (Wright 1999; Callard 2000: 23). Moreover, EM.TV and the Kirch Group have also launched two pay-TV children's channels called Junior and K-Toon on the Premiere World platform. In February 2000, EM.TV & Merchandising acquired the Jim Henson Company (see table 11.1).

France

France boasts the greatest number of children's programming out of any European country at the moment of writing. In France, thematic channels are performing well, threatened as much by each other as by the US networks. But, in contrast to the UK, children's programming is a higher priority for French broadcasters. Moreover, government-supported funding and subsidy schemes have helped to make the production of animated programming into a growth industry, with exports every year.

France's six terrestrial networks air children's programmes and six more children's channels are available to multichannel homes (Westcott 1999c: 54). TF1 and France 3 are the main players in children's terrestrial television. France 2 and M6 also fund significant amounts of programming, but their level of investment varies from year to year. Until 1997, TF1 sourced all of its children's programming from one supplier – AB – and aired mainly Japanese animation. But since France 3 has had more success with a line-up of original, French-produced programming, TF1 has changed its programming policy. The majority of programming for children on terrestrial television is animation, although many series are based on existing literary properties (Westcott 1999c: 54). La Cinquième, the educational terrestrial channel, caries a daily afternoon block of programming.

On the thematic side, Canal J is the oldest of the children's channels. It was launched in 1987 by a subsidiary of the Hachette publishing group and in 1989 Canal J was merged with Canal Enfants, a Canal Plus-backed children's venture. Thus, it was the only children's television service in France until 1996. MCM/Euromusique (91.5 per cent) owns it. Canal J spends half of its budget on programming, and since 1991 has invested in several animated co-productions, mainly in partnership with terrestrial broadcasters. It has also started producing programmes in-house. It invests a minimum of 25 per cent of a budget, which enables the producer to benefit from a public grant. Of its $23.2 million budget, Canal J devotes 60 per cent to productions and co-productions, of which 50 per cent is allocated to in-house production and 50 per cent to animation. Moreover, 80 per cent of its programming is made up of first-run shows (*Television Business International* 1998). In 2000 it launched a pre-school channel, TiJi. Relative newcomers Télétoon, Fox Kids, Cartoon and Disney Channel have also started to invest in original programming.

Canal J enjoys wider distribution than its rivals. It faces strong competition from its rivals, but in 1999 had a spectacular come-back, as its share of viewing among children increased from 8.8 per cent in December 1998 to 13.8 per cent in December 1999 (*TV International* 2000b). However, US networks have challenged the French children's channels, mainly Canal J and Télétoon. Télétoon, which was launched in 1997 as part of the TPS platform, benefits from a dominant position in homes subscribing to the TPS, and thus its ratings there are higher than in the cable systems where it faces competition. It has also invested in co-productions, but its budget is much smaller ($5.8 million) than Canal J. Télétoon aims to help its position with new product from EM.TV's Juniors library, acquired in April 2000. This was the second such accord for Télétoon after a deal with Canada's Nelvana in 1998 (see table 11.1).

More productions and co-productions

Programming a channel dedicated to children is as much a science as targeting any other audience (Glover 1993). The terrestrial European channels broadcast children's programming as early 5 a.m. in Germany and as late as 10.30 p.m. in Denmark. The majority of terrestrial channels schedule their children's programming between 3 p.m. and 6 p.m. Some allocate another slot in the early hours before school starts, and at weekends most broadcasters air an extended morning block (Ghayur 1999).

On the other hand, children are completely different viewers from adults. Although children often tend to watch 'unsuitable material' for their age (Davies *et al.* 2000), the main viewing difference between children and adults is that children do not reject older programmes in the same way as adults. Neither do they reject programmes because

Table 11.1 Children's channels in Europe's major markets

Region	Channel	Launch date	Shareholders
Belgium	Fox Kids	1999	Fox Family Worldwide
CIS, Baltic States	Nickelodeon	1998	Viacom
Czech Republic	Supermax	n.a.	HBO
France	Canal J	1985	MCM Euromusique 91.5%,
	TiJi	2000	Bayard Press 6%, Groupe Marie Claire 2.5%
France	Télétoon	1997	TPS
France	Fox Kids	1997	Fox Family Worldwide
France	Magna	1998	Groupe AB
France	The Disney Channel	1997	Walt Disney Co.
France, Belgium Switzerland	The Cartoon	1998	Turner Networks
Germany	Kinderkanal (Kika)	1997	ARD, ZDF
Germany	Super RTL	1995	CLT–Ufa, Walt Disney Co.
Germany	Junior	1996	Kirch Group/EM.TV
Germany	K-Toon	1996	Kirch Group/EM.TV
Germany	Fox Kids	2000	Fox Family Worldwide
Greece	K-TV	1996	NetMed Hellas
Hungary	Nickelodeon	1998	Viacom, HBC
Italy	Junior TV	1985	Orsini Family
Italy, Switzerland	Cartoon Network	1997	Turner Networks
Italy	RaiSat 2	1997	RAI
Italy	The Disney Channel	1998	Walt Disney Co.
Italy	Fox Kids	2000	Fox Family Worldwide
Netherlands	Kindernet	1988	n.a.
Netherlands	Fox Kids	1998	Fox Family Worldwide
Netherlands, Belgium	Cartoon Network	1997	Turner Networks
Scandinavia	Fox Kids	1997	Fox Family Worldwide
Scandinavia	TCC	1996	Flextech
Scandinavia	Nickelodeon	1997	Viacom
Scandinavia	Cartoon Network	1998	Turner Networks
Spain	The Disney Channel	1998	Walt Disney Co.
Spain	Fox Kids	1998	Fox Family Worldwide, Sogeacable–CITSA
Spain	Cartoon Network	1997	Turner Networks
Spain	Nickelodeon	1999	Viacom, Canal Satellite
Turkey	Nickelodeon	1997	Viacom
UK	Trouble	1996	Flextech
UK	Cartoon Network	1993	Turner Networks
UK	Fox Kids	1996	Fox Family Worldwide
UK	Nickelodeon	1993	Viacom/BSkyB
UK	The Disney Channel	1995	Walt Disney Co.
UK	Toon & Playhouse	2000	Walt Disney Co.

Note: n.a. = not available.
Sources: based on data collected from Westcott 1998; Callard 2000; *TV Express* 2000a; *TV International* 2000b; *Cable and Satellite Europe* 2001.

of outdated production or animated techniques. In fact, children tend to watch the same programme, if they consider it was good and fun, over and over again. Barrie Gunter and Jill McAleer (1997: 38) note:

> Children's attention to the screen . . . is neither constant nor passive. The amount of attention they are prepared to give to individual programmes is directly related to whatever the visual and audio message has meaning specific to them, and whether they are given sufficient time to absorb that meaning. In this regard, the format of programmes is all-important.

In effect, there are three important elements to successful children's programming: first, a fantastic programme that children want to watch and that their parents can see them enjoying; secondly, very strong scheduling; and, thirdly, quality marketing (Callard 2000: 23). But, because children's television has become highly competitive, offering a plethora of programmes, the tendency of young viewers habitually to watch programmes on the same channels and to repeat viewing across different episodes of the same programme has also been eroded (Gunter and McAleer 1997: 222; Abelman and Atkin 2000: 143–4). This means that having the right formula for children's television is one thing, but, since most of the channels are pay-TV, the price has to be right with parents.

However, children's channels cannot depend solely on their libraries. Thus, many dedicated children's channels started to make their own productions or branched into co-productions with other channels. The Disney Channel UK, for example, launched the distinctive and much claimed comedy drama *Microsoap* in 1998 (Price 1998). Nickelodeon UK spent 37.5 per cent of its total programming budget in 1998 on original production. This compares with just 22 per cent in 1995. *Renford Rejects* was the channel's first comedy production, which premiered on Nickelodeon UK in February 1998 and was a success.

Some, however, have doubts about the US programming investments in countries where US channels operate. For example, since 1997, US channels have announced multimillion-dollar investments in original programming. But most of this money has stayed in the USA, with of course some exceptions (Cairns 1999). Even at Fox Kids Network, which has localization as a key in its expansion strategy, there has been no original production outside the activities of the Fox production arm, Saban – which produces 300 half hours a year of animation series like *Diabolique* and *Princess Sisi* from its base in Paris (Fry 2000).

On the other hand, broadcasters around the world do not acquire all their children's programming from the USA; they also turn to the UK, Canada, France and Australia. Moreover, local production is considered a key element in most US-originated channels, because of the cultural differences across Europe. Even in the UK, US networks soon learned that 'America and England are divided by a common language' (Cairns 1999: 34). That was the main reason for looking for local partners and co-productions, as noted above. Either way, the success of US-originated children's channels with European operations has given others the motive to get involved in co-production.

European children's channels have followed the same approach. As noted above, in 1999 France's Télétoon had an output deal with Canadian Nelvana for the co-production of 200 hours of programming. Kids Plus, the Canal Plus distribution's children programming division, sold twenty-eight children's programmes outside France in 1998, amounting to 1,500 hours. Sixty-nine per cent of Canal Plus animation production is made up by its production subsidiary Ellipse Anime. The British distributor Hit Entertainment, with a library of 150 titles, has supplied programmes to the US majors (Vernet 1999).

Moreover, in terms of co-production deals, the Scandinavian countries actively cooperate with each other through their public broadcasters in the field of children's programming. They do that through the Nordvision exchange programmes and also through Nordmagi, a regional children's production venture, which was set up in the autumn of 1998. Other production companies such as Nordisk Film & TV, part of the Danish giant Egmont, and Swedish Happy Life are also becoming more active co-production partners for Scandinavian television channels (Ghayur 1999). The fact is that co-productions in Europe increasingly take the form of pre-sales where broadcasters or distributors front production cash to established producers in exchange for generous rights or an editorial role.

On the other hand, in order to face the new American challenge Europe has increased subsidies for the production of children's programming over the last few years. The EU MEDIA programme has led the way with substantial funding through its Cartoon subprogramme since 1989. In effect, with its support for pre-production finance, its incentives for studio groupings and its annual forum, the EU has played a key role in increasing the output of Europe's animation industry. During the 1990s the European animation production sector developed considerably, accounting for 25 per cent of the whole audio-visual industry.

This is because European producers have realized the economies of scale of coming up with programmes and concepts that can be sold to children from different cultures within Europe. For example, in France, animation production programming has the strong support of the Centre National du Cinéma and the domestic channels. In 1998, for instance, some 375 hours of animation were produced. Over the same period, the main French channels broadcast 3,100 hours of animation, of which 40 per cent were produced locally. Over the 1996–98 period, they invested FFr750 million in animation. In the UK, the animation production industry does not enjoy such strong support from the government as its French counterpart. Producers rely heavily on commissions from terrestrial (1,038 hours in 1998), cable and satellite channels. In Germany, in 1998, the major channels broadcast 5,886 hours of cartoons and each *Länder* has its own subsidy programme. Spain has also recently become a major producer in European animation and about fifty-three animation series were produced between 1996 and 1999, amounting to 420 hours of programming (Lecrerq 1999; Vernet 1999). This, however, does not mean that the US production companies are not involved in this production race. The main problem for European producers, as usual, is to offer their programmes at competitive prices in the international market. Again, it seems that the whole issue is more about television economics than about culture.

Children's programming: educational, fast paced and in some cases violent

While in the past children's programming was the preserve of European terrestrial broadcasters, nowadays it seems to disappear from their schedules. The results of the 1999 and 2000 *Television Business International* annual surveys on children's programming indicate that the budgets for this segment of programming at many European terrestrial broadcasters had been frozen, representing a decrease in real terms (Ghayur 2000; 2001). For example, the average number of hours broadcast per week had a nominal decrease to nine hours in 2001 from an average of 9.85 in 2000 (Ghayur 2001: 96).

The trends indicate that children's programming is gradually moving to dedicated channels for children, regardless of the fact that free terrestrial channels in Europe have always been more committed to children's programming than their US counterparts. The question, therefore, is not related to the proliferation of channels targeting the same audience, nor to how many children's channels the European market can sustain.

The question has rather to do with the quality of the content of children's channels rather than the volume of programming (see also Buckingham 2000: 147). In the UK, as noted above, the Carlton Kids' mission was to offer less violent programming. It thought that, by implementing this programming strategy, it would have appealed to the parents worried by the level of on-screen violence that their children were exposed to. But Carlton failed to attract viewers and thus advertising.

Most channels, however, strongly deny any suggestion that their output could be considered as violent or unsuitable for a young audience. They claim that their output is non-violent and suitable for the whole family or that they offer 'safe entertainment' for kids. However, many of the programmes or shows broadcast are 'action oriented'. As Ynon Kriez, managing director of Fox Kids, said to *Cable and Satellite Europe*: 'There is fighting, but it is all done with humour, there is no blood and no one gets hurt' (in Callard 2000). But some of the shows, such as *Mighty Morphing Power Rangers* and *Teenage Mutant Ninja Turtles*, have been often criticized for their violence. The fact is that action shows are starting to dominate children's channels' schedules. Action shows are on the increase and this is because they seem to have an easy appeal to viewers. Thus, TV3 and Scansat in Scandinavia had to pull an action programme (*Power Rangers*) from their schedule following an incident in Norway when a child was kicked in the playground (Price 1998: 26). In fact, Japanese cartoons are considered as violent in Europe, but until recently have dominated the schedules of children's channels in Europe (Westcott 1998). Some European broadcasters (in France, Italy, Spain) found Japanese cartoons too fast-paced and in some cases too violent. Although the issue of TV violence is not new, it always provokes the public concern. As Buckingham (2000: 123) notes: 'Among the enormous range of experiences that the media offer children, violence seems to be regarded as the defining instance – the phenomenon that somehow encapsulates everything we really need to know about the place of the media in their lives.'

In the pay-TV landscape, operators seem to an extent to take these concerns into consideration. It is not a coincidence that pay operators have started promoting or publicizing the educational aspect of their programming outlet. Nor is it a coincidence that new channels labelled as educational have been launched, such as Noggin, a joint venture between Nickelodeon and the Children's Television

Workshop, or the Kermit Channel, a joint venture between Hallmark Entertainment Network and the Jim Henson Company.

First, one has to note that what constitutes educational programming these days is subject to definition, with many broadcasters leaning towards an 'edutainment' slant rather than traditional curriculum-based fare (Wright 1998). Secondly, the increase of the educational programming outlet on children's channels is also related to the demands imposed by the US authorities after the 1996 Telecommunications Act and the concerns of the European Commission. Thirdly, and most importantly, the educational fare is used as a means to persuade parents that children's channels are also a valuable learning source for their children. For example, parents can leave their children watching such a channel without having to worry that they will be exposed to violent actions.

This is also a marketing approach since it is the parents who pay for these channels. Obviously, parents will be more willing to pay their subscription for channels with non-violent and educational programming. Therefore, educational programming, which was once relegated to public service channels, has been given a new lease of life, and is spurred by commercial interests rather than pedagogic ambitions. Needless to say, such educational programming has spawned a whole range of ancillary revenues (such as educational publications), as children's programming and channels are interconnected with the toy industry. Thus, programming evolves not from the rituals of storytelling but rather from the imperative of the marketplace (Pecora 1999).

Adding the Internet

Television programmes are much more than television programmes; they are also other media texts plus a whole range of consumer goods from T-shirts to computers. In the age of media convergence, where most activities come closer, 'children are beginning to emerge as a significant new market' (Buckingham 2000: 148).

Children's channels primarily regarded the Internet as a promotional tool. Thus they designed their web sites to promote the attractions and characters from their more popular programmes effectively. Gradually, the Internet was also used to feature games and competitions based on their programmes. For example, Nickelodeon UK created an attraction called Nickelodeon Outacontrol, at the Alton Towers theme park. It is billed as an interactive attraction where television comes to life (Price 1998: 28).

In effect, children's channels have invested heavily online because they believe the market will be huge. Children will play a key role introducing interactivity to the home. According to the research company Jupiter Communications, children and teenagers are the largest growth sectors of the online population. In 1998, approximately 8.6 million children (5–12 years old) and 8.4 million teenagers (13–18 years old) were online. By 2002, it is estimated that 21.9 million children (a 155 per cent increase) and 16.6 million teenagers (a 97 per cent increase) will be online (quoted in Schreiber 1999: 20). Thus, one can easily understand that, for the children's channels as well as for the producers, establishing a web presence is all about extending the brand. It seems that operators and producers want to benefit in various ways from the growth of the Internet. One can do it by developing properties and characters. They can then migrate their way into various forms on television. Producers can find an opportunity to launch a show online, build an audience and then sell it to television. Producers who get feedback from children can better develop the characters of their stories. Channels can exploit games and create ancillary revenues, and through e-commerce and advertising online can develop new forms of revenue. In effect, a new model is emerging combining advertising and e-commerce.

Summary

In hard contrast to the past, one can say that the children of the twenty-first century not only have the same access to information as adults (Meyrowitz 1985), but are also part of an integral component of the electronically mediated environment that constructs their social worlds. From television programming channels to computer games and then to interactive computer learning systems, 'on a daily basis children use electronic forms of communication' (Everett 1994: 30). As in the past, it remains questionable whether children, especially pre-schoolers, are well enough equipped to manage and decode this 'brave new world'. It is, therefore, necessary to develop a European, if not an international, plan that will ensure a broad range of television programming targeted to the real, especially educational, needs of children at various ages and stages of development (see Murray 1993: 19). But children's understanding of television can also be aided by parents paying attention to what their kids watch.

Conclusions
Television and its Viewers in the Internet Age

Television and Internet industries are converging, as the boundaries amongst traditional media companies, telecommunications organizations and information technology companies are blurring. The issues and debate arising from such convergence as well as from the development of the Internet in general cannot be exhausted here. But it seems important to point out the similarities in structure and content of digital television and the Internet.

The whole idea of making the huge number of TV households around the world buy PCs is very exciting for the industry. Television is seen as the only way to bring the Internet to a mass market. After all, the penetration of television is complete in virtually all households, while the PC still has a long way to go. For example, in the UK and Germany there are nearly three times as many TV sets as Internet-users, while in France the ratio is approximately six to one, due mainly to low PC penetration. As Martin Sims (1999: 4) has noted: 'It's the Internet on your television with in-built modems to access websites, not . . . television on the Internet.'

Many television channels, if not most of them, are already simulcasting their programmes on the Internet, even if, for the time being, the programming is on a limited schedule and of limited quality. Nonetheless, two thousand hours or more of live video content are webcast weekly on the Internet in the USA, while in Europe there is no channel without a web site. Additionally, in Europe most research surveys indicate that Internet use is growing rapidly, while sales of PCs are increasing at higher rates than conventional TV sets. According to a survey conducted by Jupiter Communications, it is estimated that forty-seven million European households will have Internet access by 2003, an increase from fourteen million at the end of 1998. This would represent an estimated 31 per cent of the total population (in Davis 1999: 64).

These trends create new challenges for existing broadcasters, since new channels are planning to migrate from webcasting to broadband as soon as the latter becomes digital. Broadband will not only enable faster connection to the Internet but will greatly facilitate delivery of a range of services such as VOD, e-commerce, music, e-mail, interactive advertising, online information, interactive gaming and videoconferencing. In other words, the Internet not only changes the prospects for interactivity. It also has a direct impact on what is now being broadcast. In fact, in 2000 companies like Open TV, Microsoft TV and Liberate were extremely active and competed to dominate the European market for interactive television platforms.

The *first wave* of television web sites was mostly designed as marketing tools aimed at promoting television channels. Now, channels are upgrading their sites to become extensions of the channels themselves. We have seen in the previous chapters that all thematic channels have developed their web sites.

For the *second generation* of web sites content would appear to be the key. Web sites are no longer considered as promotional tools for their television parents, and new content is being produced. Internet transmission is particularly suited to certain kinds of audio-visual content (Johnson 1998):

- *News and archive material.* It is already possible to watch a number of news services that are both up to date and available at the precise moment to suit the viewer. An archive of concerts and programmes is available, for example, on the BBC web site.
- *Distance broadcasting.* The Internet is ideal for the transmission of channels or stations of minority interest where that minority is not geographically concentrated; that could take the form of niche broadcasting for those with a shared hobby or interest and also broadcasting for those with a local interest away from locality.

The Internet, in other words, can operate as a platform not only for broadcast material but also for material designed to complement broadcasting. In the USA, the Microsoft's Web TV box enables the viewer to watch and use the World Wide Web as well as broadcast material on a television set. It is envisaged that a process of switching between them could be as easy as switching to teletext, with, of course, a far wider range of content. This has the potential of broadening the viewing experience.

In the case of television, in the 1990s it was realized that combined PCs and TV sets failed to meet expectations for a fast development, as did the set-top boxes of the late 1990s, which would give television-viewers Internet access. The US experience is indicative. In the mid-1990s, Time Warner Inc. invested millions into trying to deliver movies on demand in Orlando, Florida, but the technology proved too expensive. Cable giant Tele-Communications Inc. and Bell Atlantic Corp. announced plans to merge in 1993 to combine the promise of television, telecommunications and computers, but the deal collapsed. Even WebTV in 1997 tried to let people surf the Web from their couches, but it attracted only one million subscribers.

The set-top box is the first step along a path that might lead to a convergence in the capacity of the TV and the PC. Such a convergence is unlikely to lead to the development of one device being used universally for one purpose, as the television receiver is now. A set-top box could eventually be viewed as a low-cost personal computer. By using a new digital set-top box, America Online Inc. (AOL) delivers to TV sets across America its popular online service, complete with e-mail, chat, instant messaging and interactive content. AOL has twenty-two million subscribers who are accustomed to surfing the Internet to check out the latest basketball scores, look up stock prices and zap off instant messages. It figures that many of its customers would like to do the same thing from their TVs – if they could use the same capabilities and features with which they are already comfortable. In other words, the distinction between the PC and the television might become one of utilization rather than technology. If this becomes successful, it will certainly cross the Atlantic.

In Europe, however, digital operators are turning their attention to the transactional potential of their subscriber base. What they are looking for is a way to encourage their subscribers to buy products through their interactive services, much as people do on the Internet through e-commerce. The TV set is a ubiquitous and familiar item in all households and as such seems set to remain the primary medium for consumer electronic retailing. Moreover, the TV set, especially among the older age group, is not perceived as difficult to use as a device, and, most importantly, among the subscribers there is a critical mass of consumers to buy products through an interactive TV set. Already European digital platforms, Open (UK), Canal Numérique and TPS (France), Quiero and Vía (Spain), Stream (Italy) and Premiere World (Germany) operate interactive services.

But it is questionable whether the Internet can displace television use. This depends on whether the Web will become a functional alternative to television viewing and whether it will be used for similar reasons. Ferguson and Perse (2000: 157) have concluded that there are three major and two minor reasons why the Web resembles television viewing: entertainment, pastime, relaxation, social information and information. They also note that there are indications that the Web may not be as relaxing a use of time as television viewing. As they point out (Ferguson and Perse 2000: 169): 'The WWW [Web] differs functionally from television viewing. Watching television for relaxation is usually the second-most important reason for watching television. Web surfing, however, does not appear to be a relaxing pastime . . .'. Although the Web is a global medium, and television viewing in the last years has become stable, while Internet surfing has increased, Web channels are not being watched with the same expectations and attitudes shown to the Internet. It seems that in the near future viewers will be more attracted by the interactivity of digital television, rather than the new media world offered by the Internet. Although interactivity does not necessarily guarantee viewer involvement, it seems that the future of television lies in offering viewers a more flexible approach to their TV viewing, to enable them to decide what to watch and when, rather than surfing on the Web. And, as Ferguson and Perse (2000: 171) note, 'many computer users many not want the Web to be like TV'. However, one must also consider that the Internet may capture potential viewing time from television services, and 'whether the battle for the viewer's time is won by the Internet or by broadcast interactive multimedia applications will depend on how compelling the content is' (Davis 1999: 5).

The digital future and the viewer

The development of digital television in Europe will become a reality for the simple reason that most governments have decided gradually to switch off their analogue transmissions by 2010. This relates more to the industrial imperatives and needs of the European economic policy, intense marketing and promotion rather than the demand of consumers. In fact, consumer needs and real demand seem to have been largely ignored in the development of digital TV. This is somewhat ironic, since, as European television moves towards the digital age, it seems clear that the conventional sources of revenue (advertising and licence fee) will not remain the same as in the past. New ways of funding, mainly by the subscribers, will become the main source of income for the new channels.

In an environment in which the deregulation of European television has been associated with the emergence of neo-liberal ideologies advocating the restructuring and modernization of the economy, and, in effect, the marketization of the public communication sector, consumer demand has been taken for granted. The need for larger-scale investment and the globalization of economic systems, and not demand for services, have, in turn, brought about the deregulation of broadcasting systems in Western Europe. The deregulation of television has led to the creation of larger and fewer dominant groups. The economic dynamics of the information industries are encouraging private enterprises in the sector to become vertically integrated and to expand horizontally, thereby increasing the levels of concentration. The information industries are becoming more concentrated and populated by large multimedia groups. In fact, the European Union and its Member States have unleashed powers for mega firms and concentration in every European industrial sector, including the communication domain. As noted in chapter 5, this is due to the marketization policies adopted by the EU rather than to digital technologies.

Many argue that we have entered the 'pay-society' era, or, according to Mosco (1988), the 'pay-per-society' era. This 'new society' suggests not a new citizenship but rather a growth of privatized information-content infrastructures, which will lead to growing disparity between information 'haves' and 'have nots' (see Garnham 1990; Schiller 1996; Herman and McChesney 1997; McChesney 1998b).

An indication of this is the pay and PPV channels, especially the sports PPV channels. For many years sport used to be a trademark of the public sphere and television-viewers used to watch for free. Nowadays, viewers have to pay if they want to watch sporting events, especially soccer. The same applies to most of the thematic channels, such as movie or children's channels, which are offered by pay-TV operators in their digital platforms of programme channels. All of the channels offered by the pay-TV operators enhance viewers' choice by, as has been noted, specializing in areas of specific interest. Moreover, consumer choice is extended through the growing availability of PPV and NVOD services, allowing viewers to choose the programme they want and when they want to see it. Digital platforms offer their customers what the traditional generalist broadcasters tried successfully to offer their viewers: a diet of all types of programme genres.

In effect, the consumer-choice argument still plays a dominant role in new media developments. In the 1980s cable TV was considered as the ideal technology to end centralized television systems and as something that would encourage interpersonal communication and democracy. In the 1990s the same arguments came back, but with the terms 'cable TV' and 'wired society' replaced by 'digital TV' and 'information society'. But this digital rhetoric has paid little attention to the citizen-viewer, although the arguments tend to be on his or her behalf. As Croteau and Hoynes (2001: 207) note:

> Most of the hubbub about the new media world focuses on the benefits to *consumers*, who will gain from new innovations, lower prices, growth in outlets and new methods of shopping. With rare exceptions, the discussion of these benefits has little to say about what the new media landscape means for *citizens*. By confining the discussion to costs and benefits for consumers . . . broader questions about community, power, participation, and the public interest are either neglected or reframed so consumers and citizens are defined as one and the same.

At the same time, new media developments echo Giddens's statement on postmodernity that 'people increasingly live on a high technological frontier which absolutely no one completely understands' (Giddens 1998: 25). But these developments clearly indicate that in the foreseeable future citizen-viewers will be classified according to their purchasing power. It is not a coincidence that viewers are already called subscribers. Moreover, the arrival of thematic channels and digital television has contributed to the additional fees that European viewers have to pay. This tendency, however, has to be seen within the wider framework of the 'information society' in the EU. It seems to be a society that in practice provides access only to those who have a purchasing power to buy its products and services. It also mirrors the developments of the last decades in Europe, where poverty and inequality have been more severe. As Murdock and Golding (1999: 129) note:

> Employment opportunities created by technological change have enlarged rather than diminished income differentials within the labour market, while pressures on public expenditure, and in many countries, a neo-liberal approach to welfare expenditure have extended economic inequality. As communication and information goods and services transfer to the market, their accessibility among significant sections of the population is reduced, and their contribution to social cohesion becomes negative.

Clearly, audio-visual content is a merchandise for media companies, and in the near future most European viewers will no longer be able to watch television without paying for its content. Media companies challenge free TV access to major sporting events for every citizen and increasingly to other television content that used to be free. In other words, television content in the digital pay society has become a commodity in its more extreme form. And a handful of private media companies have used their power to buy exclusive broadcasting rights, such as films and sporting events, and to charge additional fees to the viewers who may want to watch them. The fear is that, in the long run, global media interests could undermine free broadcasting, with people being forced to link up to satellites and cables in buying the necessary equipment for receiving digital channels and paying additional fees, if they can afford it.

This echoes what Herbert Schiller pointed out some years ago that 'the transnational corporate system' would dominate the 'cultural-informational sphere' (1989: 5), since the rise of the information society constitutes a bold extension of corporate control over culture and communication (Schiller 1989: 28). The digitalization of television is, therefore, part and parcel of a developing process leading to the 'information society'. It grants dominant status to business and technological change and it pulls together divergent systems of the communications sector. It operates alongside, and gains from, the advent of a new global competition, which takes place on both international and local levels. Finally, it changes television as a public good, and, at the same time, transforms it into a highly class-divided medium.

In this new era, only state or suprastate intervention could be a decisive factor in ending this new societal cleavage, but it is uncertain whether this would be successful, since public policies in most countries favour this new 'pay society'. It is doubtful whether either the EU or the individual Member States can really control concentration and consolidation in the field. In fact, the race to a new transformation of European television started in the late 1990s, and the competitors are barely out of the convergent digital gate.

To control media consolidation, states need strong political parties. But, the television revolution has coincided with a decrease in the status of political parties. Since the 1990s, European politicians have spent more time trying to cope with the new media landscape. The so-called 'videocracy' that gives a prominent role to television and, in effect, its owners has resulted in a decrease in the power and status of politicians and an increase in the power of media owners and companies. Unfortunately, since the mid 1980s, governments have paid little attention to the television-viewer as a citizen, although they argue for him or her. All EU governments prefer market forces and have proved that they do not really consider the issues related to the social and cultural dimension of television. Neither have they really managed to tackle any of the social questions, since they have adopted an economic rationale, fixed the citizen in the role of consumer with no right other than to buy and choose services that are partially competing with each other, if he or she has the money.

The industrial perspective since the mid-1980s has been to build up the 'information societies' and to open the public domain to media conglomerates. In other words, the process started in the 1980s seems to be coming to completion at the beginning of the twenty-first century: *the European viewer has gone from being a silent citizen in the state monopoly era to a valuable consumer in the digital era of private oligopolies.*

The above thoughts reflect some of Neil Postman's questions, when he asks us to be critical about the introduction of a new technology. Following Postman's thoughts (1999: 36–57), we might ask the following questions.

- What is the problem to which digital television is a solution?
- Whose problem is it?
- What new problems might be created because we have more transmission capacity?
- Which people and what institutions might be most seriously harmed by digital television?
- What changes in society and culture are being enforced by digital television?
- What sort of people and institutions acquire special economic and political power from digital technologies.

It seems that only the resistance of citizen-viewers, mainly organized in social groups, might change the plans of large corporations, which dominate the field. This resistance would amount to an unexpected decrease in demand for service, which would destabilize market forces. Recent failures of business models for online content services, such as videotext, paid Internet, free Web, Internet/Web and Push, Portals and Personal Portals (Picard 2000), have shown that citizens, either as consumers or as subscribers of these services, were generally uninterested, and, as a result, most content providers and operators were forced to seek other alternatives. If citizens continue to resist the 'sirens' of digital pay-per-use media, media and telecommunications companies may rethink their marketing strategies. As Noam Chomsky has said, 'if you act like there is no possibility for change, you guarantee that there will be no change' (in Herman and McChesney 1997: 205).

References

Abelman, Robert and Atkin, David 2000: 'What the children watch when they watch TV: putting theory into practice'. *Journal of Broadcasting and the Electronic Media*, 44 (1): 143–54.

Achile, Yves and Miège, Bernard 1994: 'The limits to the adaptation strategies of European public service television'. *Media, Culture and Society*, 16 (1): 31–46.

Alleynet, Mark D. and Wanger, Janet 1993: 'Stability and change at the "big five" news agencies'. *Journalism Quarterly*, 70 (1): 40–50.

Alliot, J. 1996: 'La France sportive'. *Cable and Satellite Europe* (September): 28–9.

Alonzi, Tania and Burrows, Anna 1999: 'Going native'. In *Media and Marketing Europe: Pan European Television Pocket Guide*, London: Media & Marketing Europe: 5–6.

Altheide, David L. and Snow, Robert P. 1979: *Media Logic*. Beverly Hills, Calif.: Sage.

Atkinson, Claire 1997: 'Growing Up'. *Cable and Satellite Europe* (September): 22–4.

Atkinson, Claire 1998: 'Murdoch makes first move in the media wars of the new millennium'. *Independent*, 5 January: Media, 4–5.

Aufderheide, Pat 1986: 'Music videos: the look of the sound'. *Journal of Communication*, 3: 57–78.

Avery, Robert (ed.) 1993: *Public Service Broadcasting in a Multichannel Environment*, New York: Longman.

Baker, Simon 1990: 'Ma chaîne musical'. *Cable and Satellite Europe* (November): 25–6.

Banks, Jack 1996: *Monopoly Television: MTV's Quest to Control the Music*. Boulder, Colo.: Westview Press.

Banks, Jack 1997: 'MTV and the globalization of popular culture'. *Gazette*, 59 (1): 43–60.

Barber, Benjamin 1999: 'Three scenarios for the future of technology and strong democracy'. *Political Science Quarterly*, 113 (4): 573–89.

Barker, Chris 1997: *World Television: An Introduction.* Oxford: Blackwell.

Barker, Paul 1993: 'That's all folks'. *Cable and Satellite Europe* (May): 48–50.

Barker, Paul 2000: 'Let the game commence'. *TV Express*, 27 January: 5.

Barnes, Chris 2000: 'Media mergermania hits new record'. *Euromedia* (July–August): 32–3.

Barnett, Steven 1990: *Games and Sets: The Changing Face of Sports on Television.* London: British Film Institute.

Barnett, Steven 1995: 'Sport'. In A. Smith (ed.), *Television: An International History*, Oxford: Oxford University Press, 148–68.

Barnett, Steven, Seymour, Emily and Gaber, Ivor 2000: *From Callaghan to Kosovo: Changing Trends in British Television News 1975–1999.* London: University of Westminster.

Baskerville Communications Corporation 1997: 'European TV revenues to double by 2006'. Press release, 22 September.

Baskerville Communications Corporation 1999: 'Global PPV soccer revenues to reach US$5 billion by 2009'. Press release, 23 February.

Beardsley, Scott, Miles, Alan and Rose, John S. 1997: The future of direct-to-home television'. *McKinsey Quarterly*, 1: 57–81.

Becker, Wolfgang 2000: 'The introduction of digital TV in Germany: the Federal Government's initiative on digital broadcasting'. *International Journal of Communications Law and Policy*, 4 (Winter). Available at: http://www.ijclp.org.

Bell, Nick 1994: 'There is a crowd'. *Television Business International* (July–August): 34–7.

Benady, Alex 2000: 'Media alchemy'. *Media and Marketing Europe* (March): 28–31.

Bertolotti, Nick 1998: *The European Pay-TV Industry: The Full Monty.* London: J. P. Morgan Securities Ltd.

Biggam, Ross 2000: 'Public service broadcasting: the view from the commercial sector'. *Intermedia*, 28 (5): 21–3.

Biltereyst, Daniel 2001: 'Global research citizenship: towards an agenda for research on foreign/international news and audiences'. In Stig Hjarvard (ed.), *News in a Globalized Society*, Goteborg: NORDICOM, 41–62.

Blumler, Jay G. 1990: 'Elections, the media and the modern publicity process'. In Marjorie M. Ferguson (ed.) *Public Communication: The New Imperative.* London: Sage, 101–13.

Blumler, Jay G. 1992a: 'Public service broadcasting before the commercial deluge'. In Jay G. Blumler (ed.), *Television and the Public Interest: Vulnerable Values in Western European Broadcasting*, London: Sage, 7–21.

Blumler, Jay G. 1992b: 'Vulnerable values at stake'. In Jay G. Blumler (ed.), *Television and the Public Interest: Vulnerable Values in Western European Broadcasting*, London: Sage, 22–4.

Blumler, Jay G. 1992c: 'Introduction'. In Jay G. Blumler (ed.), *Television and the Public Interest: Vulnerable Values in Western European Broadcasting*, London: Sage, 1–6.

Blumler, Jay G. 1996: 'Origins of the crisis of communication for citizenship'. *Political Communication*, 14 (4): 395–404.

Blumler, Jay G. 1999: 'Political communication systems all change'. *European Journal of Communication*, 14 (2): 241–9.

Blumler, Jay G. and Hoffmann-Riem, W. 1992: 'New roles for public television'. In Jay G. Blumler (ed.), *Television and the Public Interest: Vulnerable Values in Western European Broadcasting*, London: Sage, 202–17.

Blumler, Jay G. and Kavanagh, Dennis 1999: 'The third age of political communication: influences and features'. *Political Communication*, 16 (3): 209–30.

BNP (Banque Nationale de Paris) Equities 1999: *The Television Sector in Europe*. Paris: BNP.

Bogart, Leo 1995: *Commercial Culture: The Media System and the Public Interest*. New York: Oxford University Press.

Booz Allen & Hamilton 1989: *Strategic Partnerships as a Way Forward in European Broadcasting*. London: Booz Allen & Hamilton.

Boyd-Barrett, Oliver 1998: 'Global news agencies'. In Oliver Boyd-Barrett and Terhi Rantanen (eds), *The Globalization of News*. London: Sage, 19–34.

Boyd-Barrett, Oliver 2000: 'National and international news agencies: issues of crisis and realignment'. *Gazette*, 62 (1): 5–18.

Boyfield, Keith 2000: 'Braving Europe's ad markets'. *Media and Marketing Europe* (January): 17–20.

Brants, Kees 1998: 'Who's afraid of infotainment?' *European Journal of Communication*, 13 (3): 315–35.

Brants, Kees 1999: 'A rejoinder to Jay G. Blumler'. *European Journal of Communication*, 14 (4): 411–16.

Brants, Kees and Neijens, Peter 1998: 'The infotainment of politics'. *Political Communication*, 15 (2): 149–64.

Brants, Kees and Siune, Karen 1992: 'Public service broadcasting in a public of flux'. In Karen Siune and W. Tuetzschler (eds), *Dynamics of Media Politics: Broadcasts and Electronic Media in Western Europe*, London: Sage, 101–15.

Brooks, R. and Wroe M. 1996: 'Fistful of dollars'. *Observer*, 17 March: 20.

Brown, Charles 1997: *The New Economics of Audiovisual Production: Film and TV Financing, Production and Distribution in the Digital Age*. London: FT Media and Telecoms.

Brown, David 1998a: 'Going local'. *Cable and Satellite Europe* (August): 26–8.

Brown, David 1998b: *Regionalisation and Market Positioning for Pan-European PAY-TV*. London: FT Media and Telecoms.

Brown, David 1998c: *Revenue Trends and Projections in European Pay-Television*. London: FT Media and Telecoms.

BRU 1985: Broadcasting Research Unit, *The Public Service Idea in British Broadcasting: Main Principles*. London: BRU (2nd edn, 1988).

Bruneau, Marie-Agnés 1999: 'French connection'. *Cable and Satellite Europe* (April): 46–8.

Bruneau, Marie-Agnès 2000: 'Lagardère makes TV comeback in "global alliance" with Canal+'. *TV Express*, 27 January: 1–2.

Buckingham, David 2000: *After the Death of the Childhood: Growing up in the Age of Electronic Media*. Cambridge: Polity.

Bughin, Jacques and Griekspoor, Wilfred 1997: 'A new era for European TV'. *McKinsey Quarterly*, 3: 90–102.

Bunting, Helen 1996: *The Future of European TV Industry*. London: FT Media and Telecoms.

Bunting, Helen and Chapman, Paul 1996: *The Future of the European Media Industry: Towards the 21st Century*. London: FT Media and Telecoms.

Burgelman, Jean-Claude 1986: 'The future of public service broadcasting: a case study for "new" communications policy'. *European Journal of Communication*, 1 (2): 172–201.

Burgelman, Jean-Claude and Pauwels, Caroline 1992: 'Audiovisual policy and cultural identity in small European states: the challenge of a unified market'. *Media, Culture and Society*, 14 (2): 169–83.

Burnett, Claire 1989: 'Speaking into tunes'. *Cable and Satellite Europe* (January): 38–43.

Cable and Satellite Europe 1996: 'Getting in without paying?' (October): 157–60.

Cable and Satellite Europe 2000: 'Divide and rule' (October): 26–30.

Cable and Satellite Europe 2001: 'Digital channel guide' (November): 86–91.

Cairns, Alice 1999: 'Making kids pay'. *Television Business International* (September): 30–4.

Callard, Sarah 1998: 'Breaking news'. *Cable and Satellite Europe* (October): 67–70.

Callard, Sarah 1999a: 'Reaching the converted'. *Cable and Satellite Europe* (January): 14–22.

Callard, Sarah 1999b: 'Political fall out'. *Cable and Satellite Europe* (May): 55–7.

Callard, Sarah 1999c: 'Music TV in Europe steps onto another level'. *TV Express*, 29 July: 12–13.

Callard, Sarah 2000: 'Taking candy from babies'. *Cable and Satellite Europe* (February): 20–3.

Campbell, Richard 1998: *Media and Culture: An Introduction to Mass Communication*. New York: St Martin's Press.

Cappucio, Elena 1999: 'Digital TV makes its mark'. *TV Express*, 25 March: 11–13.

Cappucio, Elena 2000: 'Broadcasters lobbying in the face of impending regulation'. *TV Express*, 10 February: 9–12.

Carlsson, Ulla and Feilitzen, von Cecilia (eds) 1998: *Children and Media Violence*. Gothenburg: The UNESCO International Clearinghouse on Children and Violence on the Screen.

Cavalin, J. 1998: 'European policies and regulations on media concentration'. *International Journal of Communications Law and Policy*, 3. Available at http://www.digital-law.net/IJCLP/1_1998/ijclpwebdoc_3_1_1998.html.

CE 1997: Council of Europe, *Report on Media Concentrations and Pluralism in Europe*. MM-CM (97), Brussels: January.

CEC 1992: Commission of the European Communities, *Pluralism and Media Concentration in the Internal Market: An Assessment of the Need for Community Action*. COM (92) 480 Final, Brussels: 23 December.

CEC 1994: *Communication to Parliament and Council: Follow-up to the Consultation Process Relating to the Green Paper on 'Pluralism and Media Concentration in the Internal Market – An Assessment of the Need for Community Action'*. COM (94) 353 Final, Brussels: 5 October.

CEC 1995: 'Directive 95/47/C of the European Parliament and of the Council of 24 October 1995 on the use of standards for the transmission of television signals'. COM L281/151. Brussels: 23 November.

CEC 1997a: *Explanatory Memorandum* (Media Ownership in the Internal Market). DG XV, Brussels: February.

CEC 1997b: *Second Report from the Commission to the European Parliament, the Council and the Economic and Social Committee on the Application of Directive 89/552/EEC 'Television without Frontiers'*, COM (97) 523 Final, Brussels: 25 May.

CEC 1997c: 'Directive 97/36/EC of the European Parliament and of the Council of 30 June 1997 Amending Council Directive 89/552/EDC on the Coordination of Certain Provisions Laid Down by Law, Regulation or Administrative Action in Member States Concerning the pursuit of Television Broadcasting Activities'. *Official Journal of the European Communities*, L 202, Brussels: 30 July: 0060–0071.

CEC 1997d: *Green Paper on the Convergence of the Telecommunications, Media and Information Technology Sectors and the Implications for Regulation, towards an Information Society Approach*. COM (97) 623 Final, Brussels: 3 December.

CEC 1998a: *The Digital Age: European Audiovisual Policy*. Report from the High Level Group on Audiovisual Policy chaired by Commissioner Marcelino Oreja, Brussels: October.

CEC 1998b: 'Summary of the Result of the Public Consultation on the Green Paper on the Convergence of the Telecommunications, Media and Information Technology Sectors; Areas for Further Reflection'. Working Document of the Commission. SEC (98) 1284, Brussels: 29 July.

CEC 1999a: *Communication to the European Parliament, the Council, the Economic and Social Committee and the Committee of the Regions: The Convergence of the Telecommunications, Media and Information Technology Sectors, and the Implications for Regulation: Results of the Public Consultation on the Green Paper (COM (97) 623)*, COM (99) 108 Final, Brussels: 10 March.

CEC 1999b: 'Relations between Sport and Television'. Discussion paper for the working group at the First European Conference on Sport, Olympia, Greece, on 21 and 22 May 1999, Version 2, Brussels: 26 April.

CEC 1999c: *The Development of the Market for Digital Television in the European Union: Report in the Context of Directive 95/47/EC of the European Parliament and of the Council on the use of Standards for the Transmission of Television Signals*. COM (1999) 540, Brussels: 9 November.

CEC 2000: *Fourth Communication from the Commission to the Council and the European Parliament on the Application of Articles 4 and 5 of Directive 89/552/EEC 'Television without Frontiers' for the period 1997–8*. COM (2000) 442 Final, Brussels: 17 July.

CES 2000: Comité Economique et Sociale: *Pluralism and Concentration in the Media in the Age of Globalization and Digital Convergence*. Brussels: 29 March

Chaffee, Steven H. and Kaniham, S. F. 1997: 'Learning about politics from the mass media'. *Political Communication*, 14: 421–30.

Chakraborty, Mimi 1997: 'Catering for kids'. *Cable and Satellite Europe* (September): 26–8.

Chakraborty, Mimi 1998a: 'Business as usual'. *Cable and Satellite Europe* (January): 17.

Chakraborty, Mimi 1998b: *News Television*. London: FT Media and Telecoms.

Chalaby, Jean K. and Segell, Glen 1999: 'The broadcasting media in the age of risk: the advent of digital television'. *New Media and Society*, 1 (3): 351–68.

Chapman, Paul 1996: *The Future of Public Broadcasting*. London: FT Media and Telecoms.

Church, Rachel 2000: *Sport on the Internet*. London: Screen Digest.

Clover, Julian 1993: 'Paying it by ear'. *Cable and Satellite Europe* (February): 18–24.

Coen, David 1997: 'The evolution of the large firm as a political actor in the European Union'. *Journal of European Public Policy*, 4 (1): 91–108.

Collins, Richard 1990: *Television Policy and Culture*. London: Unwin Hyman.

Collins, Richard 1993: *From Satellite to Single Market: New Communication Technology and European Public Service Television*. London: Routledge.

Collins, Richard 1998a: 'Supper with the devil – a case study in private/public collaboration in broadcasting: the genesis of Eurosport', *Media, Culture and Society*, 20 (4): 653–63.

Collins, Richard 1998b: 'Public service broadcasting and the media economy; European trends in the late 1990s'. *Gazette*, 60 (5): 363–76.

Collins, Richard, Garnham, Nicholas and Locksley, Gareth 1988: *The Economics of Television: The UK Case*. London: Sage.

Comstock, George 1989: *The Evolution of American Television*. Newbury Park, Calif.: Sage.

Congdon T., Graham, A., Green, D. and Robinson, B. 1995: *The Cross-Media Revolution: Ownership and Control*. London: John Libbey.

Corcoran, Farrel 1999: 'Towards digital television in Europe'. *Javnost/The Public*, 6 (3): 67–86.

Croteau, David and Hoynes, William 2001: *The Business of Media: Corporate Media and the Public Interest*. Thousand Oaks, Calif.: Sage.

Crowe, Charlie 1997: 'Head to head in Europe'. *Media and Marketing Europe* (September): 29–30.

Curran, James 1986: 'The different approaches to media reform'. In James Curran, Jake Ecclestone, Giles Oakley and Alan Richardson (eds), *Bending Reality: The State of the Media*. London: Pluto Press, 89–135.

Curran, James 1998: 'Crisis of public communication: a reappraisal'. In Tamar Liebes and James Curran (eds), *Media, Ritual and Identity*, London: Routledge, 175–202.

Davies, Hannah, Buckingham, David and Kelley, Peter 2000: 'In the worst possible taste: children, television and cultural value'. *European Journal of Cultural Studies*, 3 (1): 5–25.

Davies, Paul 2000: 'Guiding light'. *Cable and Satellite Europe* (August): 30–4.

Davis, William 1999: *The European TV Industry in the 21st Century*. London: FT Media and Telecoms.

Dayan, Daniel and Katz, Elihu 1992: *Media Events: The Live Broadcasting of History*. Cambridge, Mass.: Harvard University Press.

De Bens, Els 1998: 'Television programming: more diversity, more convergence?'. In Kees Brants, Joke Hermes and Liesbet van Zoonen (eds), *The Media in Question: Popular Cultures and Public Interests*, London: Sage, 27–37.

De Bens, Els and Knoche, M. (eds) 1987: *Electronic Mass Media in Europe: Prospects and Developments*. Dordrecht: D. Reidel.

Del Valle, David 1997: 'Spanish platforms engage in digital price wave'. *Cable and Satellite Express*, 25 September: 1–2.

Del Valle, David 1998: 'Digital platforms merge in Spain'. *TV Express*, 23 July: 1–2.

Del Valle, David 1999a: 'Strong growth potential for Spanish TV market', *TV Express*, 23 September: 12–13.

Del Valle, David 1999b: 'RTVE: Looking for a new TV model', *TV Express*, 14 January: 7.

Del Valle, David 2000: 'Leading the Spanish pay-TV back'. *TV Express*, 11 March: 5–6.

Dennis, Everette, T. 1993: 'Communication, media and the global marketplace of ideas'. *The Fletcher Forum of World Affairs*, 17 (1): 1–8.

Digital TV Group 2001: 'Hard choices for digital says Consumers Association'. Available at: http://www.dgt.org.uk.

Di Piazza, Guy 1997: *Opportunities in Digital Pay-TV: Programme Production, Channel Marketing, Transmission and Subscriber Management*. London: FT Media and Telecoms.

Dodd, Thomas 1998: 'TVS bites the dust'. *Cable and Satellite Express*, 15 January: 11.

Doherty, Catherine 2000: 'Record DTH subs annual growth for Sky'. *Cable and Satellite Europe* (August): 8.

Doherty, David 1999: 'Empires and evolution: public service content in the new media'. *Intermedia*, 27 (2): 20–3.

Doyle, G. 1997: 'From "Pluralism" to "Ownership": Europe's emergent policy on media concentrations navigates the doldrums'. *Journal of Information, Law and Technology*, 3. Available at: http://elj.warwick.ac.uk/jilt/commsreg/97_3doyl/.

Dutheil, Guy 1995: 'La France restructure son audiovisuel international'. *Le Monde*, 30 November: 28.

Dyson, Kenneth and Humphreys, Peter (eds) 1986: *The Politics of the Communication Revolution in Western Europe*. London: Frank Cass.

Dyson, Kenneth and Humphreys, Peter (eds) 1990: *The Political Economy of Communications: International and European Dimensions*. London: Routledge.

Edelman, Murray 1988: *Constructing the Political Spectacle*. Chicago: Chicago University Press.

EIM 1988: European Institute for the Media, *Europe 2000: What Kind of Television?* Manchester: EIM.

Elliot, Kathy 1998: 'TV fights to recover youth market share'. *Media and Marketing Europe* (January): IV.

Engelbrecht, Fredeline and Engelbrecht, Loefie 1998: 'EPGs: vital for television of the future'. *European Television Analyst*, (January): 11.

Esser, Frank 1999: 'Tabloidization of news: a comparative analysis of Anglo-American and German Press journalism'. *European Journal of Communication*, 14 (3): 291–324.

Eurobarometer 1999: *Public Opinion in the European Union*. Brussels: European Commission, Report Number 51.

Euromedia 1999: 'Sporting jewels' (May): 18–19.

Euromedia 2000: 'Kagan projections 2000'. (July–August): 52–3.

European Television Analyst 1997: 'Kirch loan goes ahead', 23 April: 3.

Evans, R. 1992: 'Incident exposure? Sex on TV'. *Television Business International* (June): 39–49.

Everett, C. Shu-Ling 1994: 'The endangered post-modern childhood'. *Intermedia*, 22 (2): 30–4.

Fahri, Paul 1994: 'When no news is bad news'. *Washington Post*, 10 June: F1, F2.

Ferguson, Douglas A. and Perse, Elizabeth M. 2000: 'The World Wide Web as a functional alternative to television'. *Journal of Broadcasting and Electronic Media*, 44 (2): 155–74.

Fichera, Massimo 1993: 'News as the sole content of programming'. In Claude Contamine (ed.), *The Future of Television: Generalist or Thematic Channel?*, Düsseldorf: The European Institute of the Media, 215–18.

Fletcher, Winston 1996: 'Home shopping takes a tumble from its trolley'. *Financial Times*, 2 January: 9.

Flichy, Patrice 1999: 'The construction of new digital media'. *New Media and Society*, 1 (1): 33–9.

Foley, John 1998: *Digital Terrestrial Television in Europe: The Dynamics of Transition*. London: CDG Consultants.

Franklin, Bob 1997: *Newszak and News Media*. London: Arnold.

Fry, Andrew 2000: 'Atlantic crossing'. *Cable and Satellite Europe* (April): 12–18.

Gandy, Oscar 1990: 'Tracking the audience'. In John Dowing, Ali Mohammandi and Annabelle Sreberny-Mohammadi (eds), *Questioning the Media: A Critical Introduction*, London: Sage, 166–79.

Garnham, Nicholas 1990: *Capitalism and Communication: Global Culture and the Economics of Information*. London: Sage.

Garnham, Nicholas 1992: *Capitalism and Communication: Global Culture and the Economics of Information*. London: Sage.

Ghayur, Aalia 1999: 'Growing pains', *Television Business International* (September): 37–42.

Ghayur, Aalia 2000: 'Arrested development'. *Television Business International* (September): 31–6.

Ghayur, Aalia 2001: 'Kid's programming'. *Television Business International* (April): 95–102.

Gibbins, John R. and Reimer, Bo. 1999: *The Politics of Postmodernity: An Introduction to Contemporary Politics and Culture*. London: Sage.

Giddens, Anthony 1990: *The Consequences of Modernity*. Cambridge: Polity.

Giddens, Anthony 1998: 'Risk society: the context of British politics'. In J. Franklin (ed.), *The Politics of Risk Society*, Cambridge: Polity, 23–34.

Ginneken, van Jaap 1998: *Understanding Global News: A Critical Introduction*. London: Sage.

Glover, Julian 1993: 'Kidology'. *Cable and Satellite Europe* (March): 24–32.

Glover, Julian 1997: 'BSkyB delays UK digital platform'. *European Television Analyst*, 9 May: 4.

Godard, François 1997: *Television Programming and Sports Rights in Europe: Pay-TV Rights for Film, TV and Sports*. London: FT Media and Telecoms.

Godard, François 1998: *FT Focus on Canal Plus*. London: FT Media and Telecoms.

Goldberg, D., Prosser, T. and Verhulst, S. 1998: *EC Media Law and Policy*. London: Longman.

Golding, Peter 2000: 'Forthcoming features: information and communications technologies and the sociology of the future'. *Sociology*, 34 (1): 165–84.

Gollogly, Martin and McGarvey, P. 1997: *Pay-Television: Technology, Strategies and International Market Development*. London: FT Media and Telecoms.

Goodwin, Andrew 1992: *Dancing the Distraction Factory: Music Television and Popular Culture*. Minneapolis: University of Minnesota Press.

Graham, Andrew and Davies, Gavyn 1997: *Broadcasting, Society and Policy in the Multimedia Age*. Luton: University of Luton Press/John Libbey Media.

Grant, August E. 1994: 'The promise fulfilled? An empirical analysis of program diversity on television'. *Journal of Media Economics*, 75 (1): 51–64.

Grigler, A. and Jensen, Bruhn 1991: 'Discourses of politics: talking about public issues in the United States and Germany'. In Peter Dahlren and Colin Sparks (eds), *Communication and Citizenship, Journalism and the Public Sphere in the New Media Age*, London: Routledge, 176–95.

Gunter, Barrie and McAleer, Jill 1997: *Children and Television*. London: Routledge.

Harcourt, Alison J. 1998: 'EU media ownership regulation: conflict over the definition of alternatives'. *Journal of Common Market Studies*, 36 (3): 369–89.

Hart, Roderick P. 1995: 'For the negative'. *Political Communication*, 10 (1): 23–7.

Harverson, Patrick 1999: 'Double vision'. *Television Business International* (September): 55–9.

Hatchen, William 1993: 'The triumph of Western news communication'. *Fletcher Forum*, 7 (1): 14–34.

Havermans, Jos 2000: 'Nothing compares to EU'. *Media and Marketing Europe* (March): 36–7.

Herman, Edward S. and McChesney, Robert W. 1997: *The Global Media: The New Missionaries of Corporate Capitalism*. London: Cassel.

Hess, Stephen 1997: *International News and Foreign Correspondents*. New York: Brooking Institute Press.

Hicks, B. 1996: 'Calcio's coming home'. *Cable and Satellite Europe* (September): 24–5.

Hitchens, L. 1994: 'Media ownership and control: a European approach'. *Modern Law Review*, 57 (4).

Hobsbawn, E. 1994: *Age of the Extremes*. London: Michael Joseph.

Hoehn, Thomas and Szymanski, Stefan 1999: 'The Americanization of European Football'. *Economic Policy* (April): 205–40.

Hoffmann-Riem, Wolfgang 1992: 'Protecting vulnerable values in the German broadcasting order'. In Jay G. Blumler (ed.), *Television and the Public Interest: Vulnerable Values in Western European Broadcasting*, London: Sage, 43–60.

Hoffmann-Riem, Wolfgang 1996: *Regulating Media: The Licensing and Supervision of Broadcasting in Six Countries*. New York: Guilford Press.

Holznagel, Bernd and Grünwald, Andreas 2000: 'The introduction of digital television in Germany: regulatory issues – a comparative analysis'. *International Journal of Communications Law and Policy*, 4 (Winter). Available at http://www.ijclp.org.

Humphreys, Peter 1990: *Media and Media Policy in West Germany: The Press and Broadcasting since 1945*. Oxford: Berg, 1990.

Humphreys, Peter 1996: *Mass Media and Media Policy in Western Europe*. Manchester: Manchester University Press.

Idate 2000: Institut de l'Audiovisuel et des Télécomunications en Europe, *Development of Digital Television in the European Union, Reference Report/ 1999, final report, MED 70052 C (LME), a study commissioned by the European Commission*. Brussels: June.

International Federation of Newpapers Publishers 1991: *World Press Trends*. Paris: IFNP.

International Federation of Newspapers Publishers 1994: *World Press Trends*. Paris: IFNP.

International Federation of Newspapers Publishers 1998: *World Press Trends*. Paris: IFNP.

Iosifides, Petros 1996: 'Merger control and media pluralism in the European Union'. *Communications Law*, 1 (6): 247–9.

Iosifides, Petros 1997: 'Pluralism and media concentration policy in the European Union'. *Javnost/The Public*, 4 (1): 85–104.

Iosifides, Petros 1999: 'Diversity versus concentration in the deregulated mass media domain'. *Journalism & Mass Communication Quarterly*, 76 (1): 152–62.

IP Network 1994: *Television '94: European Key Facts*. Paris: IP Network.

IP Network 2001: *Television 2001: European Key Facts*. Paris: IP-RTL Group.

Jamieson, Kathleen Hall 1987: 'Television, presidential campaign and debates'. In Joel L. Swerdlow (ed.), *Presidential Debates 1998 and Beyond*, Washington: Congressional Quarterly Inc., 27–33.

Jensen, Elizabeth and Lippman, John 1995: 'Wave of new competition may mean bad news for CNN', *Wall Street Journal Europe*, 7 December: 4.

Jhally, Sut 1990: *The Codes of Advertising: Fetishism and the Political Economy of Meaning in the Consumer Society*. London: Routledge.

Johnson, Debra 1996: 'Child's play around the world'. *Broadcasting and Cable International* (April): 24–30.

Johnson, Debra 1997: 'Ads remain biggest funding source'. *European Television Analyst*, 9 April: 11.

Johnson, Debra 1988: 'Inside the wonderful world of the Web'. *European Television Analyst*, 4 June: 14.

Johnson, Debra and Tremlett, G. (1997): 'Via digital launch triggers pay-TV price war in Spain'. *European Television Analyst*, 24 September: 1–2.

Johnston, Carla Brooks 1995: *Winning the Global TV News Game*. Boston: Focal Press.

Jupiter Communications Inc. 2000: 'Rapid DTV adoption forces European business to broaden Internet strategy to reach consumers anywhere, anytime'. Press release, 1 February. Available at http://www.jup.com.

Kathimerini 1995: 'The media promote dissident views'. 9 April: 4 (in Greek).

Katz, Elihu and Lazarsfeld, Paul 1955: *Personal Influence*. New York: Free Press.

Kavanagh, Denis 1995: *Election Campaigning: The New Marketing of Politics*. Oxford: Blackwell.

Keane, John 1995: 'Structural transformations of the public sphere'. *Communication Review*, 1 (1): 1–22.

Kilbride, Kieron 1999: 'Raiders reap sporting jewels'. *Euromedia* (September): 28–9.

Kindred, Jack 1996: 'Kids get digital'. *Television Business International* (September): 28–30.

Koranteng, Juliana 1994: 'MTV forced to dance a tougher tune'. *The European*, 18–24 March: 21.

Koranteng, Juliana 1997: *International Music Television: Opportunities for Growth in the Digital Age*. London: FT Media and Telecoms.

Koranteng, Juliana 1998a: *European Sports TV Channels*. London: FT Media and Telecoms.

Koranteng, Juliana 1998b: 'Hit and miss'. *Cable and Satellite Europe* (March): 25–8.

Koranteng, Juliana 1999: 'Fantasy football siege'. *Cable and Satellite Europe* (October): 34–8.

Koranteng, Juliana 2000: 'A question of sport'. *Cable and Satellite Europe* (July): 12–16.

Kraus, Sidney and Davis, Denis 1976: *The Effects of Mass Communication on Political Behavior.* University Park, Pa.: The Pennsylvania State University Press.

Kuhn, Raymond (ed.) 1985: *The Politics of Broadcasting.* London: Croom Helm.

Kuhn, Raymond 1995: *The Media in France.* London: Routledge.

Landy, Liz and Bridgewater, Sarah 2001: Digital TV: what's new?' *Communication Technology Decisions*, 1: 96–8.

Lang, Kurt and Lang, Glandys Engel 1959: 'The mass media and voting'. In Eugene Burdick and Arthur L. Brodbeck (eds), *American Voting Behavior*, Glencoe, Ill.: Free Press, 221–36.

Lange, André and Renaud, Jean-Luc 1989: *The Future of the European Audiovisual Industry.* Manchester: European Institute for the Media.

Lange, André and Van Loon, A. 1991: 'Pluralism, concentration and competition in the media sector'. *IDATE/IVIR* (December).

Lazarsfeld, Paul, Berelson, Bernard and Gaudet, Hazel 1948: *The People's Choice: How the Voter Makes up his Mind in an Election.* New York: Columbia University Press.

Leclercq, Thierry 1999: 'Tuning in to toon'. *TV Express*, 28 January: 3.

Lee, Paul S. N. 2000: 'Television and global culture: assessing the role of television in globalisation'. In Georgette Wang, Jan Servaes and Anura Goonasekera (eds), *The New Communications Landscape: Demystifying Media Globalization*, London: Routledge, 188–98.

Levinson, Mark 1995: 'It's an MTV world'. *Newsweek*, 24 April: 44–8.

Lewis, Elen 1999: 'Pitched battle'. *Media and Marketing Europe* (October): 24–9.

Locksley, Gareth 1989: *Satellite Broadcasting in Europe and the New technologies.* Brussels: Commission of the European Communities.

Maarek, Philippe, J. 1997: 'New trends in French political communication: the 1995 presidential elections'. *Media, Culture and Society*, 19 (3): 357–68.

McChesney, Robert W. 1998a: 'Media convergence and globalization'. In D. K. Thussu (ed.), *Electronic Empires: Global Media and Local Resistance*, London: Arnold, 27–46.

McChesney, Robert W. 1998b: 'The political economy of global communication'. In R. W. McChesney, E. Meiksins Wood and J. B. Foster (eds), *Capitalism and the Information Age: the Political Economy of the Global Communication Revolution*, New York: Monthly Review Press, 1–26.

McChesney, Robert W. 1999: *Rich Media, Poor Democracy.* Illinois: Illinois University Press.

Machill, Marchel 1998: 'Euronews: the first European news channel as a case study for media industry development in Europe and for spectra of transnational journalism research'. *Media, Culture and Society*, 20 (4): 427–50.

MacLeod, V. (ed.) 1996: *Media Ownership and Control in the Age of Convergence.* London: International Institute of Communications.

McQuail, Denis 1998: 'Commercialisation and beyond'. In Denis McQuail and Karen Siune (eds), *Media Policy: Convergence, Concentration and Commerce*, London: Sage, 107–27.

McQuail, Denis 1994: *Mass Communication Theory: An Introduction*. London: Sage.

McQuail, Denis 2000: *Mass Communication Theory*. London: Sage.

McQuail, Denis and Siune, Karen (eds) 1986: *New Media Politics: Comparative Approaches in Western Europe*. London: Sage.

Maguire, Joseph 1999: *Global Sport: Identities, Societies, Civilizations*. Cambridge: Polity.

Mancini, Paolo 1999: 'New frontiers', *Political Communication*, 16 (3): 231–46.

Mancini, Paolo and Swanson, David L. 1996: 'Politics, media and modern democracy: introduction'. In David L. Swanson and Paolo Mancini (eds), *Politics, Media and Modern Democracy: An International Study of Innovations in Electoral Campaigns and their Consequences*, New York: Praeger, 1–26.

Margolis, Budd 1999: 'Special report: home shopping'. *Television Business International* (April): 129–36.

Masters, Charles 1994: 'Europe's answer to CNN focuses on second year'. *The European*, 15–20 January: 24.

Mattelart, Armand 1994: *Mapping World, Communication, War, Progress*, trans. S. Emmanuel and J. A. Cohen. Minneapolis: University of Minnesota Press.

Mazzoleni, Gianpietro 1987: 'Media logic and party logic in campaign coverage: the Italian general election in 1983'. *European Journal of Communication*, 2 (1): 55–80.

Mazzoleni, Gianpietro 1992: 'Is there a question of vulnerable values in Italy?' In J. Blumler (ed.), *Television and the Public Interest: Vulnerable Values in Western European Broadcasting*, London: Sage, 79–95.

Mazzoleni, Gianpietro 1995: 'Towards a "videocracy": Italian political communication at a turning point'. *European Journal of Communication*, 10 (3): 291–319.

Mazzoleni, Gianpietro and Schultz, Winfrid 1999: 'Mediatization of politics: a challenge for democracy?' *Political Communication*, 16 (3): 247–62.

Media and Marketing Europe 1998: *European Planning Guide 1998/99*. London: Media and Marketing Europe in association with Initiative Media.

Media and Marketing Europe 1999: *Pan-European Television 1999*. Pocket Guide, September. London: Media and Marketing Europe.

Mediametrié 1996: *1995: One Television Year in the World*, Eurodata TV. Paris: Mediametrié.

Mediametrié 1997: *1996: One Television Year in the World*, Eurodata TV. Paris: Mediametrié.

Mediametrié 1998: *1997: One Television Year in the World*, Eurodata TV. Paris: Mediametrié.

Mediametrié 1999: *1998: One Television Year in the World*, Eurodata TV. Paris: Mediametrié.

Mediametrié 2000: *1999: One Television Year in the World*, Eurodata TV. Paris: Mediametrié.

Meier, Werner A. and Trappel, Josef 1992: 'Small states in the shadow of giants'. In Karen Siune and W. Tuetzschler (eds), *Dynamics of Media Politics: Broadcasts and Electronic Media in Western Europe*, London: Sage, 129–41.

Meyrowitz, Joshua 1986: *No Sense of Place: The Impact of Electronic Media on Social Behavior*. New York: Oxford University Press.

Missika, J. L. and Wolton, Dominique 1983: *La Folle du Logis: La Télévision dans les sociétés démocratiques*. Paris: Gallimard.

Molsky, Norman 1999: *European Public Broadcasting in the Digital Age*. London: FT Media and Telecoms.

Moragas Spa, de Miquel and López, Bernat 2000: 'Decentralization processes and the "proximate television" in Europe'. In Georgette Wang, Jan Servaes and Anura Goonasekera (eds), *The New Communications Landscape: Demystifying Media Globalization*, London: Routledge, 33–51.

Morley, David and Robins, Kevin 1995: *Spaces of Identity: Global Media, Electronic Landscapes and Cultural Boundaries*. London: Routledge.

Mosco, V. 1988: 'Information in the pay per society'. In Vincent Mosco and Janet Wasko (eds), *The Political Economy of Information*, Madison: University of Wisconsin Press, 3–26.

Mouzelis, Nicos 1986: *Politics in the Semi-Periphery: Early Parliamentarianism and Late Industrialism in the Balkans and Latin America*. London: Macmillan.

Mowlana, Hamid 1996: *Global Communication in Transition: The End of Diversity?* London: Sage.

Mughan, Anthony 1995: 'Television and presidentialism: Australian and US legislative elections compared'. *Political Communication*, 12 (3): 327–42.

Murdock, Graham 2000: 'Digital futures: European television in the age of convergence. In Jan Wieten, Graham Murdock and Peter Dahlgren (eds), *Television across Europe: A Comparative Introduction*, London: Sage, 35–57.

Murdock, Graham and Golding, Peter 1999: 'Corporate ambitions and communication trends in the UK and Europe'. *Journal of Media Economics*, 12 (2): 117–32.

Murray, John P. 1993: 'The developing child in a multimedia society', pp. 9–22. In Gordon L. Berry and Joy Keieko Asamen (eds), *Children and Television: Images in a Changing Sociocultural World*, London: Sage, 9–22.

Negrine Ralph 1985: *Cable Television and the Future of Broadcasting*. London: Croom Helm.

Negrine, Ralph (ed.) 1988: *Satellite Broadcasting*. London: Routledge.

Negrine, Ralph 1989: *Politics and the Mass Media in Britain*. London: Routledge.

Negrine, Ralph 1996: *The Communication of Politics*. London: Sage.

Negrine, Ralph 1999: 'Parliaments and the media: a changing relationship?'. *European Journal of Communication*, 14 (4): 325–52.

Negrine, Ralph and Papathanassopoulos, Stylianos 1990: *The Internationalization of Television*. London: Pinter.

Negrine, Ralph and Papathanassopoulos, Stylianos. 1996: 'The "Americanization" of political communication: a critique'. *Press*/Politics, 1 (2): 45–62.

Noam, Eli 1991: *Television in Europe*. New York: Oxford University Press.

Norcontel Ltd (in association with NERA, *Screen Digest* and Stanbrook and Hooper) 1998: *Economic Implications of New Communication Technologies on the Audiovisual Markets. A study commissioned on behalf of the European Commission*. Brussels: Commission of the European Communities.

Norris, Pippa 2000: *A Virtuous Circle: Political Communications in Post-Industrial Democracies*. New York: Cambridge University Press.

OJEC 1990: *Official Journal of the European Communities*, 'Council Regulation 4064/89/EEC on the control of concentration between undertakings'. L 257/4, 30 September.

OJEC 1999a: 'Order on the use of TV rights to events of major importance to society'. C 14/6, 19 January.

OJEC 1999b: 'The measures taken pursuant to Article 3(a)(1) of the Directive and notified to the Commission in accordance with the procedure laid down in Article 3(a)(2) by Italy are set out in the following extracts from Decision No 8/1999 of the Communications Authority adopted on 9 March 1999'. C 277/03, 30 September.

OJEC 1999c: 'Resolution of the Council and of the representatives of the governments of the Member States, meeting within the Council of 25 January 1999 concerning public service broadcasting'. C 1999, 30 January–5 February.

OJEC 2000: 'The measures taken pursuant to Article 3(a)(1) of the Directive and notified to the Commission in accordance with the procedure laid down in Article 3(a)(2) by the Federal Republic of Germany are set out in the following extracts from Article 5(a) of the fourth Interstate Treaty of Broadcasting'. C 277/04, 29 September.

Oreja, M. 1998: Address to the Spanish Parliamentary Subcommittee on the RTVE (Spanish Broadcasting Corporation). Madrid: 11 December.

Oreja, M. 1999: Speech by Marcelino Oreja, Member of the European Commission, at the Seminar on Self-Regulation in the Media, Saarbrucken, 19–21 April. Available at http://europa.eu.int/comm/dg10/avpolicy/key_doc/saarbruck_en.html.

Ouellette, Laurie and Lewis, Justin 2000: 'Moving beyond the "vast wasteland": cultural policy and television in the United States'. *Television and the New Media*, 1 (1): 95–115.

Page, Tim 1998: *Digital Broadcasting: New Services and Enabling Systems – Worldwide Technology to 2004*. London: ARC Group.

Papathanassopoulos, Stylianos 1990a: 'The EC: "Television without Frontiers" but with media monopolies'. *Intermedia*, 18 (3): 27–30.

Papathanassopoulos, Stylianos 1990b: 'Towards European television: the case of Europa TV'. *Media Information Australia*, 56: 57–63.

Papathanassopoulos, Stylianos 1994: 'Sex, deregulation and market forces – the ingredients for a new EU television directive'. *Intermedia*, 22 (1): 22–5.

Papathanassopoulos, Stylianos 1998a: 'The development of digital television in Europe', *Media International Australia*, 88: 77–86.

Papathanassopoulos, Stylianos 1998b: 'Pay per game: the advent of pay TV channels in Europe and their implications for sport', *Intermedia*, 26 (3): 21–6.

Papathanassopoulos, Stylianos 1999a: 'The effects of media commercialization on journalism and politics in Greece'. *Communication Review*, 3 (4): 379–402.

Papathanassopoulos, Stylianos 1999b: *Violence on Greek Television*. Athens: Kastaniotis (in Greek).

Papathanassopoulos, Stylianos 1999c: 'The political economy of international news channels: more supply than demand'. *Intermedia*, 27 (1): 17–23.

Parker, Richard 1995a: *Mixed Signals: The Prospects for Global Television News*. New York: Twentieth Century Fund Press.

Parker, Richard 1995b: 'The future of "global" television news: an economic perspective'. *Political Communication*, 12: 431–46.

Paterson, Chris 2000: 'International news in the twenty first century'. *Intermedia*, 28 (4): 16–17.

Pecora Odom, Norma 1999: *The Business of Children's Entertainment*. New Jersey: Guilford Publications.

Peters, Sarah, 1995: *Pay TV in Europe*. London: Goldman Sachs.

Pfetsch, Barbara 1996: 'Convergence through privatization? Changing media environments and televised politics in Germany'. *European Journal of Communication*, 14 (4): 427–51.

Picard, Robert G. 2000: 'Changing business models of online content services: their implications for multimedia and other content producers'. *International Journal on Media Management*, 2 (2): 60–8.

Plunket, John 1999: 'Sky's world of sports'. *Broadcast* (Sky Tenth Anniversary Issue), 5 February: 8.

Pons, J. F. 1998: 'The application of competition and anti-trust policy in media and telecommunications in the European Union', paper presented at the International Bar Association, Vancouver, 14 September. Available at: http://europa.eu.int/comm/dg04/speech/eight.en/sp9804.htm.

Pons, J. F. and Lucking, J. 1999: 'The euro and competition'. *Competition Policy Newsletter*, 1: 1–16.

Pool, Ithiel de Sola 1959: 'TV: a new dimension in politics'. In Eugene Burdick and Arthur L. Brodbeck (eds), *American Voting Behavior*, Glencoe, Ill.: Free Press, 141–59.

Porter, Vincent 2000: 'Public service broadcasting and the new global information order'. *Intermedia*, 27 (4): 34–7.

Postman, Neil 1985: *Amusing Ourselves to Death*. New York: Penguin.

Postman, Neil 1999: *Building a Bridge to the Eighteenth Century: How the Past can Improve our Future*. New York: Alfred A. Knopf Inc.

Price, Chris 1998: 'Kids Stuff'. *Cable and Satellite Europe* (December): 22–9.

Raboy, Marc 1998: 'Public broadcasting and the global framework of media democratization'. *Gazette*, 60 (2): 167–80.

Real, Michael M. 1996: *Exploring Media Culture: A Guide*. Thousand Oaks, Calif.: Sage.

Renaud, Jean-Luc 1998: '23 million homes switched to digital TV'. *TV Express*, 6 August: 13.

Reuters 1996: 'Murdoch unveils global pay TV sports rights'. Press Release 15 October.

Robertson, Roland 1994: 'Globalization or glocalization?'. *Journal of International Communication*, 1 (1): 33–52.

Robillard, Serge 1995: *Television in Europe: Regulatory Bodies; Status, Functions and Powers in 35 European Countries.* London: John Libbey/The European Institute for the Media, Media Monograph No. 19.

Robinson, Michael 1975: 'American political legitimacy in an era of electronic journalism: reflections on the evening news'. In Douglas Cater and R. Adler (eds), *Television as a Social Force: New Approaches to TV Criticism,* New York: Praeger, 97–140.

Robinson, Michael 1976: 'Public affairs television and the growth of political malaise: the case of the "selling the pentagon"'. *American Political Science Review*, 70: 409–32.

Robinson, Michael and Davis, Dennis, K. 1990: 'Television news and the informed public: an information processing approach'. *Journal of Communication*, 40 (3): 106–19.

Roe, Keith and De Meyer, Gust 2000: 'Music television: MTV-EUROPE'. In Jan Wieten, Graham Murdock and Peter Dahlgren (eds), *Television across Europe: A Comparative Introduction,* London: Sage, 141–57.

Rogers, Everett. 1983: *Diffusion of Innovations.* New York: Free Press.

Rolland, A. and Ostbye, H. 1986: 'Breaking the broadcasting monopoly'. In Denis McQuail and Karen Siune (eds), *New Media Politics: Comparative Approaches in Western Europe,* London: Sage, 115–29.

Rowe, David 1996: 'The global love-match: sport and television'. *Media, Culture and Society,* 18 (2): 565–82.

Rowe, David, McKay, Jim and Miller, T. 1998: 'Come together: sport, nationalism, and the media image'. In Lawrence A. Wenner (ed.), *Media/ Sport,* London: Routledge, 119–33.

Rowhwedder, Cassile 1996: 'MTV Europe seeks regional relevance'. *Wall Street Journal Europe,* 10 April: 4.

Rowland, D. W., Jr. and Tracey, M. 1990: 'Worldwide challenges to public service broadcasting'. *Journal of Communication*, 40 (2): 8–27.

Sahin, Haluk and Aksoy, Asu 1993: 'Global media and cultural identity'. *Journal of Communication*, 43 (2): 31–41.

Sankey, Amelia 1998: *Digital Broadcasting Revolution.* London: FT Media and Telecoms.

Sassoon, Donald 1986: 'Political and market forces in Italian broadcasting'. *West European Politics,* 2: 67–83.

Scammel, Margaret 1995: *Designer Politics. How Elections are Won.* Basingstoke: Macmillan.

Scammel, Margaret 1999: 'Political marketing: lessons for political science'. *Political Studies,* 48: 718–39.

Scharpf, F. W. 1997: 'Economic integration, democracy and the welfare state'. *Journal of European Public Policy,* 4 (1): 18–36.

Schiller, Herbert I. 1984: *Information and the Crisis Economy.* Norwood, NJ: Ablex.

Schiller, Herbert I. 1989: *Culture, Inc.: The Corporate Takeover of Public Expression*. New York: Oxford University Press.

Schiller, Herbert I. 1991: 'Not yet the post-imperialist era'. *Critical Studies in Mass Communication*, 8: 13–28.

Schiller, Herbert I. 1992: *Mass Communications and American Empire*. Boulder, Colo.: Westview Press.

Schiller, Herbert I. 1996: *Information Inequality: The Deepening Social Crisis in America*. New York: Routledge.

Schiller, Herbert I. 2000: 'Digitalised capitalism: what has changed?'. In Howard Tumber (ed.), *Media Power, Professionals and Policies*, London: Routledge, 116–26.

Schreiber, Dominic 1997: 'Music for the masses'. *Television Business International* (January): 38–42.

Schreiber, Dominic 1998: 'Building on the bunny'. *Television Business International* (December): 30–4.

Schreiber, Dominic 1999: 'Logging onto Kids'. *Television Business International* (September): 20–4.

Schutz, Astrid 1995: 'Entertainers, experts or public servants? Politicians' self-presentation on television talk shows'. *Political Communication*, 12 (3): 211–21.

Screen Digest 1998: 'Europe's digital platforms' (December). Available at www.screendigest.com/yp_98-12.htm.

Sepstrub, Peter 1990: *The Transnationalization of TV in West Europe*. London: John Libbey.

Shakleton, Liz 1999: 'News channels count cost of Kosovo crisis'. *Media and Marketing Europe* (June): 8.

Sims, Martin 1999: 'From aiming too high to aiming too low'. *Intermedia*, 27 (3): 4–6.

Singh-Heer, Harjinder 1999: *European Media Markets*. London: FT Media and Telecoms.

Siune, Karen 1998: 'Is broadcasting policy becoming redundant?'. In Kees Brants, Joke Hermes and Liesbet van Zoonen (eds), *The Media in Question: Popular Cultures and Public Interests*, London: Sage, 18–26.

Siune, Karen and Hultén, Olten 1998: 'Does public broadcasting have a future?'. In Denis McQuail and Karen Siune (eds), *Media Policy: Convergence, Concentration and Commerce*, London: Sage, 23–37.

Siune, Karen and McQuail, Denis (eds) 1986: *New Media Politics: Comparative Approaches in Western Europe*. London: Sage.

Smith, Anthony 1989: 'The public interest'. *Intermedia*, 17 (2): 10–24.

Smith, Anthony 1995: 'Television as a public service medium'. In Anthony Smith (ed.), *Television: An International History*, Oxford: Oxford University Press, 62–91.

Stein, Janice 1996: 'Treading carefully'. *Television Business International* (November): 21–2.

Strange, Suzan 1998: 'Who are EU? Ambiguities in the concept of competitiveness'. *Journal of Common Market Studies*, 36 (1): 101–14.

Strategy Analytics 1999: *Mergers within the Internet Industry Value Chain: Strategies for Success*. London: Strategy Analytics.

Sussman, Gerald 1997: *Communication, Technology and Politics in the Information Age*. Thousand Oaks, Calif.: Sage.

Sussman, Gerald 1999: 'The "information society": discourses, fetishes and discontents'. *Journal of International Communication*, 6 (1): 7–21.

Sutherland, Fritha 1999a: 'Local heroes'. *Cable and Satellite Europe*, (February): 30–4.

Sutherland, Fritha 1999b: 'Bargaining power'. *Cable and Satellite Europe* (March): 14–32.

Sutherland, Fritha 1999c: 'Finding your niche'. *Cable and Satellite Europe* (May): 52–4.

Sutherland, Fritha 1999d: 'Culture unbound'. *Cable and Satellite Europe* (August): 18–22.

Sutherland, Fritha 1999e: 'Windows on the world'. *Cable and Satellite Europe* (November): 24–32.

Swanson, David L. 1992: 'The political-media complex'. *Communication Monographs*, 59: 397–400.

Swanson, David L. 1993: 'Political institutions in media centred democracy'. Paper presented at the course on Parliament and Public Opinion sponsored by the Universidad Complutense de Madrid, El Escorial, Spain 2–6 August.

Swanson, David L. 1997: 'The political-media complex at 50: putting the 1996 presidential campaign in context'. *American Behavioral Scientist*, 40: 1264–82.

Swanson, David L. 1998: 'Modern communications and problems of democracy: challenges to the old order'. Paper presented at a seminar on Public Opinion and Parliament, Universidad Internacional Menéndez Pelayo, Valencia, Spain, 30 September.

Swanson, David L. and Mancini, Paolo 1996: 'Patterns of modern electoral campaigning and their consequences'. In David L. Swanson and Paolo Mancini (eds), *Politics, Media and Modern Democracy: An International Study of Innovations in Electoral Campaigns and their Consequences*, New York: Praeger, 247–76.

Syfret, Toby 1995: 'Staggering on'. *Cable and Satellite Europe* (September): 54–9.

Syfret, Toby 1996: 'Nice work'. *Television Business International* (April): 50–6.

Syfret, Toby 1997: 'Selling space'. *Cable and Satellite Europe* (November): 22–8.

Syfret, Toby 1998: 'World-wide round-up of national peoplemeter systems'. In *Television Business International Yearbook*, London; Pearson Professional Ltd: 540–2.

Syvertsen, Trine 1991: 'Public television in crisis: critiques compared in Norway and Britain'. *European Journal of Communication*, 6 (1): 95–114.

Syvertsen, Trine 1999: 'The many uses of the "public service" concept'. *NORDICOM Review*, 20 (1): 5–12.

Tabernero, Sanchez Alfonso 1993: *Media Concentration in Europe: Commercial Enterprise and the Public Interest.* Düsseldorf: European Institute for the Media.

Tehranian, Majid and Tehranian, Katharine Kia 1997: 'Taming modernity: towards a new paradigm', In Ali Mohammadi (ed.), *International Communication and Globalization,* London: Sage, 119–67.

Television Business International 1995: 'Sorry, wrong numbers'. (October): 68–70.

Television Business International 1996: 'Around the clock, around the world' (November): 18–34.

Television Business International 1997: 'PPV soccer starts to kick in' (June): 47.

Television Business International 1998: 'Not in my back yard' (November): 16–22.

Thompson, John B. 1995: *The Media and Modernity: A Social Theory of the Media.* Cambridge: Polity.

Thussu, Daya Kishan 1998: 'Infotainment international: a view from the south'. In D. K. Thussu (ed.), *Electronic Empires: Global Media and Local Resistance,* London: Arnold, 63–82.

Tillier, Alan 1996: 'Relaunch but still no anchors for Euronews'. *The European,* 4–8 February: 20.

Tobin, Anna 1999: 'Keep it in the family'. *Cable and Satellite Europe* (July): 20–3.

Tobin, Anna 2000: 'Spinning out on the web'. *Cable and Satellite Europe* (January): 22–4.

Tomlinson, John 1994: 'Mass communications and the idea of global public sphere'. *Journal of International Communication,* 1 (2): 57–70.

Tomlinson, John 1997: 'Cultural globalization and cultural imperialism'. In Ali Mohammadi (ed.), *International Communication and Globalization,* London: Sage, 170–90.

Tracey, Michael 1998: *The Rise and Fall of Public Service Broadcasting.* New York: Oxford University Press.

Traquina, Nelson 1995: 'Portuguese television: the politics of savage deregulation'. *Media, Culture and Society,* 17 (2): 223–38.

Traquina, Nelson 1998: 'Western European broadcasting, deregulation, and public television: the Portuguese experience'. *Journalism and Mass Communication Monographs,* 167.

Tungate, Mark 1996: 'Euronews fights back'. *Media International* (March): 8.

Tunstall, Jeremy 1986: *Communications Deregulation.* Oxford: Basil Blackwell.

Tunstall, Jeremy and Machin, David 1999: *The Anglo-American Media Connection.* Oxford: Oxford University Press.

Tunstall, Jeremy and Palmer, Michael 1991: *Media Moguls.* London: Routledge.

TV Express 2000a: 'Fox Kids adds Italy to its Lists'. 13 January: 9.

TV Express 2000b: 'Pace report'. 24 February: 5.

TV International 2000a: 'Movie channels score high in France. 3 April: 1.

TV International 2000b: 'Kids channels: Canal J stages comeback as competition rises in UK'. 17 April: 6.

TV International 2000c: 'German music channel hopes advertiser appeal will extend to net operations'. 1 May: 10–11.

TV International 2000d: 'After proving it's viable, DTH platform aims for soccer, interactive pay-off'. 26 June: 10–11.

TV International 2000e: 'Mass-market fiction rises in Europe as producers seek alliances'. 24 July: 1–2.

TV International 2001: 'Growth in T-commerce drives overdue growth in interactive advertising'. 5 March: 5–8.

Tydeman, John and Kelm, E. 1986: *New Media in Europe.* London: McGraw-Hill.

Ungerer, H. 1995: 'EU competition law in the telecommunications, media and information technology sectors'. Paper presented at the Fordham Corporate Law Institute, 22nd Annual Conference on International Antitrust Law and Policy, Fordham University School of Law, New York City, 27 October.

van der Rijt, Cerrit A. J., d'Haenens, Leen S. J., Jansen, Ronald H. A. and de Vos, Cor J. 2000: 'Young people and music television in the Netherlands'. *European Journal of Communication,* 15 (1): 79–91.

van Zoonen, Liesbet, Hermes, Joke and Brants, Kees 1998: 'Introduction: of public and popular interests'. In Kees Brants, Joke Hermes and Liesbet van Zoonen (eds), *The Media in Question: Popular Cultures and Public Interests,* London: Sage, 1–6.

Veljanovski, Cento 1990: 'Market driven broadcasting: not myth but reality'. *Intermedia,* 18 (6): 17–21.

Vernet, Jean-Fabrice 1999: 'Keeping the kids loyal during and after the show'. *Euromedia* (September): 20–5.

Vulser, Nicole and Callard, Sarah 1999: 'Canal+/BSkyB merger talks abandoned'. *TV Express,* 2 (5): 1–2.

Walker, Sarah 1998: 'News challenges'. *Television Business International* (November): 2.

Wall Street Journal Europe 1997: 'Media industry takes aim at draft ownership quotas'. 4 March: 1, 6.

Wallis, Roger and Baran, Stanley 1990: *The Known World of Broadcast News.* London: Routledge.

Wang, Georgette, Ku, Lin-lin and Liu, Chun-Chou 2000: 'Local and national cultural industries; is there a life after globalization?'. In Georgette Wang, Jan Servaes and Anura Goonasekera (eds), *The New Communications Landscape: Demystifying Media Globalization,* London: Routledge, 52–73.

Wang, Georgette and Servaes, Jan 2000: 'Introduction'. In Georgette Wang, Jan Servaes and Anura Goonasekera (eds), *The New Communications Landscape: Demystifying Media Globalization,* London: Routledge, 1–18.

Watson, Miranda 1996: 'Anything you can do'. *Television Business International* (April): 48.

Watson, Miranda 1997: 'Kirch left over the barrel'. *Cable and Satellite Express,* 10 April: 12.

Watson, Miranda 1998: 'Air on a d-string'. *Cable and Satellite Europe* (January): 16.

Watson, Miranda 1999: 'Ball watching'. *Television Business International* (September): 48–51.

Weaver, David H. 1995: 'What voters learn from media'. *ANNALS/AAPSS*, 546: 34–47.

Webster, Frank and Robins, Kevin 1986: *Information Technology: A Luddite Analysis*. Norwood, NJ: Ablex.

Westcott, Tim 1992: 'Cash in credits'. *Media and Marketing Europe* (December): 34–5.

Westcott, Tim 1994: 'The information circus'. *Television Business International* (July–August): 30–2.

Westcott, Tim 1995: 'Getting mighty crowded'. *Television Business International* (November): 18–22.

Westcott, Tim 1996: 'The digital economy'. *Television Business International* (October): 36–8.

Westcott, Tim 1997: 'The old and the new'. *Television Business International* (September): 37–8

Westcott, Tim 1998: 'Toon Asia'. *Television Business International* (December): 26–8.

Westcott, Tim 1999a: 'Public servants'. *Television Business International* (April): 39–42.

Westcott, Tim 1999b: 'Breaking news'. *Euromedia* (November): 16–19.

Westcott, Tim 1999c: *The Business of Children's Television: Market Definition*. London: Screen Digest

Weymouth, T. and Lamizet, B. 1996: *Markets and Myths: Forces for Change in the European Media*. London: Longman.

Wheeler, Mark 1997: *Politics and the Mass Media*. Oxford: Blackwell.

Wheeler, Mark 2000: 'The "undeclared war" Part II. The European Union's consultation process for the New Round of the General Agreement on Trading Services/World Trade Organization on audiovisual services'. *European Journal of Communication*, 15 (2): 253–62.

White Paper 2000: *Communications White Paper*. London: Department of Trade and Industry/Department of Culture, Media and Sport. Available at: http://communicationswhitepaper.gov.uk.

White, Justine 1999a: 'CNN comes of Age'. *TV Express*, 20 May: 12–13.

White, Justine 1999b: 'Short Attention Spans'. *TV Express*, 8 October: 5.

White, Justine 1999c: 'ONdigital fights back, raises prices'. *TV Express*, 2 June: 1–2.

Wiio, Osmo 1995: 'Is television a killer? – An international comparison'. *Intermedia*, 23 (2): 26–31.

Williams, D. 1976: *Broadcasting and Democracy in West Germany*. London: Oxford University Press.

Winston, Brian 1988: *Media Technology and Society*. London: Routledge.

Wolton, Dominique 1992: 'Values and normative choices in French television'. In J. Blumler (ed.), *Television and the Public Interest, Vulnerable Values in Western European Broadcasting*, London: Sage, 147–60.

Woodman, Chris 1999: '15 years of intelligence'. *Cable and Satellite Europe* (May): 30–8.

Wright, Emma 1998: 'Learning difficulties'. *Television Business International* (September): 34–6.

Wright, Emma 1999: 'Trading up'. *Television Business International* (April): 62–4.

Zelizer, Barbie 1992: 'CNN, the Gulf War, and journalistic practice'. *Journal of Communication*, 42 (1): 66–81.

Zenith Media 1999: *Television in Europe to 2008.* London: Press Release, 2 September 1999.

Index

Index Compiled by Zeb Korycinska